# Conversations
## *with*
# Great Teachers

For Margie

Bill Smart
6/15/10

# Conversations *with* Great Teachers

BILL SMOOT

Indiana University Press

BLOOMINGTON & INDIANAPOLIS

This book is a publication of

Indiana University Press

601 North Morton Street
Bloomington, Indiana 47404-3797 USA

www.iupress.indiana.edu

*Telephone orders*     800-842-6796
*Fax orders*           812-855-7931
*Orders by e-mail*     iuporder@indiana.edu

MANUFACTURED IN THE UNITED STATES OF AMERICA

Library of Congress Cataloging-in-Publication Data

Smoot, Bill.
  Conversations with great teachers / Bill Smoot.
    p. cm.
  ISBN 978-0-253-35491-4 (cl : alk. paper) 1. Teachers—United States—
Interviews. 2. Teachers—United States—Biography. 3. Teachers—Job
satisfaction—United States. I. Title.
  LA2311.S56 2010
  371.100973—dc22
                              2009054108

1 2 3 4 5 15 14 13 12 11 10

This book is dedicated to the memory of my mother, HELEN ROZAN SMOOT (1918–2002), who was my greatest teacher.

# Contents

## 4  Teaching the Creators and Performers

## 5  Teaching the Fixers and Makers

## 6  Teaching the Athletes

## 7  Growing the Body and Spirit

## 8  Teaching at the Bottom and on the Edge

# 9 *Teaching the Protectors*

# 10 *Teaching in the Corridors of Power*

# Introduction

One of my most memorable moments in preparing this book occurred during my interview with Arthur Lane, a retired fencing teacher in his nineties. In response to one of my questions, he instructed me to pick up a fencing foil. He cradled my hands in his and adjusted my grip. Then he had me move the foil this way and that, explaining why this grip was the best, and I understood in both my hand and my mind that it was. The understanding was embodied, literally. When he removed his hands, I could still feel their touch. The lesson lingered as a physical sensation.

That moment is emblematic of what I have come to think of as the education triad: the teacher, the student, and that which passes between them. But what passes between them? And how? What happened in my hand when the old fencing teacher held it and explained the grip? How does that metamorphosis we call learning happen? What do great teachers say about their teaching?

These were the questions that led me to my project of interviewing fifty-one great teachers about their teaching. I am a long-time admirer of the late Studs Terkel's work: his books of interviews with people about their jobs, their memories of the Great Depression, their experiences in World War II. My wish that he had done a book of interviews with teachers morphed into an idea, then an intent, and finally a commitment—I would do one myself.

Classroom teachers were a logical start, but I soon realized that teaching takes place in many corners of society. So I sought great teachers everywhere, and everywhere I found them—an inspirational group of men and women who generously granted me conversations about their teaching. Among them were teachers of first grade and college physics, teachers of firefighting, fiction writing, exotic dancing, brain surgery, and circus arts.

I did the first interview in June of 2007 and my last in January of 2009. Though these teachers comprised a diverse group, I began to see qualities that their teaching had in common. Not that they had a single way to teach—far from it. But among this diversity of people, disciplines, and styles of teaching, I found universals. More than once I heard a phrase only slightly different from something said in an earlier interview, though one teacher instructed first graders in reading and the other taught adults how to wrestle alligators.

One commonality is that they all regard teaching as not just as a job but as a calling, a combination of serious purpose and sacred commitment to that purpose. Lynette Wayne, a first-grade teacher, says simply, "Teaching chose me." These are people with a mission, and that metamorphosis we call learning is their cause.

There's the old joke about the person who, when asked if he likes his job, replies, "If I liked it, it wouldn't be a job." The teachers with whom I talked love their work, using words like "passion" and "joy." Teaching is more than what they do; it is who they are, and it defines their place in the world. Several of the teachers now retired kept slipping into present tense when they talked about teaching—not because they wish they were still teaching, but because in their teaching they had been so deeply themselves.

John Faggi, a prep-school English teacher, quotes his former headmaster as identifying in great teachers "an authentic presence in the classroom." I often thought about that phrase in doing these interviews, because the teachers with whom I spoke seem in their teaching to be so deeply in their element. They have not always felt so from the beginning of their careers, but when they remember their first years of teaching, they realize that what they acquired over time was that sense of belonging in the classroom.

This authentic presence is important because the teaching triad is fundamentally a human relationship—in all of its multi-layered depth, complexity, richness, and challenge. Every act of learning involves a change in the learner. Acquiring a fact is a small change; learning to act, to perform surgery, or to be a soldier or a writer is a larger transformation. The student who once did not understand poetry but now loves it is a new person. To allow oneself to be taught—to be changed—requires trust. The teacher must be deeply authentic in the classroom because that authenticity is the basis of trust.

A central building block of trust is care. These teachers spoke of their care for students and of the importance of students' knowing they care. Teachers care about their students as people, and they care that they learn. Such care is not just a feeling or a wish. "Care," like "love," is an active verb; it manifests itself in the long hours and great effort that these teachers devote to what they do—from a middle-school phys-ed teacher's "toe talks" to students (she talks to them about their behavior while they look at their toes), to a philosophy professor's great effort in making his lectures clear. The triad is the teacher, the student, and that which passes between them; and what passes between them both constitutes and depends upon a human relationship. The teacher's care is the current that carries what passes between them. Teachers think about students, ponder them, observe them carefully, and try to determine what they need. In teaching other teachers at the FBI Academy, Kathy Mitchell says that her first principle of teaching is that "it has to be about the student." When asked to account for his success in teaching both undergrads and medical students, a world-renowned neurosurgeon says, "I connect."

Great teachers have a sense of their students as individuals, and they know that each individual learner is unique. One inherent challenge of teaching is that it is usually done in groups, and yet the teacher has to know students individually, and to understand their inevitably different ways of learning. The teacher also needs to recognize possibilities in each student that may not be apparent. Fourth-grade teacher Steven Levy says he used to pray "to always see what is the genius in each child that makes him or her absolutely unique."

Great teachers have humility in knowing that they serve a purpose larger than themselves. Even when I interviewed teachers in whom I detected a touch of ego—though they were few—it was clear that they leave their egos behind when they teach. Nor did I find anyone who cultivated disciples. What the teacher ultimately gives to students is the ability to make their own way forward. Pastry chef Dieter Schorner wants his students to be better than he. More than once, my conversations with these teachers called to mind the words of the great Haiku master Basho: "Don't follow in the footsteps of the old poets; seek what they sought."

These teachers are not only passionate about their students but also about the content they teach. Vince Dunn is passionate about understanding fires: he investigates them, studies them, and writes books about them. Paul Karafiol believes that math is beautiful. Suki Schorer does not just teach ballet; she has written a book on Balanchine. Many others spoke of their passionate love for their subject matter—from physics to circus arts. Teaching does not so much complement their expertise as it completes it. For them, knowing a subject fully is being able to teach it.

The great empiricist philosophers of the eighteenth century believed that the mind was empty at birth, later filled by experience. For John Locke, the mind was a "blank slate"; for David Hume, "an empty cupboard." But that's not the way Ron Washington teaches major leaguers to play the infield. "I never just put it in you," he says. And exotic dance teacher Catherine Rose tells her students, "This is inside of you." The teachers with whom I spoke do believe that knowledge is transferred, but for all of them, what is transferred between teacher and student in the education triad goes beyond information.

Kant studied those eighteenth-century empiricists and concluded that the mind was no mere passive receptor but an active organizing agent, giving understandable form to sensory input. In this way, these teachers seem to be Kantians—or post-Kantians. They believe that they are not so much imparting information as teaching ways of thinking, modes of awareness, and habits of mind. They are developing abilities already present, actualizing potential already there.

In the Platonic dialog *Meno,* Socrates teaches a slave boy the Pythagorean theorem not by stating it, but by asking questions that elicit from the boy geometric insights, through which he discovers the theorem for himself. Basketball teacher Tom Nordland says simply, "What sabotages learning is to give answers." And corporate consultant Michael Ansa says the most important element of his teaching is asking good questions. The name most often invoked by these teachers is Socrates.

Many teachers speak of engaging their students in *doing.* In teaching women executives, Hannah Riley Bowles uses the case study method to draw the women into mock scenarios. Steven Levy taught the curriculum to his fourth graders by having them make bread (beginning with growing the wheat), and he now teaches interactive techniques to other teachers. Physics professor Eric Mazur says, "Learning is not a spectator sport."

All of this calls to mind Confucius: "I hear and I forget; I see and I remember; I do and I understand." No one I spoke with quoted this or mentioned Confucius, but many of them live his wisdom in their teaching.

And yet, we should not be too hasty. In my twenty-two years as a student, the best teacher I ever had—also interviewed in this book—merely lectures. But these "mere" lectures were cathedrals built of language, rendering the best philosophies of the ages with a clarity that made them beautiful. While some dismiss lectures as passive learning, can "passive" be a true description for what occurs in a mind rocked to its core by what it hears? While teachers make thoughtful choices about their techniques, teaching is never reducible to technique, and while dull lectures abound, there are also teachers who can raise the lecture to such an art that the receptive student, hearing such a lecture, is forever transformed, as four decades ago the philosophy lectures of William Gass transformed me.

Teachers teach more than the subject they teach. They also teach meta-lessons, and while facts may fade from memory, something deeper often remains: the form of what the student learned, the excitement of thinking beyond the given, the means by which he or she learned, or the passion the teacher felt. When the dates, the chemical formulas, or the names of characters fade, it is these deeper lessons that remain.

The education triad exists in objective time, in *chronos*, but it has its own temporality, its *kairos*. There are periods of slow and steady learning. There are periods of no learning. There is drill and repetition. And there are lightning flashes of understanding—the "aha" moments of which many teachers spoke. The slow and steady periods are hard work, for both students and teachers, and the teachers know it. Suki Schorer's ballet students must acquire strength and muscle memory. It does not happen fast. Nor should it. Arthur Lane, the fencing teacher, says "speed is the enemy of learning."

So teaching requires patience, not just in the sense most people assume—of remaining calm when a student misbehaves or persistent with a student who is slow to "get it"—but patience in the sense of being wise about the nature of time. Great teachers know that each moment is part of a larger journey, a journey drawing from the deep past and stretching far into a future largely unknown. Teaching is an act of faith in the future, a high-stakes wager. The fireman and the drill sergeant know that how they teach may save—or cost—lives. The photography teacher hopes his efforts will bring art into a student's daily existence and—in a different way—lives are at stake there, too.

Great teachers are natural curriculum designers. They are not only experts in their subject areas, they also have a keen sense of what is more important and what is less: what elements are most essential, how to divide learning into steps, and how to present those steps in a sequence. Those public schools that have taken course design out of the hands of teachers have degraded the education triad, and, in those circumstances, some of the best teachers have fled to charter or private schools where they are allowed to function fully as teachers, not as delivery boys for a pre-packaged curriculum.

Great teachers have a quiet confidence in what they do, a solid sense of their purpose and how they are pursuing it. And while they are contemporary in that there is little new that escapes their awareness, and while they are distinctive for retaining at any age a vibrant spirit of youth, they are never trendy, and when they talked about their teaching, I was struck by the absence of educational jargon or buzzwords. Such words seem particular to administrators and educational spectators who do not teach. And when these teachers use technology, it is with the attitude that technology is no more than a tool. First-grade teacher Lynette Wayne doubts she would miss her interactive white board if it were taken away, and her common-sense conclusion is that "technology is no better than the teacher who uses it."

I came of age during the sixties. Having grown up in a small town, a Boy Scout, a son of a World War II veteran, I went off to college believing that America stood for truth and justice. Like many of my generation, I was deeply affected by the war in Vietnam and the lies by which the government defended it, by corporate exploitation, by our clandestine undermining of governments around the world, by the assassinations of our noblest voices for change, and finally by the moral sleaze of Watergate. These eroded my faith in my country and left me with an angry sense of betrayal that would remain for decades. I joined the movement to change things, but our successes seemed outweighed by our failures. But interviewing these fifty-one great teachers, coinciding with a season of changing political leadership in America, gave me a pride in these teachers and a belief in America greater than any I've felt since I was a student in high school. Theirs is indeed a fierce humanity, and, experiencing it, I have felt inspired and filled with hope by the importance and the value of what they do.

In my conversation with Rhodessa Jones, a vibrant, soulful, and charismatic performance artist who teaches incarcerated women, she observes, "If we can really be present, then we can go anywhere." Her wisdom reminds us of the precious promise of the teaching triad for the country and the world. It may also explain why, at the end of these conversations with great teachers, I was left with a sense that the triad of teaching is both elemental and miraculous. It is elemental as carbon is elemental to life—foundational and necessary. It is through teaching that knowledge, skill, and wisdom are passed from one person to another, one generation to another. Through teaching, the knowledge that elevates the level of our humanity is preserved, built upon, expanded, and reborn. We ask what makes us human: That we grow our food? Build our shelter? Make art? Wage war? Practice religion? Whatever it is, it gets taught.

Teaching is also miraculous. It is not a miracle of the rare sort, like a weeping statue or a person who survived a hundred-foot fall, but miraculous as creation always is, like the germination of a seed or the birth of a child. Someone did not understand, and then the teacher came; something passed between them, and now that someone does understand. The teaching triad is the daily miracle: teacher, student, and that which passes between them.

# Conversations

*with*

# Great Teachers

# 1 | *Teaching in the School Room*

*"Good teachers have to have a sense of where they are."*

# John Faggi

## PREP-SCHOOL ENGLISH TEACHER

*John Faggi has taught English for over twenty years at the College Preparatory School in Oakland, California, one of the preeminent private high schools on the West Coast. Graduates from those years frequently identify him as their best and most memorable high-school teacher.*

*He attended Andover as a scholarship student and later received his BA from Princeton and his MA from Harvard. After serving in the Peace Corps, he taught at the Athenean School in Danville, California, and at Choate.*

### What do you really teach?

What I hope to teach is pleasure. Maybe it's because I am at a school where the kids are pretty able, but I think the teaching of skills is really secondary. It just happens with the work they have to do.

What I just want them to do is really see how literature is a way to enjoy life, and to live a better life, because they're more sensitive to feelings and ideas and the depth of life—you know, as T. S. Eliot said about Dante, the "heights and depths of human emotion." And when Holden [*Holden Caulfield is the narrator in Salinger's* The Catcher in the Rye] is watching Phoebe go around and around on the carousel and he's crying, that moment is . . . teaching literature is filled with moments like that, in which life stops and we can look at it.

What I really love is when kids at any skill level seem to have a fire lit under them and get excited about something and love it and really enjoy it. I love it when they come into class wanting to say something, wanting to ask something about what we have read—something that isn't about getting a good grade, that isn't about how to write the five-paragraph essay. The older I get, the more bored I am with that stuff—it just doesn't seem very important to me. Sometimes I think I don't teach certain things as well as I should because I don't think they're very important.

So I want the kids to enjoy and appreciate and find pleasure. One of my best students ever reminded me of this. Liza is a TA for me in Partners [*a summer program to give an academic boost to middle-school-aged underserved students*]. When my Partners students were discussing a poem, I heard her say, "Well, what do you like?" And I realized that although I had put several questions on the board, I had not included that one. And I felt a little sheepish. So at the end of class, I said to students, "I overheard Liza say, 'What do you like?' and I want to make that the first question you should ask. What gives you pleasure? What's fun and interesting?"

And then when kids get more sophisticated, they can ask a question, and be intrigued by what they don't understand, and enjoy that. I think that's another thing I want to teach—a kind of balancing act in which you can learn to appreciate what you don't understand. Art is not an exact science and it never will be. When it's taught like one, it's taught poorly. That's why I don't like the five-paragraph essay—because it's so mechanical. In terms of appreciating literature, the sooner they can live with techniques like paradox and irony, or a consistent contradiction where you can't decide—it's this or that, no it's both—the sooner young students can get to that point, the happier I am, the better I feel I can teach.

I think I also want to teach . . . "reverence" is not the right word because it sounds a little sanctimonious, but a kind of appreciation that makes them stop. Because I think life is increasingly fast. The high-tech world is a world that doesn't encourage concentration of the kind we value, that we've grown up with. They don't grow up with that in their lives. I think I want to teach them slowing down, whether it's for poetry or anything else.

I also believe in certain kinds of principles of life—clarity and simplicity and patience—that are values that I don't see much of in the modern world. Those are values I hope would come out of emphasizing enjoyment, pleasure, slowing down, looking—even silence.

*Putting modesty aside for the moment, can you tell me what you think has been your secret to success? One of the paradoxes of education is that it's hard to educate educators in how to educate. Suppose a beginning teacher asked how you do it.*

I think it has to do with—this is not my phrase, it's actually Robert Baldwin's phrase [*a previous head of Faggi's school*]—an "authentic presence in the class-room." The kids see through sham—not just sham, but they see through somebody who's over-prepared, someone who's trying to hammer certain points home in an inauthentic way, somebody who comes in with an axe to grind, somebody who's not flexible or open. The kids are brilliant at seeing through all the ways that we hide inauthenticity.

It doesn't mean that I don't make use of a persona in the classroom. Sometimes I put on certain roles. But most of the time . . . I don't know if it's correct to say I'm myself, because what does that mean? The reading I'm doing in Jungian psychology suggests that we are not one person but many, many selves, and part of what's fun about teaching is these different selves can come out. But underneath all of that, kids feel the authenticity or they don't. And once they feel the "authentic presence," then they trust. Without trust, nothing can happen.

One of my colleagues used to say, "We have to earn the trust of our students." Sometimes on the first day, I say to the ninth graders, "Many of you respect me because I'm a teacher and this is a good school, but I challenge you to hold back on that a little bit and see whether I'm gong to earn your respect and earn your trust." I think that without trust, the kids will be more likely to fake it or to try to cheat in some way . . . not cheat, but not try, not let themselves go and experiment. I don't think you can learn anything ultimately without being willing to fail. I encourage them to the extent that I can. Sometimes students are so concerned with grades and succeeding that they don't try something that they don't think they can do. But if they trust me, and also each other . . .

On the first day, I put the word "civility" on the board and I talk about what that means, from the Latin "citizen." If we are good citizens of the community around this table (at my school we actually have Harkness tables), then it's not just trusting me but trusting one another. [*Harkness tables are large oval seminar tables named after philanthropist Edward Harkness, who donated them to Phillips Exeter Academy in 1931.*] Also, the process is much larger. It's a tradition that goes back to Socrates in the West, and in the East, too; we have this tradition of an older person teaching younger people in small classes. I revere that tradition. One of the few times I get angry is when I think kids have violated civility—not by being silly and acting out, but by being rude or saying something ad hominem, something that gets in the way of the whole Harkness-table approach.

So if someone were to ask me how I do it, I would say that it really has nothing to do with the books I've read or the schools I've attended—this is hyperbole, of course, but I'll say it anyway—but you walk into the room and you give off an aura of someone who is in the right place.

I remember a great book by John McPhee about Bill Bradley—when Bradley was a college basketball player at Princeton—called *A Sense of Where You Are.* It seems like good teachers have to have a sense of where they are. A good high-school teacher at a good school is not a martinet, not somebody out of ed school with a grab bag of technological tricks. It is somebody with an authentic presence, who will nourish and cultivate the respect of the students.

*"I don't think there's any greater joy than teaching in a first-grade classroom."*

# Lynette Wayne

**FIRST-GRADE TEACHER**

*Lynette teaches first grade at Christa McAuliffe Elementary School in Hastings, Minnesota, a town of twenty-two thousand on the upper Mississippi*

*River. She has taught elementary school for twenty-eight years, ranging from kindergarten through fifth grade.*

*A lifelong resident of Minnesota, she received her bachelor's degree from Winona State University and her master's degree from the University of Minnesota. In 2008, she received an award for teaching excellence from the National Education Association.*

I think there is an important factor in every grade. One of the most significant things in first grade is that's where a majority of the children are first learning to read. But that's not always the case, because the students are at varying levels when they come into first grade. Some are coming in already reading, and some are coming in not knowing letters and sounds. So differentiation of instruction is important in first grade.

*There are probably readers of this book who haven't been around first graders since they were one themselves. What is the mind of a six-year-old like? What is that stage of development about?*

Oh, my goodness. I think that's really hard to say because the children are unique and have their own differences. It's a very curious age. They're eager to learn. They love being in school, for the most part. They love learning. I find that their little minds are like sponges. They just want to absorb everything that you can give them.

I think that if somebody hasn't been in first grade for a long time, he or she would be surprised at the rigor of the curriculum that is now in the schools. We are expecting more of our children now, and we're finding that they are able to do quite a bit, so I'm seeing tremendous growth in the children that I'm teaching. The rigor of our curriculum has certainly increased over the past few years.

We now have homework at every grade level here. It may be reading a book nightly from our reading program. It may be a review of the math activities. At first grade, there is not as much homework as at higher grades. We need to tell parents—and we need to have these honest conversations with them—that if their child is going to learn to read, they have to spend time reading to their children, because they're not going to learn to read if they haven't heard the word first. And they're going to have to spend time listening to their child read once their child begins to read. If they just depend upon technology and learning games . . . that's not going to work with reading, because reading is a very hands-on kind of thing where parents need to listen. The parents also have to turn off the TV and turn off those computers when they need to have that time to read.

I don't have grandchildren yet, but when I do . . . I think we have to be really careful that technology doesn't take over all the responsibilities of teaching our children.

*What has prompted the higher standards?*

I think the state standards. You know, every state has a set of standards—expectations of what children are supposed to learn. I imagine that the Elementary and Secondary Education Act—what they call "No Child Left Behind"—has a played a part in it, too. So I think it's the standards that are coming down to the schools, whether they be national or state—and of course, your district's expectations, also, and the curriculum that's chosen for your district.

*Do you feel that these higher standards are good, or do you sometimes feel that we're asking too much of kids?*

I think that in the standards debate, you're going to get a different answer from everybody you talk to. I think it's important that we—as teachers—know what the standards are and know what's expected of us. Sometimes expectations that are put upon us by groups that are not in the classroom sometimes can be a little . . . I don't know if I want to say "frustrating" or . . . [*she hesitates*]. I want to say this correctly. I think we want to have high standards for our children. I think we need that. Because if we don't have high standards, they're going to face greater obstacles later. So how a district will use those standards and implement them into the district will vary from school to school. We're fortunate here because we're able to have professional conversations around those standards, and that makes it easier for us.

No matter where you teach, you have to know your content well. I think that's vital no matter whether you're a preschool teacher or a college professor. But I also think that, especially at the early childhood level, you have to know a lot about child development and how to teach that content.

Your curriculum has to be child-centered and developmentally appropriate. So content is important, but pedagogy and how you deliver the content are also critical.

When I'm teaching reading, and teaching letters and sounds, I may be able to do it with some children visually, but other kids may need something more tactile— where they're touching and doing it in a different way. So I think the curriculum has to be delivered in different ways— sometimes in multiple ways—for children to understand it. You can't just talk through it; you're going to have to use a variety of approaches in order to hit every child's level of understanding.

We now have SMART Boards [*an interactive whiteboard with a touch screen feature connected to a computer*] in our classroom and everybody says, "Isn't technology great!" Well, technology is only as good as the person who is using it to teach the lesson. You can have all the pieces there, but if you're not using them effectively, it's not going to be any better than anything else.

*At the end of the day, is there any advantage to high tech aids like SMART Boards over, let's say, a blackboard and chalk?*

I think a good teacher, especially a good early-childhood teacher, can use a variety of things: I can use a wall, a chalkboard, a SMART Board. I think what the technology piece gives us is a new way to deliver information. So could I teach without this technology? Absolutely. But the technology gives me some new and different ways to bring information to my children.

*In addition to a couple of things you've mentioned, such as differentiated teaching, what are your keys to success?*

First of all, I absolutely love what I do. I often tell others that I don't think I chose teaching; I think teaching chose me. I knew from a very early age that I was going to be a teacher.

I've wanted to stay in the classroom. I haven't wanted to go anywhere else. I think I'm very passionate about issues—issues not only for the children I teach but for the profession itself. So I think having that love for teaching and that passion about issues related to children and education have helped to keep me current and always looking for ways to grow within my own practice.

Also, I became nationally board certified in the year 2000. [*The National Board for Professional Teaching Standards offers a rigorous process by which teachers can become certified.*] What that process did for me was allow me to put my practice under a microscope and examine it against high national standards. It allowed me to deconstruct what I'm doing in the classroom to see if it's effective, and that's kept me also looking at how to improve my practice as I continue in my career.

*Was your college and master's degree work in education valuable? There are people who don't think very highly of ed schools.*

Since I knew from a very early age that I wanted to be a teacher, I absorbed everything I could in college. I even graduated in three years. I was so ready to get into the classroom. I was fortunate in that my undergraduate program allowed us to get out into the schools. Back then (I graduated in 1975), it wasn't as typical to get people into the schools early. Often you didn't get into a classroom until you did your student teaching. But I was able to get into the classroom and do a variety of activities ahead of time. I think nowadays, more people in education programs are actually getting into the classroom earlier, and that helps them to decide if this is really the career that they want.

I also am very active in working with new teachers who come into our school district. We know that too many teachers leave the classroom within the first five years. I think that happens more if a person hasn't had much experience in schools before teaching.

*So you teach at two levels. You not only teach your first graders, but you also mentor new teachers.*

Yes, I am really active in that. About ten years ago I started, with another person, a new group called the Teacher Support Network. It was a way of bringing teachers who are new to our district together and . . . so that they had a safe place where they could talk about what was happening in their first year of teaching. We created this to give our new teachers the support that we felt they needed. Since then, our district has added a one-on-one mentoring program that we are paralleled with. I think it's just critical to support teachers in their first years of teaching so that we keep our best and our brightest in the classroom.

### What are the keys to the successful mentoring of new teachers?

I think the key is giving them all the support they need, whether it be with curriculum, pedagogy, or just offering a shoulder when they're feeling frustrated or overwhelmed. Personally, I grow as much when I meet with newer teachers as they do. I'm energized by them. I think we need to have those connections, and I think all of us need to have professional conversations about what we're doing in our classrooms. Teachers really have so little time in their day—because we're always getting ready for the next thing that we're going to teach—that we don't give ourselves time to have those professional conversations with each other.

### Are you the same teacher you were twenty-five years ago, or do you feel like you've changed much?

I've changed. And I continue to change. I'm continually looking at how I'm going to change things in my classroom. And even though I know I want to change things, I won't know exactly how I want to change them until I meet my students and I know what their needs are.

I think as a teacher you need to keep growing and learning and changing. I'm not the same person I was twenty-nine years ago when I left college. You continually grow as your students come and go.

I think a lot of my philosophy about teaching has remained the same, but my practice has changed. Going through the national board certification was such a rigorous process. I think what that teaches you is that when you're looking at the high national standards for an early childhood classroom, those standards stay with you, and you realize it is all about student achievement and taking our students as far as we can in those few months that we have them. Going through the national board process really made me focus more on what it is that I do in my classroom, what happens as a result of what I do in my classroom, and what happens next because of what I just taught. My assessment informs my instruction. Then I instruct and I assess, and my assessment informs my instruction again. I think those are really critical pieces that I was reminded of going through national board certification. I don't think they were new to me, but I was able to revisit those concepts that sometimes we forget.

### Sometimes in teaching—or parenting—there's a tension between giving praise and trying to instill high self-esteem on the one hand, and giving criticism and trying to improve students on the other hand. How do you strike a balance?

I think that children do need to feel valued and feel good about what they're doing, but they also need boundaries and they need explicit instructions. I have a very strict standard for my room, but I think if you were to walk into my classroom you would see that it is a very warm and caring atmosphere, where the children not only respect me but they respect each other.

*Minnesota and its classrooms, I assume, are not as racially diverse as many states . . .*

We're finding that our percentage of minority students is increasing as the years go by. But there is a lot of diversity in our classrooms, even though it may not be racial. There is diversity based on poverty, special needs, academic needs. I have a son who has cerebral palsy. He's now twenty-five. He just got married last October. He went to St. John's University and did very well. As a parent, I was always worried—could he find that special person who could look past his disability and see the person within? I think every parent wants that for their child, no matter what their differences are—whether it be skin color, whether it be the amount of money that family has, whether it be the academic needs of the child. Every parent wants us to look past their child's differences and find a way to make their child feel successful and good at school.

*When you teach, do you ever hear in your own voice the echo of a teacher you had when you were young?*

My first-grade teacher was probably the teacher I adored the most. When I won my NEA award for teaching excellence, the newspaper in my hometown picked up the story. They interviewed me for the story, and when they asked about teachers I remembered, I mentioned her name. I got a letter from her congratulating me on the award, telling me she remembered me. So I don't know if I imitate her, but I remember how she made me feel, and that's what I want my students to feel. I want them to feel valued, and loved, and appreciated for what they do.

I was fortunate. I grew up in a small town—New Richland, Minnesota—of a thousand people, and I had excellent teachers all the way through.

*What was it about that first-grade teacher that made you so adore her?*

I think she just made all of us feel like we were the most special people in the world. She was so kind and caring, and she just had this manner about her. You didn't want to disappoint her because you adored her. As a result you'd be sitting on the edge of your seat waiting for anything that she would tell you. It was the way she made you feel that just remains with me to this day . . . and it was well over forty-five years ago that I had her.

*And now you're a first-grade teacher, and a happy one, it seems.*

I absolutely love what I do. I love those "aha" moments when you can just see children lighting up because they've learned a new word, they've learned how to read a book, or they're gaining confidence in themselves—not only as readers or as learners. I don't think there's any greater joy than teaching in a first-grade classroom.

*"I . . . wanted to do something that's new and pioneering . . . so the kids can have that sense of the adventure of being a learner."*

# Steven Levy

## FOURTH-GRADE TEACHER

*Steven Levy has taught every grade level from kindergarten through college in twenty-seven years of teaching, mostly fourth and fifth grade. He was recognized as the 1992–1993 Massachusetts Teacher of the Year and honored by the Disney American Teacher Awards as the national Outstanding General Elementary Teacher in 1994–1995. In 2001, Mr. Levy was the recipient of the Joe Oakey Award for his national impact on project-based learning. He received the John F. Kennedy Prize for the teaching of history. He has written various articles for educational journals, and his book, Starting from Scratch: One Classroom Builds Its Own Curriculum, was published in 1996. He currently works as a consultant for Expeditionary Learning Outward Bound. We spoke about his teaching of fourth graders.*

I think about the age of the fourth grader as the golden age of childhood, like the Greeks before the Romans. They still live in a bit of an ideal world. They have enough of their intellectual faculties to really do important and serious work, but at the same time they have not fallen into cynicism and defiance, and the adolescent hormones have not yet kicked in.

*What were your primary goals in teaching that age?*
The goals, I think, are as much determined by the local setting as by the developmental level. And it's changed over the past ten years, so that now the academic preparation for doing well on high-stakes tests has taken over much of teachers' thinking, even at that grade level. Now content and skills are heavily part of one's objectives.

I taught in the town of Lexington, Massachusetts, which is a fairly well-off community, so some of my most important goals came from the kind of children that I was teaching. I found that we had a different kind of poverty in Lexington than you might find in the city: in Lexington, the poverty was what I called the poverty of gratitude. These kids are somewhat privileged and have a lot of blessings in their lives, and I came to see that if those blessings didn't wake up some sense of compassion and service, if they didn't see the gifts they had as opportunities to make a better world, and if they used those gifts just to boost their own station in life, then those gifts would become negative things and a sense of entitlement would emerge. They wouldn't be willing to work very hard if it didn't come easy or the first time, and then you wouldn't see perseverance that you might find in people who have to struggle in their lives.

So I would do projects that would force them to create things that they took for granted, and really come to appreciate all that it takes to make them happen.

### Could you give some examples of these projects?

I made them grow wheat and go through all the steps that it takes to turn that into a loaf of bread. In the process, we studied a lot of our curriculum. We did lots of science experiments in terms of how to get the wheat seeds to germinate. We studied simple machines while we looked at how the grinder works to grind the wheat into flour. We did work with fractions in math as we figured out recipes, because we baked about eighty loaves of bread from the wheat that we ground. We studied colonial life and the Pilgrims. I thought that if I could give them some experience of what it's like not to get something immediately, just because you want it, then I've done these kids a good service.

I also did a similar project with wool, where I gave them a raw piece of wool and they had to figure out how that became an article of cloth. Sometimes it took months for them to learn how to card and knit and weave and dye and spin. So giving them experiences like that, I hoped I would challenge the expectation that everything comes easy in life.

The ultimate project I did with them was that I emptied out the entire classroom and they arrived on the first day of school to an empty room. Their challenge was to design, fund, and then build their classroom. This was my favorite of all projects because I love to take stuff away from these kids, and then they get nothing except what they worked for and figured out how to get on their own.

### Did you do this every year?

I did something different every year. But there were some, like the wheat project, that I did every year. It's nice to do something over and over again because you can really refine it and deepen it and tie it more directly to content and skills. But then I also wanted to do something that's new and pioneering that no one has ever done before so the kids can have that sense of the adventure of being a learner.

### In the year that they started with an empty room, what did they come up with?

We had to study the Pilgrims. That was a big part of our curriculum. So every time we came to a problem, that was our excuse to go do research about Pilgrims to see if they met that problem, and if they did, how they solved it.

The first problem was about getting money, so we looked into how the Pilgrims got the money to fund their voyage. We found out that they got it from companies investing in them. So we tried to use the model we learned from the Pilgrims for our own work. We learned what investment was, and the kids wrote hundreds of letters to every business in our town inviting people to buy a share. They sold forty-four shares. A carpenter bought a share, so we asked him if he would come and design a desk to build. An accountant bought a share, so we asked her to come in and show us how to set up books to keep track of all the money we had. We had banks buy a share, so we had the banks explain to us how interest worked. A retired handyman bought a share, so he came in and helped us build the desks. We didn't finish building the desks until February. They were these beautiful desks with tops that flipped up. That was a pretty exciting year. That was a pinnacle year in my teaching.

*Did the increase in testing and the requirements of "No Child Left Behind" legislation make project-based learning more difficult?*

It made it tremendously more difficult. In fact, the more high stakes the testing became, the more the teachers would put aside any kind of engaging work, or work that was not directly related to standards. So I feel that my mission now is to go out and try to help show people how you can continue to use projects. When projects are designed carefully, and when they have rigorous components, they'll do a much better job in preparing kids even for the tests they have to take, and certainly a better job in preparing them for life. So a lot of my work now is showing teachers what those kinds of projects look like.

*Did you ever get resistance to your projects from parents or administrators?*

I think there's always resistance when you do something new. I anticipated resistance, particularly from parents, so I had meetings with parents over the summer before the school year began, and I laid out my plans. I showed them how I would be able to cover all of the curriculum and how ultimately this would help their kids get into Harvard. If they had had serious reservations, I wouldn't have done it.

As for the administration, I think as long as the kids are producing, they keep hands off and let you do what you want to do. Of course, it was essential that my kids did well on tests. If the kids had done these projects and then bombed the tests, I'm sure it would have all been over. But in fact my kids did as well or better on the tests as the other fourth-grade sections in our school. I think that was because of the qualities of thinking and problem solving—of doing this kind of work. If the test is at all worth its weight, it's going to ask kids to do those same kinds of problem solving that my kids became practiced at.

Project-based learning is a challenge in this country, and it rightly has been criticized for being very fluffy. They spend weeks building a pyramid out of sugar cubes to show their understanding of ancient Egypt—which might be a lot of fun—but the kids don't learn anything doing it. So there has to be a mind shift in terms of how to design these projects so that they really are addressing content and skills that kids need to learn.

*How did you evolve this method of project-based learning?*

It started small. It started with an instinct toward doing cool stuff and then writing about it and thinking about it. I think my instinct was always to teach through projects. At first, I don't think they were very rigorous or tied to the skills as they later became.

A lot of the work I've done recently as a consultant has been trying to articulate the processes and strategies that go into this kind of work.

*It often seems that in creative endeavors one develops something first by instinct and only later is able to fully account for it and theorize about it—whether you're talking about an artist, a scientist, or a teacher.*

Yes. It's like a phrase I heard used by another educator—ready, fire, aim. A lot of it is jumping in and doing stuff and then figuring out how to make it better, how to describe it, and how to share it with other people.

*To go back to your aim of addressing the "poverty of gratitude," do you think your teaching has an effect on students in that regard? The tests can measure skills, but the shaping of attitudes is harder to measure.*

I think I had a significant impact in that regard. It is a real question about how you get any kind of evidence about that. One of the ways is through keeping journals, and it was always tremendously rewarding to read the kids' journals where they reflected on some service they had done or something they had taken for granted but now appreciated.

It's a challenge for teachers who have goals in terms of character development to find ways to measure whether we've made an impact or not.

*Teaching in one small town for a long time, you must have had a lot of contact with your students as they got older.*

It's exciting now because a number of students I taught are now teachers. I actually have a mentoring relationship now with some of them who are entering the classroom.

I've also been very curious about the long-term effect of the way we learned in my class. I brought the class who did the empty classroom project back together for a reunion when they were sixth graders. I asked what, two years later, had lasted? What followed was two and a half hours of the most fascinating educational conversation I had ever experienced in my life. Then that same group had another reunion when they graduated high school, and they once again reflected on what they felt they had learned. At that reunion, the most common sort of "amen" experience that they gave voice to was that learning doesn't have to do with school—it's just something that people do in their lives.

*Aside from your projects, what do you think were your keys to success as a teacher?*

I think it's something about seeing in all students their particular genius: something about their particular spirit, something that was fully formed for them even though it was trapped in a nine-year-old's body. It's about seeing the potential— well, "potential" is kind of a trite word—but just seeing qualities that are sometimes not at all represented by their behavior. So in miserable kids that are haughty or bossy you see qualities of leadership, or in people who are whiny and always complaining you see a depth of ability to turn suffering into something golden. I used to pray a lot about that, to always see what is the genius in each child that makes him or her absolutely unique. If I could practice seeing and talking to that part of them—and not just seeing the one with the snotty nose or the one who just slapped some other kid—it's like seeing into being the possibilities that I could discern in their spirit.

I can think of a number of kids who kind of descended into a kind of beasthood when they entered seventh and eighth grade, and then at some point they began to emerge, and they decided to become human beings. At that point they are able to reflect on themselves, and once the light begins to shine inward, they see two things. One, they see, "God, I was really a jerk." And two, "Wow, and he really liked being with me day after day." I've had several kids come back later and express that in one way or another to me. So there are those troubled kids whom you didn't think you were having any impact on, but then they come back later and you realize you did have an impact.

When you teach these kids, you have no idea what they are going to become. You don't know who's going to become a fireman or who's going to become a neurosurgeon or who's going to work in a factory. But what you hope for them is that whatever they become, they will somehow be able to see all of life, and learn the lessons of life, and relate that to bigger principles of who we are and how we are related to each other. That would be my hope for the kids I've taught: to see that everything we do is somehow connected, somehow there's a spirit behind it. That we need to be able to see through the earthly artifacts to the principles that are behind everything.

I was lecturing at a college a few days ago, and a woman asked me how, as a teacher, you keep a life. It sounded to her like teaching took so much time. And when you consider the statistic that after three years, 50 percent of the people who start to teach leave the profession, I realized that in my generation, we went into teaching because that was how we thought we could save the world. We had no trust for politics, no trust in religious institutions, and I think we saw the best way was to be training a new generation of people who could think in a different way—who could have compassion and stand for justice and equality and truth. And we went into it with that passion.

It's such hard work that if people go into teaching as they would any other job, if they don't have at their core this moral commitment, then they won't survive the challenges and the difficult work and the long hours it takes to succeed—particularly in challenging educational environments like urban settings, and with kids who don't have a lot of advantages. I sound like an old man now telling people, "Don't come into this profession if you just think it's a nice job and you like kids—because you won't last."

*You're right. It's a calling.*
Yes.

*"I ask for order. I pound on doors. I never give up."*

# Kathleen Engle

## MIDDLE-SCHOOL PHYSICAL-EDUCATION TEACHER

*Kathleen Engle has been teaching in Newcastle, Wyoming, a town of three thousand, for twenty-four years. She received bachelor's and master's degrees from Black Hills State University in Spearfish, South Dakota. She has received a number of awards for her teaching, including the Milken Foundation Educator Award and the Disney Salutes the American Teacher Award. She was Wyoming Middle School Physical Education Teacher of the Year in 1994, and in 2008 she was inducted into the National Teachers Hall of Fame.*

I teach sixth-, seventh-, and eighth-grade physical education: the basic skill movements, fitness concepts, and social behavior. We do two days of fitness every week, and for the other days go through a cycle of four units: we have nine weeks of sports, nine weeks of organized games, nine weeks of concentrated fitness, and nine weeks of outdoor activities.

*With regard to "social behavior," the middle school years seem crucial. Recently there's been a lot of attention given to the so-called "mean girls" phenomenon in middle school. Do you see that at your school?*

I think that it's a self-esteem issue. I think people who have to put others down or are mean to others don't feel good about themselves—so to me that's a self-esteem issue. I think that's everywhere in society, and adults have it too. If you constantly set good examples for students and give them guidance on their behavior, you can hold them responsible for their behavior. If they're being mean to someone, there's a consequence for their behavior.

*Are there particular ways in which you try to teach that?*

I'm famous for what we call "toe talks." These came in response to kids being mean to each other and not even realizing it, because it had become such a habit. So they can be in the classroom or the gym or even the locker room, and I have them stare at their toes and listen. We talk to them about their behavior, how it looks to others, and whether they realize what they're doing. Because they're staring at their toes, they can't play off of each other with the rolled eyes and the shrugs and touching each other. Because when they're looking at each other, they're not listening to me. But it really makes them think. So the toe talks have been very productive. Often kids will come back to me and say, "I really didn't realize what I was doing."

If the kids aren't getting along, I might have them do a team-building exercise where they have to work together to solve a problem. For example, it might be walking across a river (that really isn't a river) but you have to work together to get across the river. A lot of times you'll find the kids that have the most animosity toward each other actually work best together, because they're probably competitive with each other. But it makes them become more team oriented and think about others as well as themselves.

*Over the long run, are those kinds of exercises effective?*
I'm fortunate in that I have the kids over all three years, so I can definitely see the effect. There's a consistency of our programs and what we expect from the children. I just believe that if you hold them accountable, you set high expectations, and you keep demanding that those expectations be met, then they will rise to the occasion. They would rather do that than disappoint—if you gain their love and respect.

To me that's the key. They need to know you are going to set fair expectations and to realize that even when I get upset with them, I still love them. And I tell them that—that I'm upset at their behavior, not at them as a person. Young kids want you to hold a grudge and be mad at them, so then they can be mad at you and have a reason for their behavior. I believe we need to set the example and hold them accountable.

*You mentioned self-esteem. Are there other things you believe are especially key at this age?*
I believe parent involvement is huge at this age. This is the time when the child is trying to break away from the parent and the child is struggling with that. Kids want to go be with their peers, and mother and dad aren't actively involved in every movement. Parents play a huge role—as do teachers and any other adult they know and can trust.

*You teach in a very small town, a population of 3,000. Do you think that's a blessing, or do your students have most of the problems of young people in a city?*
I definitely believe our culture is a little different, but I also believe kids are pretty much the same everywhere, especially with the influence of the media. They see the same things as anyone in a city. So a lot of their acting out—talking back to adults, being disrespectful—I think a lot of that comes from media, from some of the computer games they play, and the aggressiveness of those. I think parents—and schools—need to play a role in monitoring that.

But as far as being a small town, maybe there's the advantage of—you know—I may see Johnny's parents at the post office that afternoon and address some issue, where I assume in a big city I would not. But I hope those city teachers are calling home and holding kids and parents accountable for the behavior of the child.

*We've talked about social behavior. What about the physical aspect of the physical-education curriculum? When I was in junior high, P.E. meant being sent out to the playground to run around on our own.*

I have fought very hard—as have many others I work with—to remedy the situation of the military-type physical-education classes: the roll-out-the-ball classes, the athletes-only classes. I really strive to bring the whole child in, to develop the whole child in physical education—mind, body, and emotions. It's been really hard to put the old-style P.E. approaches to rest, because we have to defend P.E. every day. I believe that if you set a good program, and you set it so that you are helping a child be a whole child, then our school district will support you much better.

In my program, my passion is fitness. I was an overweight child myself, and activities—especially sports—saved me. So I believe if we can bring our society out of its problems of obesity and diabetes through even just walking thirty to forty minutes a day, then I will at least have given kids tools for a lifetime.

A lot of the statistics show that by sixth grade kids have decided whether they like movement or not. So hopefully our program will never allow going back to the games of dodgeball or murder ball or whatever it was called—where children are eliminated and where someone is always left out. We provide activities and fitness for all body types, and we provide things that kids can take enjoyment in, so that it will become a lifetime activity.

To avoid the elimination games, we play what we call continuous games. So in a version of dodge ball, if a child is struck—and it's a foam ball—they then get to go to another part of the court for another kind of activity. So we make sure they're going all out for the whole thirty-five minutes. We have 100 percent participation, even by our special-ed students.

*So your classes are coed?*

We split only when we go to the fitness center, because we have found that for middle school kids, especially seventh and eighth graders, the girls will work harder when boys are not present. Their bodies are developing and they are just more comfortable in all of the movements if boys are not around. But when it comes to a mass game, they want the guys there. They want the challenge.

*Do you also teach about nutrition?*

We have a health teacher, but in P.E. we try to reinforce anything that they're teaching in health, so that students get a double dose of it.

*In much of the country there's great concern about the diets of young people. Is it a problem in rural Wyoming as much as it is in the cities and suburbs of the rest of the country?*

Definitely. It's always easier to grab junk food and the highly refined sugars and the high-glycemic-index foods. It's killing us—literally. We are trying very hard to provide the kids with the knowledge and the skills to refrain from junk foods. I think it's so important that we continue to fight the battle of obesity and insulin. It's just crazy what we're doing to our bodies through food. But it's also the production of food in general—with all the preservatives we're putting in our food, and the sprays we're putting on our food.

I think if we can establish areas where kids can get nutritious snacks through-out the day—which we're trying to do—and offer them salads and fruits and veg-etables, it will help. We also need help from the parents.

Also our physical-education program is so rigorous that halfway through their sixth-grade year they realize that we're serious about fitness, and that good eating is one way to help get fit. The elementary school sends home all kinds of informa-tional packets on nutrition.

*You've won a lot of teaching awards. As a teacher, what are your keys to success?*

I believe I'm innovative. I've always been a hard worker. And I believe that if you have a passion, you should go after it. I love change, I love seeing children become who they want to be, and hopefully I've helped them do that. I ask for order. I pound on doors. I never give up. I believe teaching is my calling, and I have no desire to do anything else than to continue to provide opportunities for young kids in the physical world, and hopefully to have them gain value from it.

I don't know that I'm the best, but I hope I'm an effective teacher. I want to be a teacher that makes a difference. I've come to realize that the middle school child really doesn't understand the message until they're older. I get many cards and let-ters years after, thanking me for teaching some skill correctly or making a student understand the value of exercise or the value of eating correctly. For middle school kids, they are so involved in growing that they're really not paying attention to you, so if you get those letters later on, you definitely know you've made a difference.

*And you mentor younger teachers . . .*

Yes, I have mentored probably twenty teachers, and they are like my extended fam-ily. Many of the teachers I have mentored call me all the time and ask me what they should do about something. I'm solution oriented and action oriented. I think they know that if they call me, we're going to find a solution.

*Was the mentoring in the context of a formal program, or did it just happen naturally?*

It just happened naturally. As a first-year teacher, I had the most amazing principal. And my mother was a teacher, my grandmother was a teacher, and both of my daughters are going into teaching. I believe that if you make the right things simple and the wrong things hard, you'll always do the right thing. I live by that, and I think people see that. Hopefully, I have sunshine above my head and that keeps the clouds at bay. I think people feel that, and I think that's how I've been able to mentor others. I have open arms and an open heart. Many times when I'm late for supper, it's because I've been talking to someone who needs an uplift, and it's usually a younger teacher. And I had great mentors, too.

*So many of the teachers I talk with have had at least one parent who was a teacher. As did I.*

I can remember my grandmother who taught in a one-room schoolhouse. She would take me with her and I would sit in the corner and watch. She had about twelve or fourteen students, all ages, and they came from ranches. She would stoke the fire and make the lunch and teach the kids. And kids would teach the other kids. I thought that was so amazing as I sat there.

When I think back about that, I believe I always knew that I was going to do what Grandma did. Also, I had a learning disability, and that's why I excelled in the physical realm. Later, I overcame some of those issues. I can remember Grandma saying to this one kid, "You need to go help little Johnny do his multiples, because he's struggling today." And that kid just popped up and went over to help the other student. It was just the most amazing thing. And in the physical world I get to do that because if some student is struggling with a skill, I can put a more highly skilled person with that student and he or she becomes the teacher. And that's always been something that I've loved to do.

*"Helping them to feel good at school is really important."*

# Deirdre Grode

### SEVENTH- AND EIGHTH-GRADE LANGUAGE ARTS AND SOCIAL STUDIES TEACHER

*Deirdre Grode teaches at the Hoboken Charter School in Hoboken, New Jersey. One of the cornerstones of the school is service learning. Students apply for the school and are then admitted by lottery. Enrollment is capped at twenty-two students per grade.*

*Deirdre has taught in Costa Rica and in the Bronx. She is in her seventh year at Hoboken Charter School. In 2007, she received the Outstanding Young Educator Award from the Association for Supervision and Curriculum Development.*

In my freshman year at college I volunteered to teach twice a week at a prison in Boston, where I taught classes in ESL and GED preparation all day. That's when I decided to become a teacher. Sometimes when some of my friends say they feel burned out from teaching, I say, "Teach in a prison." Because the students want to be in class; they realize they're in prison because they made bad choices—some of them around education—and they're very committed. I remember one of them once saying to me, "Keep piling on the homework, because we've got all the time to do it."

***And now you're teaching at a charter school.***

Yes. Before, I taught in a regular public school for one year. Now I teach at a charter school, so there's a lot more freedom for teachers to write their own curriculum than at regular public schools, where things are a lot more standardized. Especially since "No Child Left Behind."

Here we don't use regular textbooks. In language arts we read books like *Of Mice and Men* and *Macbeth*. We also do a lot of writing. In social studies I can do things like a human rights unit where I focus on the UN and NGOs [*non-governmental organizations*]. I take the students up to the UN. I do a unit on apartheid, and right now we're studying land mines around the world. I do projects on awareness building. Students research topics on land mines and become more engaged citizens.

One of the pillars of the school is service learning. So in language arts we read excerpts from novels like *The Kite Runner* and *The Breadwinner,* and in social studies students learn research skills, and they research some aspects of land mines such as the Ottawa Treaty. In language arts they write persuasive essays, and they choose from topics like "why the United States should or should not sign the Ottawa Treaty" or "why Americans should or should not care about land mines even though they don't affect us directly." So in doing that we are able to teach a number of skills and also encourage students to become more engaged citizens and participate in the process of being informed and effecting change.

Because of the freedom teachers have, we are able to keep really great teachers here. They don't want to teach at a regular public school where they're given scripts and a pre-set curriculum that would bore them and bore the students silly and allow for no creativity.

We still have the same accountability as regular public schools and our students have to take the same state tests, so you have to be sure to incorporate everything that the tests test. But at this school, teachers are respected more, and there's a trust that they'll figure out a way to incorporate the state standards. At some schools, I think administrators don't trust that teachers can figure that out.

### What is your own teaching style like?

I try to be adaptive to the students' needs, so what I teach one year may be different from what I teach the next year. If I see a student struggling with a concept, I might try to teach it in a different way the very next day. I like to have students working as much as possible. I think if I'm in the front of the room lecturing, they won't be as engaged. Of course, a few times a year I may end up lecturing for forty minutes because the kids are really engaged and there's so much information I have to get across. But then another day they're working for fifty minutes, and I'm just facilitating. So it can differ from day to day.

I'm not so rigid that I would need to stick to a plan that I created before—I'm always open to suggestions from students. And if I see that something is not working, I recognize that the problem might be with the way I've structured the lesson, and I might need to try something new.

I think the kids know that I care about doing a good job and about their success. They know that I hold high expectations for me and for them. When you set higher expectations, students work harder, and they want to meet those expectations. They appreciate that you respect their intelligence and their abilities.

*Do you have a wide range of abilities in your classes?*

Yes. We have a lot of special-needs students, but we also have a lot of students whose parents felt they weren't being challenged enough in the other schools. So we've got kids who are gifted and kids who have special needs all in the same class.

*How do you deal with that? In the books you mentioned,* Of Mice and Men *is more accessible, but* Macbeth *is a challenging read for a middle school student. In fact, it's not an easy book for most American adults to read.*

Right. With *Macbeth*, for example, I teach it in a way that's largely performance-based. We read the whole text, but we do a lot of activities around it and a lot of group work. Before we start each act, everyone has to learn maybe ten famous lines from that act, and everyone has to memorize their lines. We have this Macbeth doll that we pass around, and when a student catches the doll, they shout out their lines. Students can memorize one line—or if they can't, they can look down at their book—so then there's more of a familiarity with the language. Then they get into groups and predict what's going to happen in the next act and what kind of tone is being set. So things like that get everyone to some understanding before we start. As much as Shakespeare is difficult, plays are much easier for kids who struggle with literacy because there's less description, it's just dialog, and each character is short and to the point. So there's a lot of visual and performance parts to how we approach it. Two of the years it's been a special-needs kid who's played Macbeth and memorized all the lines.

I've also done *Night* [*Elie Wiesel's holocaust memoir*], and that's a difficult book, so I've given weaker readers *Maus* [*Art Spiegelman's graphic novel about holocaust survivors*]. Then we come together and discuss the themes that are found in both texts. What I've found is that the kids who read *Night* think that the graphic novel is really interesting and keep asking the kids who were reading it about it, and then they borrow it, and then a lot of the kids who read *Maus* end up borrowing *Night*. Then they ask each other questions as they are reading. So it works.

*What do you think is most essential about the middle school years as a stage of education and a stage of life for a young person?*

It's a really important age. They're experiencing so many changes and they're losing confidence and they're caring about new things. I think it's a really important age to capture their interest and make sure they're buying into school and the values you want them to have. Helping them to feel good at school is really important—to help them feel successful and smart. I think service learning is really effective at doing so because they are passionate and opinionated, and they want to go against the status quo. There are these controversial things going on in the world that they want to develop strong opinions about, and they want to fight for these things, and they see the relevance of their schoolwork for once. They may not realize that this is test prep or skill development, but they care about writing these letters or these essays that educated the community, so they're doing their best work. Engaging them with ways that build their confidence and getting them engaged with civic action is really important.

Some of the problems at that age—the teasing and the "mean girls" thing—come from feeling insecure. They're going through these changes, and they feel insecure, and so much revolves around looking cool—so we try to address it as much as we can, in homeroom and in classes. When we read *Of Mice and Men*, we talk a lot about trying to pull others down to build yourself up, and is that an honorable thing to do. We often look at Nobel Peace Prize recipients or we discuss who in history exhibited characteristics that we should try to adopt. I've heard kids say, "Oh my God, you're acting like Curly" [*a character in* Of Mice and Men]—so they can see the parallels.

*Have you changed much as a teacher since you first started?*
Service learning has been the biggest thing. I wasn't familiar with it before I came here. I was mentored in it, and now it has become the lens through which I create my lessons. Also, teaching just becomes easier. I've become more organized. Also, after you've taught for a while, you start to realize what will work and what won't. Now I'll see a new teacher experimenting with something and I'll realize it's not going to work, but I wouldn't have known that when I was new. You kind of just learn. . . .

*I know what you mean. Through experience you acquire instincts.*
Definitely.

*"A lot of the beautiful stuff is hard."*

# Paul Karafiol

### HIGH-SCHOOL MATH TEACHER

*Paul Karafiol teaches math at Walter Payton College Prep, a selective-enrollment public school in Chicago. Previously he taught at Phillips Academy, Andover, and Providence St. Mel School. He received his bachelor's degree at Harvard and his master's degree at the University of Chicago. He is a recipient of the Edith May Sliffe Award for Distinguished High School Mathematics Teaching given by the Mathematical Association of America.*

*We spoke on the campus of Walter Payton College Prep during summer break. He warned me that he didn't have any "big theories" about teaching.*

I find that if you present the math that's really cool and interesting, in the best way possible, the kids want to learn it. If you keep moving and try to make the class challenging and fun, so they're actually discovering and figuring things out every day, they like that.

**The key phrase there must be "cool and interesting." Not all math classes seem to earn those words. You probably had a couple yourself along the way. So how do you teach math in an interesting way?**

I think you have to back up one level. The first thing that's important is that you're teaching neat, cool mathematics—mathematics where there may be surprising connections or ideas that follow from one another. Maybe in a sort of predictable way, but it's not just the same old thing every day. You're not saying, "This is the fifth day we're going to talk about this topic that we talked about last year for a week and also the year before that for a week." Even if you're doing review, you've got to present it in a way that is going to make it fresh.

I think you've got to present the mathematics that you think is beautiful. I look at a chapter or a topic that I feel is important to teach, and I say, "What are the most beautiful ideas in this, what is the most interesting stuff in this lesson?" Then I say, "How can I bring that to my students?" Now, a lot of the beautiful stuff is hard. I think a lot of the time we look at students who are not at the very top, and we say, "They can't get this and so we're not going to teach it to them." So they end up not ever learning any mathematics that's beautiful. Then they hate mathematics. And we're surprised. If we taught English the way I think we teach mathematics, nobody would ever get to read a real poem or short story until they were a junior or senior in high school, and then we'd wonder why they hate reading so much.

So after you decide that this is really beautiful, the next question you have to ask is, "How can I make this accessible to my students?" That's a complicated question. What ideas does this theorem depend upon? What skills do my students have to be really good at on this particular day when I do this thing with them, so that they won't be stopped in their tracks because there's something they're missing? So you have to know really well what their strengths are and what their gaps are. You know some of that by teaching a course many years in a row. The first time you teach a course, you think, "Wow, that was really hard. I had no idea that some of my students would not be able to do that." So then the second time, you know that they don't know it, and a week ahead of time, you do a little activity where you practice it or you review it. Then the next year that lesson goes better.

The other thing is that through the course of the year you get to know your class better. Every class is different, so some things that my class may have a lot of trouble with one year they're not going to have trouble with another year, and vice versa.

Now I'm ready to actually answer your question about how you present math in a way that makes it exciting. Watching math is really boring. So I think you have to present activities and lessons that really get the kids thinking about mathematics, trying to develop their own ideas, to make some conjectures, to test their ideas, to make connections, to engage in reasoning, and to look for patterns. None of what I just said is "practice the same thing fifty times." Practicing the same thing fifty times is almost never successful—in my experience. There are teachers who can make that work, maybe, but for me, I feel like it's better to practice the same thing a couple of times over a bunch of different days and then come back to it in a month. I don't ever want to say, "Today we're going to solve fifty linear equations." Because either you get it or you don't get it early on, and if you don't get it, it's like being hit over the head with a blunt instrument, and if you do get it, a lot of practice isn't particularly interesting.

*Do students ever ask what you mean by saying math is beautiful? A sunset is beautiful—but math?*

They don't ask that—at least not of me directly—but they should. I get so excited about it, and I think that excitement conveys what I mean by saying it is beautiful. If a kid were to ask me that, I would say that mathematics has a certain economy so that you only need a few ideas to go from point A to point B. That it shows connections between things that might not have appeared connected before, that understanding those connections leads you to other insights, and then there's an "aha" quality that I couldn't even capture . . . that you look at something and say, "Wow. That is just so neat." And you have it on a smaller scale when you solve a problem, or on a larger scale when you suddenly understand a theorem or a proof of that theorem that you never understood before.

*Do you try to bring in real-world examples and physical embodiments of math? A lot of math can be done without reference to the real world.*

It can. I think the more ways you give kids to get into math, the better it is. Again, for me a lot of math is finding connections. So connecting different representations or different ideas together is intrinsic to doing math. So an origami way of folding a parabola isn't just a cute thing, but it helps you to understand what a parabola is. I always look for stuff that kids use their hands with, though it's not always applications.

*Do you ever feel, especially when teaching more difficult topics in math, that a student has a limit to his or her ability that you're bumping up against?*

I haven't encountered that much. There are definitely differences among students in how quickly they can absorb what's going on, but even saying that—it's a gross overstatement. It's not just that kids absorb things at different speeds, but one kid may be fast on one topic but slow on the next topic. Or it might be one single thing they don't get.

Sometimes when I talk to those students I tell them about what happened to me in the sixth grade. My father tried to teach me reciprocals. You know, 3/5, 5/3, multiply and you get 15 over 15, and it equals one. What's so hard about that? It's not complicated. And my students don't find it complicated. But I couldn't understand it. I was in tears because it made no sense to me. So when they hear that, it gives them hope, because I got past it.

Usually when I have a student who can't understand something, it's a function of my own impatience rather than a question of the student's ability.

When I first started teaching, I had more of a hard and fast answer to the question of what might be a student's limit of understanding. But now . . . I guess now I just don't find it a useful question to ask.

*So it's like a math teacher's version of Pascal's Wager. You're going to have faith that they can do it.*

Right. That's a nice way to put it. You have to go into class that first day with the deep belief that every student is going to learn a lot of great math that year. And if you don't believe that, the kids will figure out that you're not in it all the way, and they won't come with you. But if you really do believe it, they'll trust you.

*You said earlier that you're always trying to make things new and exciting. But if some students are slower than others on a given lesson, how do you keep the faster ones on their toes without leaving the slower ones behind?*

That's something I'm always trying to improve on. I don't think somebody is helped by having three days in a row of forty problems a day on the same topic. But I don't think it's wrong to give that person 120 problems on that topic over the course of a year—well, 120 might be a lot, but certainty 50 or 60 wouldn't be excessive on a topic that was really important.

Here's an example. The first year I was here, I was teaching Algebra I, and by the end of a lesson on graphing lines, 70 percent of the class could graph a line. But of course 30 percent couldn't, and that's a really important topic for freshman algebra. So every couple of days another line graphing problem came up, and I would pick the next kid (out of that 30%) that I was going to "fix." I would go to that kid and I would sit with him and we would work through it. And I might say, "Come by at lunch and we'll do a couple more." Then I'm up to 72 percent, and then a couple of days later I'd pick the next kid I was going to fix. So if you pick one every couple of days, the kid's not bored by it. And the day after you fix the kid, it's really great to look over at his or her face and the kid's like, "Wow, I can do it." And you choose an advanced problem that requires graphing lines, so the kids who can already do it are really thinking about the new issue, and not about graphing lines.

By including this review and trying to preview topics, I'm always thinking to myself, "What will they need to know a week from now, and what do I have to do today so they're ready for that lesson?" That keeps the pace moving without leaving some of the kids behind.

But I'm never satisfied with what I do in this regard. I feel a little uncomfortable giving these pat answers because I'd be the first person to tell you my class is not perfect in this regard.

*Though you teach mathematics, your undergraduate major and your master's degree were in philosophy. Has that affected your teaching in any way?*

It's influenced a lot the way I work with students. My fields in philosophy were ethics and logic. I think it's made me better at listening to students and more inclined to give students autonomy. I mean at one level I'm very autocratic—when you come into class, you must have your ID on. [*In the Chicago public schools, all students have to wear an identification badge.*] But at another level, I really want the students to own the mathematics. So there are a lot of classroom procedure things I don't really care about. What I care about is that the students are doing math, that they're listening to each other, that they're sharing ideas . . . if that's happening, I don't care so much about whether it's organized. If a lot of people are talking in their groups and it seems kind of raucous, then that's good.

I guess another influence is that a lot of the philosophers I read were by and large very suspicious of making big theories. And I don't have a lot of theories about education. I think a lot about what I do, but not in a "big theories" sort of way. I maybe don't read as many education articles as I should. If I go to an education conference, I just go to the sessions about mathematics as opposed to math education.

*So you're more inductive than deductive.*

It's funny, because intellectually, I'm a more deductive person. But I think it's hard to be a deductive thinker as a teacher—and maybe this is a theory [*we laugh*]— because, I mean, for any big theory, you have 120 counterexamples at any moment. You have all of these kids and not one of them exactly matches any theory you have about math education.

Here's an example. I just told you how important discussions are. I had two sections of the same course this year. And they were scheduled in such a way that I could teach one section one day and then reflect before teaching the other section the next. One of the classes was large and very talkative, and we had great discussions every day. I walked out of that class going, "Yes! This is why I'm a teacher! This is the best class ever." Even kids that didn't much like math would come out of class and say, "That was really fun, Mr. Karafiol."

The other class was smaller and had some very strong students, but everybody in the class was quiet. I told them why I wanted them to be vocal, but even by the end it was still quiet. Some days I felt like a comedian who was bombing. But this class did better on every test. Now this is a small sample, and it's hard to generalize, and there were lots of variables. But if I had a theory, it's that kids learn math best by discussing it. So what am I left with?

I teach one course where discussion is especially important. It's a course where I present ideas about the foundations of mathematics to juniors and seniors who really want to go another step. I said, "I'm presenting ideas," but that's actually wrong.

I adopted a method known as the Moore method [*named for University of Texas professor R. L. Moore (1882-1974)*]. I give the students a list of major definitions and theorems, and their job is to construct proofs for these theorems, and the classes consist of their presenting solutions to those problems.

On the first day of class I very deliberately sit on the student side of the room and I tell them that the reason I'm sitting there is that they're the ones who are going to do the math in this class. It's sort of my aspiration to do that in all of my classes. But in this class it's very appropriate—the kids are very advanced mathematically and they're very comfortable being up at the board and talking about mathematics. In other classes you have to bring students along to the point where they're willing to do that. In this class, they're there already. They are developing independence of thought, so that instead of relying on me to say this proof is good or this proof is bad, they can critique each other's work. My goal is to talk as little as possible, and when I talk it's mostly to ask questions.

We start out with number theory—which I describe to laymen as all the math you learned in third through fifth grade but your teacher never explained why it worked. And then we do the theorems that underlie calculus. Partly we're able to do this because there's no set curriculum; it's not an AP class where we have to cover a certain set of things. So if I give them a set of problems and it takes us three weeks to do them, that's fine. We talk about math that I think is incredibly beautiful and that the kids are really interested in. So their interests guide the explorations we make. It's a really fun class.

### Is there anything else you want to add?

We've talked about math teaching, but it's just a piece of what I do. When I went into math teaching, it was because I really wanted to work with young people.

I started an organization here five years ago where juniors and seniors run freshman orientation. That's one of the most rewarding things I do, and there's no math in it.

I love math and I love math contests, but if you ask me for my favorite memories of math contests, they're riding on the bus with the kids. Sometimes we have totally silly conversations about what counts as a bagel, and sometimes we have very serious conversations. A couple of years ago on an overnight trip to the state math contest, four boys ambushed me and the other math coach and dragged us into their room for "guy talk." It was really cute—they wanted to know how we got girls. It brings tears to my eyes now thinking of it. It was one of those things I think I'll remember most in my entire career. They needed someone to talk to about that and they saw me as someone they could talk to. That's incredibly validating. In addition to the ego boost—wow, they like me—I think I was actually useful. They all had girlfriends by the end of the year!

So that's the personal side of teaching, but in the big picture, it's important, because a lot of the kids I teach are never going to go on in math. Of course, they'll do math in college and I want them to be prepared. I would say that for my students, my goal mathematically is that their math ability will never be an impediment to something they want to do. More generally, I'd say that what I want for my students is that they grow up to be healthy and happy adults. And to be part of that is really a privilege.

*"It's about building trust."*

# Mike Auerbach

## HIGH-SCHOOL BIOLOGY AND CHEMISTRY TEACHER

*Mike Auerbach teaches biology and chemistry classes at Brattleboro High School in Brattleboro, Vermont. He teaches both on the regular campus and at the alternative school campus for students at risk for dropping out. He was awarded the CIBA Foundation Exemplary High School Teaching Award in 2008.*

I am the science teacher for our alternative high school, an off-site location for kids who have difficulty in the mainstream environment, usually for behavioral or psychosocial reasons. Also a lot of them have very poor skills, so they get sent to this school for about an eighth-grade curriculum, to remediate some of their skills, with the idea that they would return to the main campus and do better. But actually, most of them remain at the alternative school for their entire high-school career. I also teach regular and honors classes, but my strength is considered to be working with marginal students.

I am able to talk pretty successfully and pretty directly and candidly with teenagers. I'm a little coarser than the average teacher. I've been everything from a house painter to a waiter to a demolition man—and a lot more unsavory things [*chuckles*] at other times. So I guess I relate to them a little better than people who went to college and came right out and became teachers. They know that I'm telling it like it is, I guess.

I guarantee you that I'm the only science teacher in the state of Vermont who will play "your mom" with students.

*Your mom?*

It's the verbal game of insulting each other's mothers. Like "your mother is so ugly . . ." It's all in good fun. It comes out at the right time and we have some fun with it. I let them break the rules a little bit.

*What's the secret of being playful like that but also getting some real teaching done? Often young teachers struggle with that.*

That is a risk that I run every single semester, and sometimes I end up more on the bad side of that line than I would like. It is a danger of teaching the way I teach. But at the same time, I would say that usually they know when it's time for business; they know they have to do what they have to do. They do show respect.

One of the things I often do is tell them about myself or tell them a story. Almost every day, that's how we start. Or maybe I'll ask them about their weekend, or I'll ask if anybody has a good story to tell. Or I'll tell them a story—I've got a lot of stories and I've done a lot of things. What I remember from when I was that age is that we really liked to know about our teachers. We liked it when they revealed themselves as human beings. So I might tell them a story about when I was a teenager and had my first job and made a $2,000 mistake from just being stupid. Or when drinking and driving comes up, I've got a really tear-jerking, stop-you-in-your-tracks story that was part of my life. That's always how we start.

**Do you do that in all of your classes, or only in the class at the alternative school?**

That's really true of all of my classes. Now in the higher-level classes, we get down to business a little more quickly, because we have more to do. But the way I like to start class is to let them ease into it, to let them be themselves a little bit, talk to them, see what's going on—because it makes them feel more comfortable in the environment and less resentful for having to be there.

**Is the class at the alternative campus successful? By the end, have the students learned some science that will serve them well in life?**

The honest answer is no. The whole design of the program is to keep these kids from being dropouts. They take kids who have a 100 percent chance of dropping out and they put them in an exceedingly easy environment, where they can get up and make themselves an English muffin in the middle of class and sit on a couch. The only hurdles for them are to show up and not be extraordinarily disrespectful. And even at that, two-thirds of them will fail. They will get sent out of the building enough times or they'll show up stoned enough times that that's it for them.

The learning is all right. I make it as engaging as I can. I give them very hands-on stuff: Can you count the number of bugs you caught? Can you identify what kinds they are? Can we try to put them together into some kind of food web?

But no, these are not kids that reach for something and grasp it, and I'm not Jimmy Smits and this isn't a good movie. There's no soundtrack and there's no magic moment in which these kids decide to be present in their lives. And that's really unfortunate to watch. I make it more palatable and more engaging and more accessible to them, I think, than any teacher they've had—and they still fail to thrive.

The program really isn't designed to have them achieve greater success. There are a couple of students here or there who are just a couple of steps out of the mainstream, and they have some chance of succeeding. And some of them will have a positive experience in my class and go on to gain a little confidence—that has happened. But I'm not going to tell you that there's great success. What I do is keep these kids alive academically. I'll have one or two a year who will do well, and some will graduate—and that's worthwhile—but not many of them. It's not where I do my best teaching.

A lot of what I try to do is get them to think about their behavior day to day, because they're combative, and they're difficult, and they rationalize things to death. Most of these kids are white, and they want to be urban, and talk ebonically, and use the same slang they hear on TV. And they want to be gangstas, and they act like it.

I try to role model how a person acts—how a person who gets a paycheck and has worked there for eight years acts. For example, when someone says *no* to me, professionally or socially, I try really hard not to storm around and throw things and yell obscenities, because this is the sort of thing they will do, and I try to point that out. So even though I experience frustration, I will tell them what I did instead.

**Does teaching this alternative class have its rewarding moments, or is it mostly frustrating and depressing?**

In some ways I dread it as a semester-long prospect, because I know what will happen. Last year, out of ten students I began the semester with, two boys had been expelled by the end of the year, one boy went into drug treatment, and three of the girls became pregnant. So I dread it, because I know that despite my best efforts, it's going to be a disaster. You try to break it down into baby steps for them, and then you realize that even in baby steps there are ways to blow it if you have absolutely no dedication to being successful. If there's nobody at home who will wake you up in the morning, or bring you to school, or even ask you if you're doing your work; if nobody at home works—or has worked—for generations; if people at home are mentally ill, or just as drunk or stoned as you are, then there's not much chance of success.

But at the same time, as far as sitting around and just talking with them, they tend to be in some ways the wisest among all my students. The scales have dropped from their eyes as far as what reality is all about. They're very quick and very observational, and they keep you on your toes.

**With these kids at this campus, do you have any sense of how the cycle can be broken?**

The difficulty is that the cycle perpetuates itself generation after generation. It's not something that can be easily broken, and I don't have any great ideas. But my sense is that it would help if these kids developed useful skills before it's too late. You don't want to be a guy looking for a job who can't really do anything, and maybe has a criminal record besides. If these kids could learn to do something . . . I guess that's really the ticket.

The place to start would be teaching them how to control themselves and how to act around people. Their greatest deficit is that they don't take anything or anyone seriously—including themselves. They don't see themselves as having any potential and they don't see the legitimate world as having anything to offer them—and in a lot of ways it doesn't; it's already written them off.

The school wants to show on its "No Child Left Behind" records that their dropout rate is ten kids lower than it is, and that's what they spend that budgeted amount of money on—seeing that those ten kids graduate. They're not trying to make scientists out of any of those people; they're just trying to get them through with a certificate of completion. Which is not to say that they abandon them—they send the counselor out to talk to them about their feelings, and about drugs and alcohol. But the kids just play the person like a puppet. They think he's funny. So they say provocative things just to get him going, and then they laugh at him. So without these kids being in some sort of serious environment, that really offers them a reward at the end of really being somebody, you're not going to have any success with them. And most of them go home to the worst examples you can imagine.

So I don't know how you break that cycle. Maybe you break one kid at a time by modeling some sort of good behavior, just being a person to them. And point out to them that they could take their lives more seriously and that they really would get a reward for that.

*So let's talk now about your other classes at the regular campus . . .*
I would love that.

*You have been identified as a very successful teacher. What do you think are your keys to success?*
I try to use objects, events, and analogies to teach science. For any scientific concept that I'm trying to teach, there is something analogous either in a daily event or an object they're familiar with. So I might use the example of a student struggling to get out of class to discuss diffusion and osmosis, or I might have them do a little dance to learn mitosis. I might use a coffee cup full of forty-six labeled popsicle sticks to represent chromosomes. Or I might use Play-Doh, which seems silly, but the silliness of it gets them to focus. It's not that I'm doing happy playtime.

I have a big felt periodic table filled with cards that I can take off and put back on instead of just pointing to the periodic table and saying blah, blah, blah. That's not my original idea; it's something I saw in some other teacher's book on how to teach chemistry. So a lot of the things I use I've invented, and others I just pick up from other sources. I like to put things in their hands that they already have a sense of, that they already understand, and then use those things to teach them something new. They already know how a CD changer works, and if you can use that to show them how a protein is made in the ribosome, that's great. So I tell stories and use analogies and objects. A lot of it is just using an engaging style. For me, that's what works.

I don't think I have anything that I could write a book about, except for some of the specific things I've mentioned, but it's just my style. We like each other, we laugh with each other, and when it's time to listen, they do. I can get forty-five minutes of effective listening out of an eighty-seven-minute class, which is as much as anybody can realistically expect.

*Does your familiar and informal manner in the classroom ever make administrators nervous?*

Often I think to myself, "Boy, I hope no one mentions that conversation we just had to an administrator or a parent." And that's not because I was nasty or did anything unethical but just because something was a little racy or I allowed a little innuendo to fly around the room to get the point across—but it was effective. It made it a better class to be in for that period of time. I'd just as soon never have to defend it before the school board, but the students learn better for it. Hopefully they'll walk out thinking about science in a more interesting way because it was made more interesting for them.

When I first started, one of my colleagues said something to me that has stuck with me ever since. I was begging him for help. I was new and I was in over my head. I had no idea how to manage a class or design a curriculum or do anything. So I asked him for help and he basically shot me down. He said, "I've got nothing to offer you. You are your own gunslinger in there." And he walked away. But that's really true. It's you and thirty kids and what you make of it.

*How did you acquire your style of teaching? I assume trial and error was one important ingredient.*

Trial and error was *the* important ingredient. I did receive some very sage advice from my department head, and he did work with me regularly in my first two years. And I've taken some education courses along the way. But trial and error really is the thing. I have, through the years, gathered strategies and tricks and activities that work for me, and then discarded ones that don't.

I myself was not a top science student. What happened, though, is that in the course of taking it, I realized I was good at it. And ten years after I graduated from high school, I finally went to college in science. So I think it's important to help students identify when they do have talent and don't realize it—because that is a service. For a kid to realize, "Hey, I am good at science"—that's important. I had one student who lived in a trailer park and was basically heading nowhere, and I told her she was good and suggested she take a two-year radiology technician program at the local community college. And she's doing that now, and that's a tremendous thing for me.

If somebody wants to mention me in their Nobel Prize acceptance speech, that's fine, but what's important to me is helping students identify their talents and pointing out to them why they succeed and why they don't succeed.

Someone said that a successful teacher, like a successful coach, will, in front of an entire team, point out to a player, "Hey, you're not carrying your weight as far as this or that is concerned, and you need to work on that." There's no judgment—it's just calling it what it is. It's important, just like it's important for people to realize when they've done well.

The worst feedback in the world is a teacher who says, "Good job." Because that doesn't tell a student anything about what he or she did well. I like to point out exactly what a student did well. It might be that they're a C science student but they write clearly, and I like to point that out. And on the opposite side of the coin, I point out why they didn't say what they think they said.

What I feel I have to get most of my students past is the wall of frustration or the tendency to give up. So I think another important thing I do is talk them through that, walk them through that. They say, "I'm not good at math. If there's math involved, I can't do it." I say, "Yes, you can." I feel it's important to be engaging with them, because if they just see you as somebody who's droning on, they're not listening to you in that attentive, in-the-present way that you need in order to follow you through a complex, but ultimately rational, process. You're walking them through a minefield, but most of the mines they've thrown in front of themselves (like "I can't do math"). And you have to walk them through it.

The style I have allows me to get them to follow me through that minefield because they understand what I'm talking about, and that I'm using real words and trying to break it down for them. It's about building trust. If they trust you—that you're not just droning on to hear yourself talk, that you're really starting where they're at and trying to walk with them step by step—then they just might take the steps. And then you have that moment that every teacher talks about, that "aha" moment. Nothing's more satisfying than that.

*"I am an opportunity provider."*

# David Lazerson

## SPECIAL-EDUCATION TEACHER

*David Lazerson teaches special education in the Broward County, Florida, public school system. He holds bachelor's degrees in divinity and American studies and master's and doctorate degrees in education. He has taught for over twenty years in New York and Florida. He has received numerous teaching awards, and he is widely published in the field of special education. In 2008, he was inducted into the National Teachers Hall of Fame. In conversation, he exudes warmth, generosity, and boundless energy.*

I work with students from preschool to age twenty-two. These are individuals with what we call "profound special needs": students with various forms of autism, Down syndrome, cerebral palsy. Some are in wheelchairs; many are completely non-verbal. There's another group referred to as "medically fragile."

A lot of times these kids are sort of in their own world. When they come into the classroom, some sit in a chair and start to pick up things and play with them. Some might lie down on the floor on mats because they feel more secure there. Others walk around and don't like to sit down. A bunch are in wheelchairs.

Sometimes you wonder what, if anything, is getting in there. It's a very challenging, but a very rewarding, kind of work.

Before I can even think about academics, there are issues like how do they feel: Are they hot, are they cold, are they tired, are they angry, are they upset? Are they happy, are they sad, do they have to go to the bathroom? So many issues that we take for granted, but these are huge issues between the kids and the caretakers who work with them. So it's a real challenge.

*You teach music to them . . .*

My use of music did not really start as a conscious decision. I just happened to bring my guitar to school one time, and I was just doing kid songs with them, and I had passed out some percussion instruments. These were teenage students with profound autism. They responded pretty well. The principal happened to come by, and later she said, "Wow. That was the only time I've seen so many really engaged in a group activity."

So I started doing music every day, and pretty soon other teachers in the school started bringing their kids by for music. The principal then said that she wanted me to start doing music for the whole school, so we set up the music program. With her giving me the green light, the creative juices started flowing.

She was a remarkable administrator. It's a rare breed of administrator who will figure out what your strengths are, then let you go with them. I felt able to find my niche and flourish under her.

Before, I was at a school in another district, and the young assistant principal felt threatened by me because I had been teaching over twenty years and I had a Ph.D. I could care less about that, but he felt threatened. He didn't know a blithering thing about special ed and special needs. So we always butted heads. At one point he said to me, "You are the worst teacher I've ever worked with." I eventually resigned from the school district in order to move on and see what else was out there.

Then this job came along, and it was a godsend. That showed me that sometimes you just have to take risks. My resigning was big thing; it meant that I was jobless for four or five months. You begin to question yourself. But now I feel like I've died and gone to heaven.

I'm a rare breed, having a Ph.D. in this system as a teacher. Sometimes people ask why I don't become an administrator. I'd make a lot more money. But I tell them that my love is not sitting at a desk and pushing a pencil or going to meetings—I hate meetings. I love working hands-on with the kids. That's my first love.

*Concretely, what is your teaching like? What are some of the things you do with music?*

My biggest challenge was—and *is,* because it's an ongoing challenge—to find ways to get the students involved. For the most part, they really seem to be stuck in their own world. The challenge is how to get them to make meaningful connections with what's outside of them and to participate more. One of the things that I've found to be phenomenally successful is music. If you could put this in a formula, it would be this: music equals magic. Music has an effect on certain areas of the brain, and it helps the kids to focus better.

So I went to our tech person and I said, "I've got lots of kids with very poor motor control. But they can operate a head switch or a knee switch. Help me so that when they hit that switch, a drum is going to activate." Some of the stuff we made, and now there's even some commercially produced stuff. So now when a kid hits a switch, an arm will go up and down and move a shaker or a tambourine, or activate a drum machine. Then I tried the same thing with lighting effects.

Now if you come into my room, you would see maybe twenty different switches. So you push a button and music will come on, or drums—or a bubble machine will activate. So here are students who before would just sit in their wheelchairs like blobs, or would come to the table but would not interact, and suddenly they're pushing these buttons.

For some of them, it takes a while because they're just learning cause and effect—they hit a switch and lights come on. Kind of funky, psychedelic lights. They realize, "Wow. When I hit the switch, something cool happens."

So I taught the kids a couple of songs. I got on my guitar and they played along using their switches—adaptive switches, they're called. I got the speech therapist to help some of them learn American Sign Language. These are basically kids that are non-verbal. And they'll get up there and perform. I've developed PowerPoint presentations for each of our songs. So our concerts are now a multi-sensory experience for people in the audience, because it's a multi-sensory experience for us performing. The kids are activating light shows and drumming effects from their wheelchairs. So every time the kids in their wheelchairs hit a switch, a different image comes up on the screen. We now have wireless switches. One kid uses a head switch, and one uses a knee switch.

Let's say I'm singing, "I can see clearly now, the rain is gone. Look all around, there's nothing but blue skies . . ." They hit the switch at that point to make the blue skies come on the screen. Some of these kids have normal intelligence, but because they are non-verbal and have little motor control, you'd never know it until you take the time to figure it out. Other kids are much lower functioning, and they just know that every time they hit the switch, something happens. And there are times when it doesn't matter what's coming up on the screen, as long as it changes every three or four seconds. Even those very low-functioning students can do that and run a slide show. So we have live music, a visual presentation from the computer that the kids control—and so the kids comprise a performing troupe. By now we've got a repertoire of fifteen songs.

I had a girl this past year, someone with what is known as profound autism. She would come and sit in the back of the room. She would rarely say anything—maybe one or two words. She was mostly in her own world. Sometimes she would suddenly scream out something. So I gave her a microphone, and she started to sing, word for word, a Disney song, "A Whole New World." Her pronunciation wasn't great, but I recognized the song right away. The teachers and aids in the room—our mouths just fell open. This was only two or three months ago. Since that time, she has performed at our student talent show. I play the music in the background and she sings these two songs that are musically complicated. So where had the problem been? The problem was with us, the teachers, who did not know she could do that. A lot of the time we, as teachers, put these kids into a box. We make a list of their limitations and we begin to internalize this. We teachers in special ed have this saying, "Labeling is disabling." But sometimes we are the worst offenders.

We've taken them to senior centers and other schools. We did two shows at the Center for the Performing Arts to over a thousand people. They're like heroes when they perform at these places. Kids will come up and ask for their autographs. They have an honesty about them, a sweetness that really touches other people. They're so inspiring. It was cool to see their growth. Some had been too shy to get in front of anyone and do anything, and now they've become complete hams. It's been an incredible thing for their self-growth and self-confidence.

One of my mottos is, "There's nothing special about special education. It's just good education." All of the things that work in special-education work in regular education. It's figuring out what works best for each child, how to motivate kids. And how to get them involved.

I had a great professor in my master's program in special ed. I remember the day he wrote on the board: GOK. He said that when we've picked apart this kid; when the parents, psychiatrists, the teachers have had their input; and the principal, the behavioral specialists have all had their input; and they've all decided this is where the kid is at, this is what the kid can do, and this is what the kid can become, just remember GOK: God only knows.

### *Your teaching stands as a testament to that.*

Once I got this idea—I don't know how I ever got the school to agree to it—of bringing teenagers in from a detention home to tutor our younger special-ed kids. These were kids who had been told for years, "You can't be responsible. You cannot give to others. You're just takers. You're just society's rejects." Suddenly, we're saying, "We're giving you responsibility. We're putting you in the position of being a teacher, and these are going to be your students." It was a pilot program that started with three teenagers from the detention home. They had to be driven and their detention officer had to stay in the room with them because he was afraid they might make for the door and run. Eventually, these kids earned the ability to take the bus or ride their bike to the school on their own. I remember I had this one kid. One day there was a terrible storm, and I figured he wouldn't be able to come that day. He rode his bike and arrived at the school soaked to the bone, saying, "I can't miss teaching." These three eventually got out of the detention system by being tutors for my special-ed kids.

### *How did you get the idea to do that?*

When I graduated college, I went to a rabbinical school and got a bachelor's degree in divinity. I remember when they were giving me a tour of the campus, I went into this one big room. There were tables there, people had books open in front of them, but it was really loud, man, really loud. I asked what this was, and the tour leader said it was known as the "house of study." In Hebrew, it's *beit midrash*. It literally means the house of study. He said, "I guess in English the best translation would be the library." But the library was a place where you're quiet, and this place was noisy. He explained that the effective Jewish system of learning was one-on-one peer learning. It's called *chavruta,* the term for friendship. So it's a friendship way of learning.

At this school, let's say you have a class for an hour. For the next two hours you learn with your colleague, your partner. It's much more interactive. I went from learning maybe eight hours a week in college to learning eight, nine, ten hours a day at the rabbinical school. I would wake up in the middle of the night so happy with how much I was learning. Later I thought, if this could work with me, it could work with anybody. Because before that, I had been turned off to learning. I just did enough to get by. I got low 80s and I was happy with that. It drove my parents nuts. I was bored, I was unmotivated—but hey, I was passing. In rabbinical school, I attributed the fact that I was learning so much and enjoying it to this system of learning, this peer-interactive learning.

After rabbinical school, when I went to get my master's degree in special ed, I decided I wanted to try it with kids in the public school. I went on to use it with students with behavior problems as well as with those who are withdrawn—both the hyperactive and the hypoactive—and it worked really well. I used the same technique with high-school students at risk for dropping out. These were students with horrendous attendance and nothing was working with them. I used the peer-interactive learning with them—I had them tutoring students a few years younger, and it worked phenomenally well.

This is a system where the teacher is not so authoritarian with the learning—not so much the attitude of, "I am the almighty giver of knowledge and you're just the sponge here to absorb it." To me, that's the old-school, military model that a lot of administrators use against teachers. There's no trust. And that's the way some teachers run their classrooms. But if you put students in charge of a section of the learning, it means the teachers have to relinquish control a little bit. But more happens when that takes place. The kids turn on to learning. The students respond to being given responsibility, to working with others. When we let loose and give up a little bit, I think so much more is able to happen.

So I leave you with that, my brother.

# 2 | *Teaching in the College Classroom*

*"Learning is not a spectator sport."*

# Eric Mazur

## PHYSICS PROFESSOR

*Eric Mazur was born in Amsterdam and educated at the University of Leiden. He came to Harvard to do a postdoc in 1982, and two years later he joined the faculty. He is currently the Balkanski Professor of Physics and Applied Physics at Harvard. He is a world-renowned researcher who has made significant contributions in spectroscopy, light scattering, the interactions of laser pulses with materials, and nanophotonics. He is the author or co-author of over two hundred scientific publications and holds twelve patents.*

*Professor Mazur is also renowned for his work on teaching methods in physics and the sciences. He has written a book on teaching (*Peer Instruction: A User's Manual*) and given workshops on teaching across the country and around the world.*

**From what I've read of you, you were a highly rated lecturer at Harvard, probably imitating your former professors who had lectured you, but then you underwent a paradigm shift and developed a new way of teaching physics.**

You hit the nail right on the head when you said I was basically emulating the people who taught me. I was appointed as an assistant professor at Harvard in 1984, and I got the big premed physics course. They are basically premed students who do not want to learn physics. They were there because they had to be. I never asked myself how I was going to teach the course. It was clear—I would do what everybody does and the way I had been taught, never even questioning whether that method works or not. In hindsight, I think there are many holes in my own education because that method doesn't work.

So I started teaching and the feedback I was receiving was extremely positive. I got very high end-of-semester ratings. And my students did very well on their assignments and tests, so obviously I was a very good teacher. Then in 1990, I came across a series of articles that claimed that students learn very little in introductory physics courses. It had a test that consisted of twenty-nine questions, and they showed that if you give the test at the beginning of the semester and again at the end of the semester, the score hardly changed.

I thought, "No way. Not my students." So I gave that test to my students, and when the test had been completed and I looked at the results, they were nowhere near what I wanted. So that was the first sign that my students, in spite of doing well on my assignments and giving me high ratings, were not really learning. They were doing rote memorization and regurgitation. They were coping with the assignments without internalizing any of the information—in one ear and out the other.

One of the things you learn as a scientist is the value of data. Here I had data that disproved my belief that I was a good teacher.

*Can you give an example of one of the questions on that test?*

Most students taking introductory physics can recite Newton's third law. It says that if two objects are exerting forces one on one another, the force on one is equal in magnitude but opposite in direction to the other. In other words, if I push on the wall, the force is equal to the force the wall pushes back on me.

On that test there's a question that says a truck and a car collide head on. Is the force of the heavy truck on the light car larger than, equal to, or smaller than that of the small car on the heavy truck? The car will get dragged back, while the truck just slows down. The effect on the car is much bigger than the effect on the truck. The forces are the same, it's just that the mass of the car is smaller and therefore the effect is bigger. A large percentage of the students—at Harvard, in spite of being able to recite Newton's third law—stated that the force of the truck on the car was larger than the force of the car on the truck. So they can do the physics in an abstract way, but when applying it to an everyday situation, they failed to make the connection.

*Wait. I think I'm failing this too. I seem to remember from my own intro physics class that F=ma. Isn't the mass of the truck much larger?*

You're correct. So for a given force, if you make $m$ larger, then $a$ becomes smaller. So bigger mass, smaller acceleration. When the two collide, if one has a larger mass, the car will be dragged backward and the truck will just slow down.

This is stuff that gets covered in the second week of class, and what you cover afterward builds on it. So for students at the end of the semester not to understand this means they haven't been able to follow anything that came after the second week. And the fact that they were able to solve problems just indicates that they were following recipes, without any correct mental model of how the world actually works.

So my data had disproved that I was a good teacher, and I struggled with that for a while, wondering if maybe I should just teach graduate courses. I wondered if that test was bad, but after some time I concluded that it was my test that was bad, because it allowed students to pass the test by mindlessly applying a recipe. But that's not what science is about.

That's when I realized that the culprit was not the test, nor the students, but the way I taught. In spite of my high evaluations, I was a pretty lousy teacher. At first I didn't know what to do about this, because there was nothing in my experience that indicated a solution to this problem.

But then the solution appeared serendipitously on my doorstep—not quite my doorstep but in my classroom. I had been worried that my students would find that test too simple because it didn't involve any math. But they didn't regard that test as simple because they knew they hadn't done well. In fact, the end of the term and the final exam were coming up, so they were actually concerned. They asked me to organize a class to explain these questions to them. I booked a classroom at night and I started answering the questions. When I got to the truck question, I explained it as well as I could, I made a drawing on the board, and when I looked around, the students looked totally confused. I asked for questions, but they were so confused they couldn't even verbalize a question. I explained again, and this time I thought I'd nailed it, but again I saw many confused faces. I thought, "Why isn't this going in their brains?"

I knew that about half the class understood it now, so on the spur of the moment I did something that even now I don't know exactly why I did it. But I said, "Why don't you turn to your neighbor and discuss it with your neighbor?" Something happened in my class that I had never seen. The classroom erupted. Everyone was talking: the car this, the truck that, gesticulating . . . they wanted to understand. So after a few minutes of this, they had it figured out.

And I thought, "Wow. I've got to find a way to incorporate this into my classroom."

I had been lecturing for years, two hundred students in a class, and when I would pause to ask if there are any questions, there would be stony silence.

If you and I are two students in a class and you are trying to explain it to me, you may do a better job than the course professor for the following reason: you have only recently understood it, whereas the professor learned this years ago. Because the professor is the expert, it may be difficult for him to understand the difficulties the beginning learner faces. But the student may know what the difficulties are—what the conceptual roadblocks are—and how to avoid them.

So the next year I taught that course I said, "I'm going to teach by questioning rather than telling." That's not such a surprising idea; Socrates said that over two thousand years ago. I like to think of education as two things. One, education is a transfer of information. That's why we have amphitheater seating. Before books became a commodity, the only way to transfer knowledge from one generation to the next was to lecture. But is education just the transfer of information? No, it isn't. It's much more. As a student, you have to take that information and assimilate it: make sense of it, connect it to what you already know, build mental models. It's not just storing facts in your head, especially in the sciences.

If I look back at my own education, I think that most of the learning took place outside the classroom. I went into the classroom and got the information, but then I wanted to figure it out. But then I became a physicist; most of my students at Harvard are premeds or engineers. They don't want to be physicists. They don't have the time and the energy to figure it out.

If you see education as, one, the transfer of information, and two, the assimilation of information, and you ask yourself which of those two steps is the hardest, I think we all agree that it's the second one. Information is very easily gotten—from the internet, from printed material—you name it. So we should really take that information-gathering stage and throw it out of the classroom. Since you have a humanities background, this will make sense to you. If I taught Shakespeare, I wouldn't go into class and open the book and start reading the play to them. I would have assigned them to read the play for that day. But that's not what we have done in the sciences. We basically read them the book, which is a lot less interesting than Shakespeare.

So I decided that I was going to throw that information-gathering stage out of the classroom and focus on the assimilation. I now tell my students to read before coming to class and then to tell me what parts of the chapter they found difficult. So the night before class, I get on the web a list of what they found difficult. The next day in class I don't explain those parts to them; instead, I say, "Some of you had this question so I'll give you a minute to think about it." I usually phrase it as a multiple-choice question so I can quickly poll them. Usually they have clickers in the class, but you could also use a show of hands. Then I know where the class as a whole stands on the question. I try to aim the question so that about half get it right and half get it wrong. Then I say, "Try to find someone around you who has a different answer and try to convince them of your answer." And the one who is right is more likely to convince the one who is wrong. I call this method peer instruction. So the students teach one another.

There is continuous engagement: there is reflection, commitment, argument, and the recommitment—because after two or three minutes of discussion, they vote again. There is also continuous feedback to me. I don't have to wait until the exam to find out how they're doing. In a way that is non-threatening and is not part of their grade, they can continually assess their own knowledge. It allows me a flexibility, because I find out if we need to spend more time on a topic or whether I can move on to the next one.

So that's the essence of how I've taught since 1991, and I've never looked back.

*Did you ever get out that old test that started all of this to see how they do now?*
Of course. They tripled the gain. By gain, I mean the difference between how they did on the test on the first day and how they did at the end.

Thousands of instructors have now adapted this method—teachers of chemistry, psychology . . . I have been flabbergasted by how this method has taken on a life of its own. People asked for materials, so in 1996 I wrote a book on this method [*Peer Instruction: A User's Manual*] and then the thing took off beyond my control.

*Do you use this method in your classes other than introductory physics?*
Yes, because people learn so much more when they're engaged. You don't learn how to play the piano by watching someone play. You have to do it yourself, play scales and sweat over it and move your fingers. It's the same with learning any discipline. Learning is not a spectator sport. You've got to do it.

Now I've said that education is the transfer of information followed by assimilation. I focus on the assimilation, but that assumes that the students can get to the information. But if I teach a very advanced graduate course where there are no books or papers available, then I have no choice. So I have to give them the information before we can work on assimilation. I teach at a summer school in Italy every other year where there are seventy participants. Thirty-five are professors and thirty-five are graduate students and postdocs. We talk about advances in my field of physics, which is optics and lasers. If you're a lecturer there, you give seven lectures, and for the rest of the two weeks you sit in the audience as a participant listening to other people's lectures. I noticed that it was really hard for me to listen to people talk for so long. And if I derailed in hour two because something was said that I couldn't follow, then the remaining five hours would be totally lost on me. So I might open my laptop and catch up on e-mail. So I started using my new method there, and I did it with some trepidation, because these were not students but my colleagues. But it worked beautifully.

*It seems we've been talking about getting human beings to understand what other human beings understand. But in science we arrive at that point where there's the quest for new understanding. Civilization depends upon that—for everything from convenience devices to cures for terrible diseases.*
Absolutely.

*At that point, is the teaching different? How does one teach scientific creativity? Or can it be taught?*
How do you teach musical creativity? I really think that artistic creativity is not too different from scientific creativity. In all of those, I think you learn by doing, not by being told. Science is really looking for underlying laws that explain a lot of different, disconnected things. If you explain something here in the universe and then you see something that happens over there that looks very different, they may both obey the same principle. You don't need to explain this separately from that; there's one reason for both. That's the beauty of science.

So the creativity in science lies in discovering these deep unifying patterns. That type of creativity consists of some pattern recognition first of all, but also some thinking skills that can be developed. I think every human being possesses these thinking skills. You don't have to be a scientist to have them. You only have to observe children at play or doing a science project in kindergarten to discover that every human being is a little scientist who wants to understand how the world works. People are interested in magic—why? Because it appears that things are happening that they cannot explain. But unconsciously, we're always thinking, "He must be doing this or he must be doing that," and we want to find out because we know there can't be real magic. Every human being has the innate drive to rationalize the world and understand the things around us. That can be taught, but it's a thinking skill. By asking students questions in class, and asking them to reflect and then talk to one another, you're basically training those thinking skills. The thinking skills are much more valuable than physics per se, because the students in my class are premed. Who cares if they remember Newton's laws? It's not going to make them better doctors. On the other hand, having good thinking skills is important—so that when they see a seriously ill patient but haven't seen those exact symptoms before, they can analyze what they're seeing and draw a logical conclusion. And that can make the difference between life and death, right?

*It seems as if the motto of your method might be "learn by doing."*

I would rather say "learn by thinking" than "learn by doing." I'll tell you why I'm making that distinction. Going around the country talking about science education, I see that a lot of people are talking about "hands-on" activities where students get very prescriptive instructions of what they need to do—you know, pour this into that, turn this meter to that and write down the number. That's very hands on, but it's brains off. It should be brains on.

I had to change my own labs to make them more discovery-based: here's some stuff; figure this out. I found that those labs were much more frustrating for the students, but the results were much more lasting because, as one student said, "Once I've figured something out, I've figured it out for the rest of my life." Not only does it build confidence—*I* figured it out; no one told it to me—but you know that if you figured it out once, you can figure it out the next day.

In kindergarten and elementary school, you see a lot of activities where students figure things out on their own, but then in middle school and high school we go to a very prescriptive way of teaching and there's no more figuring it out. There's just cramming the information in.

I have students who come to my class and they are very disturbed by having to figure it out. They'll write evaluations at the end of the term where they say, "Professor Mazur is not teaching us anything. We have to learn it all ourselves."

I no longer see myself as the "sage on the stage." I'm the "guide on the side." I help them learn, but I cannot do the learning for them. The best I can do is coach them and create an environment that is maximally conducive to learning.

*So many teachers worry about "coverage." Do you cover less with your method?*

I probably used to cover more, but it didn't stick, so what good is it? I have discovered that I have to reduce what I cover, because I was trying to cram in way too much information. Now I find that much more sticks. So which is important—how much I cover, or how much stays with my students?

*"If you don't love teaching, you ought to be doing something else."*

# Ellen Peffley

## HORTICULTURE PROFESSOR

*Ellen Peffley has taught horticulture classes at Texas Tech University since 1984. She is widely published in her field, and she has received numerous teaching awards, including the Chancellor's Outstanding Teacher Award in 2005.*

Horticulture is a discipline within agriculture. Most people think of agriculture as being field crops: cotton, sorghum, wheat, and things like that, with tractors and huge equipment. Horticulture is more of an applied botany or an applied biology where we deal with vegetable crops or fruiting crops or ornamentals.

What I do in my classes is give the students the basic science and then apply it to various crops. I introduce them to the various disciplines within horticulture: vegetables, pomology [*fruits*], and ornamentals. My goal is to proselytize, because while I would love for them to be horticulturalists, more than that I want them be educated, because a lot of our laws in Congress are made by people with no experience in agriculture. I want them to be informed citizens when they leave my class.

The Principles of Horticulture class is a four-credit-hour class that meets three hours of lecture a week, and two hours a week in the lab. We try to have the labs correspond to the lectures. The labs are structured so that they can take the science they have learned in the classroom and apply it. They learn to propagate plants by seed and by asexual cuttings, they make bonsais, they make topiaries, they learn about transpiration [*water evaporation from plants*]. We have a hydroponic lab [*growing plants in nutrient solutions rather than soil*] where they grow and harvest cucumbers. The latter has been part of a NASA grant I've had for a number of years.

I also teach other classes. I teach a vegetable crop class, for example, where they learn more about vegetables than they probably thought existed. I take them to farms. The students get off campus and go beyond the textbook. We see cucumbers being harvested mechanically and processed. We go to watermelon growers and squash growers. They see people harvesting, and so they gain an appreciation for the labor that is required, and the specialization of each crop in terms of how it's grown. In that class as well, we talk about society and politics—because immigration is such a big issue now, especially in horticulture, because it's so labor intensive. In that class, fieldwork is a major component. So they not only learn about the plant scientifically, but they learn about the industry as well.

I've never taken a poll, but I would guess that 90 percent of my students do not come from agricultural backgrounds or intend to go into agriculture. Most of them are urban kids. The ones who do come from an agricultural background are more than likely those that come from a large farming practice—that would be growing wheat or cotton or something like that. Very few have come from a horticultural background.

*In recent years there has been increasing attention to food, especially its nutritional and health value. Has that impacted your teaching?*

It's impacted the content of my teaching, yes. Style, no. For the past ten years or so I've facilitated a course on phytochemicals. Those are plant-produced compounds that are used by the body in ways other than nutritional. The class on phytochemicals is quite an advanced class, and it has a lot of chemistry in it. We study the clinical aspects of how antioxidants work, anti-tumorogenic compounds, things like this.

And then in the lower-level classes we just introduce them to the basic compounds and how to choose foods based on color—the most intense the color, the more healthy they are for you. I bring that into my class always, because they do need to know how important it is to have a good diet. Many of our students don't. For example, in the lab where we grow cucumbers, some of them have never eaten a cucumber. All they eat are hamburgers and French fries. They taste cucumbers and decide, "Oh, these are good." Then they learn that not only do they taste good, but they're good for you. We used to have a billboard advertising watermelon in Lubbock that read, "Have you had your lycopene today?" So they learn how lycopene is good for you—men especially, since it reduces the risk of prostate cancer. Students say, "This is really cool. We're going to start eating our tomatoes and watermelon." So it has impacted the students.

*What are some of the things you think of as keys to success in your teaching?*

I had very good teachers myself, so first off, I credit my very good teachers. And one thing I was taught is to try to answer every question positively. And that's something that I have tried to do.

So if I ask them a question, "What do plants need?" and someone answers, "Oxygen"—well, as far as making photosynthesis, that's the wrong answer. But instead of saying, "No, that's not right," I turn it around and say, "Oxygen is used in respiration, but what else would plants need to make sugars?" So I lead them to realize for themselves what the correct answer is. So I try to answer positively. That's something I was taught, and it's something I try to do.

*Other tricks of the trade you have devised?*

I don't allow hats in my class. And that's a big deal because girls now wear baseball caps as well as boys. And in ag school, you've got boys wearing cowboys hats as well. Years ago, if a man was wearing a hat, he would take it off in the presence of a woman. I began to see that students don't have social courtesies any more. So part of what I do in my class is teach etiquette. And part of that is that they don't wear hats in class. I tell them that if they don't like it, they can drop the class and take something else.

Another thing that I learned from one of my old professors at New Mexico State was to learn the names of the students. I teach lecture sections that have around 100 or 120 students, and I make it a priority to learn all their names. I have a seating chart and I take attendance every day. I try to at least know their names and maybe something else about them.

In my freshman class—the Principles of Horticulture class—I give quizzes frequently, and they are given at the beginning of the class. The quizzes are not meant to be punitive but to reinforce something that we had or to make them think about something I am going to be lecturing on that day.

So I track attendance, and for those who miss a quarter of the classes, I write them a letter and tell them that they're going to be dropped from the class unless they come in and talk to me. Almost always the students will make their way in and say, "I'm sorry, I didn't know I had missed that many." I give them an analogy: "What would happen if you were working. Would your employer allow you to miss that much? Well, this is your job, and you have to decide if you want to work at school or not." I've had students who have told me that they've never had a professor who cared enough to call them in and say, "You know, you need to get your act together and start coming to class."

Hopefully it's made some of them more successful students at college. I do that only for my freshmen. But I teach them that that's a life skill—you show up. And if you don't show up for class, you're already failing.

### *Have you seen changes in the students over your twenty-four years as a teacher?*

Their skills are not as good. Their writing and speaking abilities degenerate every year. It's really alarming how many students can't write a paragraph. They can't write complete sentences. I think our students today don't write as well or comprehend as well as students twenty years ago. They expect everything to be given to them. They'll say, "You don't have an outline for us to study?" I say, "No, I've given you everything in lecture." So I think they come out of high school having been spoon-fed.

### *What do you think the reasons are?*

I can tell you that the students who come from smaller communities are better students. The ones from larger school systems do not write as well, so I guess that reflects on the large public-school systems. I really don't know that much about what happens in public schools, but I don't think they write like we used to write.

Something else is very alarming. On every test I have given in the last fifteen years, I give a bonus question, and the bonus question is always a geographic question. For instance, if we have been talking about carnations grown in Colombia and then shipped to the Netherlands, or Israel developing a drip system, I might ask them on the next quiz to put an X on Colombia or Israel. What I find is that about four students out of a hundred can locate the country on a map. Many won't even know what continent it's on. It's appalling.

### *What would you most want to tell others about teaching?*

You have to love it. If you don't love teaching, you ought to be doing something else. At the university level, there are people who teach because they have to teach, and they don't do a good job of it. You have to love it, and if you love it, you love the students.

I love it when the lightbulb comes on. You sort of look out in class, and if you're teaching a new principle or concept, a student might have that deer in the headlights look, where it's like, "I have *no* idea what she's talking about." And then, it clicks, the lightbulb comes on, and it's just wonderful.

*"God protect us from dumb ministers."*

# Father Thomas Buckley

## THEOLOGY PROFESSOR

*Father Buckley teaches in the Jesuit School of Theology, one of the schools in the Graduate Theological Union, a partnership of seminaries and graduate schools of theology in Berkeley, California. His research interests are in American religious history with an emphasis on church-state relations and the interaction of religion with social policy.*

We have students who are getting ready to be ordained priests. But we also have ordained men who are doing advanced ecclesiastical degrees. Then about half of our students are men and women who are preparing for non-ordained ministry in the church. Some of them will become teachers. The church is so different today from what it was fifty years ago in terms of available opportunities for people to do active ministry in the church—men and women, ordained and lay. There's all kinds of work to do. We prepare people for that—academically and pastorally. I'm the academic end.

I teach religious history, which is a branch of social history. I love teaching religion and politics because those are the two subjects that my mother said we are never supposed to talk about.

I love teaching church history. It deals with a subject that is very much at the core of a person or a group. So we're not talking about peripheral stuff—we're not talking about the history of furniture or dress. Religious history is talking about what people's deepest values are, their core beliefs.

*What is the role of the academic side for someone who is going to become a priest? One might even wonder if it's necessary.*

It's absolutely necessary. God protect us from dumb ministers who are not prepared, ignorant people teaching scripture they don't understand, ripping things out of context. It's absolutely essential for an ordained minister to be really well-grounded academically. And we can't even do the whole job here in three or four years. What we can do is lay the foundation and give them some of the tools, so they can continue to educate themselves after they leave here. It's really important that people who get up in the pulpit know what they're talking about.

We have had enough dumb ordained ministers and priests. We don't need any more. They're a menace. They're bad for the people—because they're dealing with issues of belief that are absolutely central in people's lives. It's one thing if they give bad political advice. It's much worse if they give people bad spiritual advice.

*You must have moments of frustration when you see in the media some of the things that are said in the name of Christianity or in the name of what the founding fathers intended.*

So often they have axes to grind. Are they using the founding fathers to prove their point or do they really understand? Can they put themselves back in that context and understand the debates, issues, and concerns of that time? And can they understand to what extent those issues are applicable today? That's really important. Jefferson never envisioned America the way it is today. To say that Jefferson said such and such and that's applicable today—that's really stretching it.

I think church and state separation is absolutely essential for a healthy society—especially a modern society. I think the intrusion of religious figures into political decisions is a huge mistake. But I think the church has something to say to the state about moral values.

It seems to me you can get two very opposing views. One says that religious values and concerns should dictate political action. The other opposing viewpoint is that you have nothing to say. I think both are wrong.

### What is the proper balance?

Let's take the abortion issue, the most controversial case. Let's take the bishops who say that a Catholic shouldn't vote for a politician who favors pro-choice.

I would prefer to say that life is a tremendous value—from the moment of conception. How do we best preserve that value? It's more than abortion. It's life. It's life at every moment. It's the life of somebody on death row. It's somebody who doesn't have enough food, who doesn't have medical care. The life issue is part of what Cardinal Bernardin called a seamless garment. If you respect life in the womb, respect it out of the womb. Respect it in peace, and don't be making weapons of war and destruction. Make it the seamless garment.

John Courtney Murray was a Jesuit priest teaching in the second half of the twentieth century. The cardinal principle for him was the dignity of the human person. He wrote a wonderful little book called *We Hold These Truths* and he made a very telling point when he argued that everything that is immoral should not necessarily be illegal. We Americans tend to conflate legality and morality. The prohibition of alcohol is a great example of that. He said that sometimes the more you try to make the great social evils illegal, the more in fact you promote them.

I rather like what Governor Tim Kaine said—I hold that life is precious from the moment of conception, but I don't favor criminalizing abortion. The way to stop abortions is birth control, sex education, prenatal care, postnatal care, decent job opportunities for people, child care for women—all those things are important. And it strikes me, Bill, how in the second half of the twentieth century we have moved toward a culture of death. The gap between the rich and the poor is enormous and it's getting worse, and the differential between what CEOs make and what the people working in the factory make is just astronomical. Why are people making these enormous salaries? They have no right to that money, it seems to me. I think that's corrupt. I think that's wrong.

I think the bishops' pastoral letter, "Economic Justice for All" [1986], was a superb statement of the right balance in the economy. Everyone is entitled to a decent job and an education. The best piece of social legislation we've had in the twentieth century was the GI Bill. Educate people to their best potential. Give everybody the best health care we can. Everybody. Those are life issues. We get all tied in a knot over the abortion issue, but I think it's just one in a whole series of life issues.

*What is your preferred method of teaching—discussion, lecture?*

It depends on the course. My preferred style for lecture classes is lecture with lots of questions and discussions, lots of give and take.

I have a wonderful class I'm teaching right now on American religious history, and it has four students. It's just delicious, and I love it. They read original sources. For example, today when they came into class they had read a sermon by John Wesley on "free grace" and a long published letter by George Whitfield attacking John Wesley, his friend. So we had a great discussion of those two texts and the points they're making theologically.

I'm doing a seminar now that is great fun. It's a class on Vatican II and U.S. Catholics. This is mainly for those students, men and women, Jesuits and non-Jesuits, who are getting ready for ministry in the Catholic Church. It's very important for them as they leave here to understand what happened at the Second Vatican Council and the way it impacted the population of this country. So what I want them to understand is how the church was transformed between 1950 and 1980.

*Your courses involve a lot of controversial issues. How do you handle the issue of expressing your own positions? There's a wide range in how professors handle this. Some "profess" their own views while others keep theirs hidden—or try to.*

I can't keep them hidden. I'm too transparent. And I love a good argument. Sometimes what I'll do is take a contrary position. On the graduate level, sometimes I'll simply sit back and let them take a position. If they ask me, if they push me, I'll tell them what I think. Or sometimes I'll volunteer it. The graduate students are less impressionable than the undergraduates. And the undergraduates are less impressionable than high school students. When I taught high school students, they did not know where I stood on issues, and I tried to keep it that way. Of course, as they got to know me better, they learned where I stood. But in class, they know I'm a Catholic priest, and they know I'm a Jesuit. So when we do the Reformation, they know where I stand. But I can sometimes surprise them with what I say about this or that figure in history. I try to be fair. So I will say to the Lutheran students after I do the class on Luther, "Was I fair? Was there anything I left out?" When I teach my course on the English Reformation, I send the syllabus, with the readings, to friends at the Episcopal school and ask them to comment on it—whether it's balanced. I can have a point of view, but I have to be fair to the other side.

*Over the span of your teaching career, have students remained the same? Have you seen changes or trends?*

You know, in the eighties, I noticed the Reagan revolution taking hold. I think today it's shifted again. But I'm not so sure about undergraduates because I'm not in touch with them, and the graduate students here are a very select group—they're totally committed to going out in the world and making a difference.

I must say, there were times at Loyola Marymount [*a Catholic university in Los Angeles*] when I'd be out for a walk in the morning and see the BMWs, Porches, and Mercedes in the parking lot, and I'd wonder if this was the crowd that I really want to be part of. On the other hand, I have students from those days that I'm still in touch with.

**So they turned out all right?**

Well, they are more conservative than I would like. But it reflects American values today, which I think are kind of lousy. I don't think there's nearly the commitment to the common good of society that needs to be there. So if I push anything, I will push that. And of course, I'm preaching to the choir here.

*"That's what teaching does. . . . It teaches the teacher."*

# William Gass

## PHILOSOPHY PROFESSOR

*William Gass taught college philosophy for fifty years, retiring in 2000. After teaching at Wooster College and Purdue, he was appointed David May Distinguished University Professor in the Humanities at Washington University, where he taught from 1969 until his retirement in 2000. His works of fiction and criticism have won numerous awards, among them Rockefeller Foundation and Guggenheim Foundation grants and the Lannan Lifetime Achievement Award. He received the National Book Critics Circle Award for Criticism three times. For his novel, The Tunnel, he received the American Book Award. He also won teaching awards at Purdue and Washington University.*

*On a personal note, I took four of his classes when I was an undergraduate at Purdue in the late sixties, and he was the best teacher I ever had. Over the years, I have met an uncanny number of people who had him as a teacher—usually at Washington University—and who called him the best teacher they had ever had.*

**Setting modesty aside, what made you so good as a teacher?**

[*Laughs.*] Well, it's hard to set modesty aside here.

I wasn't very good at several aspects of university teaching. One was the tutorial. Another was leading the seminar.

The other aspect of university teaching is the lecture hall, and there I thought I was OK. If I was any good in the lecture hall, it was because I was concerned about the material itself. This is what always moved me and made me interested in making it as clear as possible. I did have the artist's advantage of being able to look at philosophical positions as conceptual structures and admire them whether I agreed with them or not. Often students thought I preferred a position that I didn't at all, just because I expressed it fully and with some enthusiasm.

*If we recall the grammar we learned in middle school, the verb "to teach" can take two kinds of direct objects. One teaches students, or one teaches a subject matter, like mathematics or philosophy. For you, the latter was primary. Is that fair to say?*
Yes. And I was teaching it to my own profit, too. That is, I was talking about it—not teaching it—but talking about it aloud so other people could hear. But I was also trying to get it to say something to me, or enlighten me. Often in the middle of teaching a passage in Plato, say, which I had gone over a hundred times, my attempt to express what was going on in the passage would allow me to see something for the first time. So it was quite selfish in many ways.

I was in the company of these texts and was able, for my good fortune, to really enjoy the company. So I could be as enthusiastic about Aristotle as I was about Plato because listening to them is quite a treat. What I was really doing was sort of channeling the texts to the students through my attempts to understand them.

*Is it fair to say that for you teaching was akin to creating a work of art?*
Well, teaching was akin to *examining* works of art, because I regarded most of these texts as works of art—works of conceptual art. That's what makes valuable certain philosophical systems, which we recognize now as totally wrong. I mean, like Plotinus. [*We both laugh.*] But Plotinus's system is gorgeous. To teach it, then, is to teach a kind of vision that has the substance of intellectual fiction.

*But in constructing a lecture about Plato, let's say, there's a point at which the lecture itself becomes so good that it is a work to be admired in itself . . .*
Well . . .

*. . . or am I testing your modesty again?*
The lecturer doesn't know that. Because he's the performer there. So if that is the audience's feeling, fine; but the performer can't stop in the middle of his broad jump to admire his style.

*But over the years, surely you were aware your teaching had a great effect on a lot of students.*
No, actually I was very unaware of that. It wasn't that my teaching didn't receive awards and approval and that sort of thing, but I didn't cultivate the students as

many people do. So I wasn't aware that I was having a profound effect; in fact, I think the opposite. One of the comforting things about teaching philosophy—now if I were teaching anatomy it would be different—is that it's hard for you to do harm. Even if you teach some idea and your notion of that idea is nuts, nobody's going to be hurt. Most of the students—99 percent—are going to forget it anyway, so you haven't damaged somebody's soul or skills in any deep sense, and that was very comforting. I often played a little German thought game about that: Suppose people really believed what you said? That would be terrifying. I would shut up completely.

*I remember that at Purdue—and I imagine this happened at Washington University—students would often line up outside your office door. Surely you were aware that through your teaching, students became more attuned to and more enthusiastic about ideas or maybe even the life of the mind. You must have known that.*

Well, that would have been my hope. What I would have loved to have given to students is not so much the subject matter itself, but the relation of somebody to that material. That's what I think people take away. Because unless they major in something, it's going to fade. A lot of the so-called factual material won't be remembered. But what may remain—certainly this was true for me in the teachers I had when I was going through school—was their approach, their commitment, their way of dealing with the subject.

My thesis advisor, Max Black, was a difficult person. But when he got in class, the clarity and brilliance of his lectures was so immense that you just couldn't resist them. He made difficult things transparent; it was amazing. The things that bothered you about him as a person—his immense ego, for instance—were given up in his approach to the subject. And that was a great lesson.

I had a lot of really terrific teachers in my educational career—Wittgenstein was one of them—but the real deep intellectual pleasure, excitement, and belief in the importance of their subject always held the thing together.

*Were there teachers earlier in your career, in your undergraduate years or even in high school, who were influential?*

Yes. I had wonderful teachers at Kenyon, almost everybody. There was a Jewish-refugee history professor named Salomon [*Richard Georg Salomon taught at Kenyon College until his retirement at age seventy-eight in 1962*], and he taught a yearlong course in ecclesiastical history. Of course I was not a church person *at all*, but he was said to be so good that I signed up for the class anyway. It was marvelous. It was one of the best things that's ever happened to me. He elevated one's taste as well. He was an enormous snob, and so you suddenly abandoned Tchaikovsky and embraced Bach. You had to get rid of that later, but at the time it was very important to do it.

And in high school I had some very good teachers, particularly in English. They were the traditional American woman, and I didn't agree a lot, even then, with their enthusiasm for James Fennimore Cooper—I hated Cooper—and that sort of thing, but I admired *them,* and I read the books with great excitement. They enjoyed my immature judgments and my getting into the swim of things and saying, "I don't think this is any good because . . ." I was of course stupid, but they wanted me to engage. They were good people. That was extremely important to me.

*There is something about philosophy that is outside the mainstream of the currents of American energy. It's not what occupies most people's minds.*
That's certainly true.

*Did you think of it as your purpose, then, to shock people or be in some ways subversive?*
No, not with students. I think people got that impression, and certainly from my writing they would get that impression. But the sense of subversiveness that I might have had (and I certainly did have some) was not so much in terms of what students might do—because that would worry me—but rather in terms of how the academic world thought was the best way to present things, to say things, to be on the right side, and so on. I've always had that sort of problem.

I may have been one of the first people to use obscenities in an academic lecture. Also, my hatred of decorum. And I think I have a playfulness on serious subjects that a lot of people find upsetting. My kind of reverence for the material was often deemed inappropriate for the climate I was supposed to be in.

*When you got your chair did you continue teaching philosophy?*
I was given a chair in the humanities, not in philosophy. That meant that I could teach any subject in the humanities I wanted to. That allowed me to wander around. I did courses in contemporary French philosophy, the philosophy of architecture, the philosophy of literature.

*All of these new courses must have taken quite a bit of work on your part. Did they dovetail with your own writing?*
When it was philosophy of literature, I was often teaching authors I was writing essays about. The essays usually came out of the teaching. I would often decide to teach a certain novelist—Calvino, for example—before I had read a great deal, knowing that this would get me to do it. I would have to make the time. That was a chance to educate myself, because that's what teaching really does—it teaches the teacher. You learn by teaching. In preparing that material, you're really just indulging your own passions.

*When you planned a lecture, did you think of it as a whole, as if a lecture is a kind of literary genre?*
Yes, very much. And I tried to give a sense of development, especially with philosophy. It was nice to be able to show the student how ideas unfold, how they lead from one thing into another, especially when it's not obvious on the surface. It's also fun

when you could start out with an argument and make it sound very attractive to your students and then suddenly they would realize the consequences of this argument were things they felt they shouldn't like at all, and it would produce this kind of, "Uh-oh, I've been led down this trail of reasoning and now I'm here where I don't know that I want to be." That kind of experience is sort of jazzy in philosophy.

I wanted also to be as clear as possible. The goal was to get the ideas as clear as possible without falsifying them. And I wanted to conclude my coverage of a particular subject with a sense of what comes next. So most of my courses were taught in a historical manner, even when they were not history of philosophy courses.

*Having taught for fifty years, did you see any changes in students over the years?*

I noticed a number of changes. At Washington University, there was a steady increase in the number of foreign or foreign-born students. Also, the quality of students was going up very rapidly.

Among so-called standard-issue American students, I had an epiphany one day in class. Almost none of the students in this class could hope to surpass the social and economic level of their parents, whereas when I was growing up, almost everybody was coming from a family of a lower class and striving upward and could expect to have a better life—a more luxurious life and a more cultured life—than their parents. But not any more. I had many students whose parents were physicians, let's say, and that changed the tone.

*In what way was the tone different?*

Well, they were more worried about trying to get into med school, or law school, or whatever, because they were expected to do that. It made them more anxious students, but not better ones. The earlier students were eager, hungry for the material. The later students were hungry for the grade rather than the material.

I remember that when I came back from the navy after four years [*at the end of World War II*], I was so eager just to study. I loved every minute of it. We were GI Joe kinds of people—and we were all like that—just so grateful not to be doing what we had been doing. That was true of a lot of my friends when I was a freshman: that eagerness and excitement of just being at college, the real adventure of every day finding something new. But now students are jaded but anxious . . . fearful . . . a little of the sort who know that the more success they have, the more success they will be expected to have. And that was a kind of horrible fret: so it was going to be bad if they didn't do well, but it was going to be worse if they did do well. The exception is the immigrant population and the minority students; they have the old-style push.

Of course, I might be quite wrong about this, but that was the impression I got.

*I wish you were wrong, but a lot of teachers have similar perceptions . . .*

Education is so basically important, but now it's expected. It's something they're used to. You can come from a family of, let's say, musicians, and there's music everywhere. And you come to school and you already know a lot of that and it's important in your background and that sounds great. And it is. But you never have the experience of suddenly coming from a background where there wasn't any such thing, and then having that world open for you when you were ready for it. It was harder to get students to suddenly say—as I did—"Oh, my God, there are Greeks!"

Nowadays, it's like finally reading Kafka after you've heard about him and encountered the ideas assigned to him for years. You can't have the experience of running into Kafka like a stranger on the street and just having your mind blown.

### Do you miss teaching?

I don't miss it at all. It's because, I think, I have my own sense of having to get things done while I still have time and can work. And that fills my psyche, and I don't need the teaching. And teaching was very demanding, and it asks for a lot of your energy. That was good because it was worthwhile. It's obvious because I've been far more productive in my seventies and eighties—since retirement—than I was at any other time.

> "What carries the teacher through is his or her passion for the subject."

# Susan Moeller

### JOURNALISM PROFESSOR

*Susan Moeller teaches in the Philip Merrill College of Journalism at the University of Maryland, where she is the director of the International Center for Media and the Public Agenda. She is also the co-director and lead faculty member of the Salzburg Academy on Media and Global Change. She has received the Board of Regents Teaching Award.*

*She is the author of* Compassion Fatigue: How the Media Sell Disease, Famine, War and Death *and* Shooting War: Photography and the American Experience of Combat. *She has been interviewed on* Nightline, ABC News, CNN International, The NewsHour with Jim Lehrer, NBC, *and on radio programs on National Public Radio and Public Radio International.*

*You teach a class to undergraduates on media literacy. Could you give me an example of what you do in that class?*

One of the topics we cover is the business of media—media mergers, and how commercial pressures have shaped information. So I give students a homework assignment in which they are asked to look at fifty of their own MP3 files or CDs, and they are given a website that will identify who owns what labels. Now there are four major music labels that control at least 90 percent of the music that comes out around the world.

Most students, when we talk about the music industry before they do the assignment, believe that the music they like is cutting edge, that they are consumers of independent music, and that the musicians they like are "working against the system," as it were. So they are frankly flabbergasted to learn that even the most outraged music that they own is almost always owned by these four major music labels. Because they've already learned about what such mergers do in terms of identifying and packaging talent, there's the shock of understanding that the music they listen to has been shaped not entirely by the artist they thought was the sole creator, but also by an industry that sees the music as a commodity and not purely as artistic expression.

The other shock of recognition comes when we talk about advertising and we look at body image and how advertisers use women—but increasingly use men, too—to market products. Sometimes we do a homework assignment that basically replicates what others have done, in which students are asked to answer a few questions, and then they're given a time period to look at one of the women's magazines—*Vogue,* for example—and then they're asked another set of questions. Almost universally, what the before and after questions illuminate is that women students, particularly, feel less good about themselves as a result of looking at the women's magazines. And not only in terms of, "Oh, I need to go out and buy a new pair of jeans because I'm wearing the wrong kind of jeans," but in terms of how they feel about themselves as a whole person. They tend to be happier about their lives before they look at the magazine than after.

When you show them the results of the test, that tends to be revelatory for the students because many students pick up such magazines, they believe, in order to take a break. It's something they give themselves like going to a movie or getting themselves an ice cream. It's something that they believe makes them feel good. But what they learn is that actually, no, it doesn't make them feel good. Then we talk about why could that be.

*That sounds like a course that every student in the country should take.*

It's a fun course, and it usually gets good reviews from the students. We usually have about six hundred students who try to get into a course of two hundred.

*What do you think makes you a good teacher—for example, in this course? Is a lot of it curriculum design, or is it how you teach?*

I think it's probably both. It's important to think about the curriculum design, the organization of the class, and how to present the material in ways that are going to be both engaging to students but also going to create the kinds of outcomes we want to create.

I'm trained as a historian, and in the arts and humanities, I don't think a lot of teachers think about outcomes, about what they want their students to come out knowing. If you're teaching twentieth-century American history, for example, you may say that you want students to understand the causes of World War II and what has evolved as a result of World War II. But it's the unusual teacher who gets more specific than that. And maybe you don't need to in those kinds of courses. But when you're teaching something like media literacy, yes, there are facts you can teach, but it's less about facts, and more about getting students to think about the information you're presenting, and getting students to get comfortable with the kind of analysis they can bring into their classes and into the rest of their lives.

I get e-mails from students two and three and four years later who say, "I still can't watch a prime-time TV show without thinking about product placement"—or without thinking about why the women are so skinny, or why the lead-in teaser was this rather than that. Well, that's great to hear, and it's great that they learned a method of analysis that two months—or two years—later they're still thinking about.

In order to do that, you can't talk at students. You have to engage them. I have taught at Harvard and Princeton, but at Maryland—the students are very bright, but many of them are the first people in their families to go to college. So they are really committed to being there. So they do show up at the beginning, but you're going to quickly lose them—in a class of two hundred, you can end up teaching to ten kids—if you don't make the lectures interesting and if you don't convince them that what they're learning in the lectures is something they need to know. So you've got to deliver information that they—independent of the tests that you give them—perceive as being important or, at the very least, interesting. The information has to be compelling. And the way you deliver it, frankly, has got to be compelling.

Every teacher has his or her own style, and you can only teach in your own style and be authentic. But there is a performance quality to being a good teacher, and you can't minimize its importance. Performance matters. It's the language you use, the speed with which you speak, it's the examples you choose, it's how you speak to or with the students . . . but I think above all, it's passion for the subject. I say that thinking about the teachers I know. The best teachers are the ones who are able to communicate their passion about the subject to you.

Just this week I went to the back-to-school-night at my own children's middle and high school. They have a fabulous school. We walked in the algebra teacher's classroom, and the very first thing she said to the parents was, "I just love algebra—don't you?" And she clearly did. So she threw up an equation on the board, and though most of the people in the room couldn't follow her, we were riveted. We wanted to hear what she had to say because she clearly loved it. And she wanted to make us understand.

I find that in . . . the classes where I have students rushing down the stadium seating aisles to get to me are the classes where I've gone from laughing, to crying, and the whole range of emotions in between, because I really care what I'm talking about.

Teaching is like writing or any other skill—like music or language acquisition. There are no doubt people who are by inclination and talent better teachers than others, just as some people are more gifted musicians. But teaching is an acquired talent and it takes a tremendous amount of practice—like music—and you get better and better at it. Maybe like those other skills, too, you have to continually reassess what you're doing before particular audiences and over time. A lot of that is acquiring techniques. If you're trying to deliver facts, then speaking in bullet points can be helpful. If you're trying to tell people about decision processes, then telling stories can work.

The reason I identify passion being the most important is that what carries the teacher through is his or her passion for the subject. I think we've all had teachers in our lives who we are convinced are using the same yellowed lecture notes as they used twenty years ago. Those are not necessarily the worst teachers in the world, but what you get from those teachers is maybe a command of the subject—but you rarely get from those teachers a continuing passion for it. And if you're that teacher, it's hard to get excited about something and keep your enthusiasm up for it if you yourself are not getting something out of it.

One of the reasons I love teaching media literacy is that even though it's a tremendous amount of work . . . Literally on that day that I'm teaching, I'm frantically putting together my PowerPoint—not because I don't plan ahead but because I want to use something that happened that day, or the day before. That means that I have to continually be aware of what's happening in order to put it in my course, so for any information that comes over my transom, I'm thinking, "Can I use that in this week's class?" And that keeps me engaged in my surroundings and interested in the class and keeps my passion fresh.

*"My method is based on the give and take of discussion."*

# Jack Metzgar

## TEACHER, ADULT EDUCATION

*Jack Metzgar recently retired from teaching in a bachelor's degree program for adults twenty-five and over at Roosevelt University in Chicago. He grew up in Johnstown, Pennsylvania, where his father was a steelworker and his mother was a teacher. He did his undergraduate work at Ohio University and the New School, and he received his PhD at Northwestern. He has published articles and books in the fields of labor history and working-class studies.*

Usually I don't identify myself as an "adult educator" because it just confuses people. Adult education to most people means English as a second language, remedial

English, or a variety of non-credit courses. But I taught in a highly structured bachelor's degree program. My typical course would meet on a Monday night from 6:00 to 8:30 and a Wednesday night from 6:00 to 8:30 in a seminar, defined as twenty or fewer students in a discussion-based class. So basically, for thirty years I got paid to organize material and then discuss it with adults in the city of Chicago or on our suburban campus.

The content of each course we could make up. Teachers taught wildly different things in their classes. I did different things in my humanities or social science seminars. One of my humanities courses was on the three theories of art: realism, formalism, and expressionism. The students would read—struggle with—some theory, and then we looked at painting, we looked at architecture, we looked at literature, we looked at movies. They tried to apply different theories of art to what they saw or read. It was just wild. I would take them to the Art Institute—in those days, there was a free night. They weren't allowed to see representational art. [*Laughs.*] They had to go to the modern section. For many of them, it was the first time they had ever been inside the Art Institute, even though they were lifelong Chicagoans.

Years later, I would meet some of these students and they would say, "You know, I remember when we went to the museum. I've never gone back, but I want to go back some time." [*Laughs.*] So for some, the course opened a door that they never walked through.

*But did some of them did go back?*

Yeah. People have told me that. And there were people who had extraordinary gifts, and I pushed them along. They went back. And the course had a bigger impact on them in the sense that they continued with it. But I think they would have found those things anyway. Our program at Roosevelt has over the years found some jewels who would never have discovered they were jewels without us.

Many people go into the program thinking they are not "college material." College material is an old-fashioned phrase, but it comes up. Students wonder whether they are college material. You get to be there as people realize—even while you're correcting all their comma splices—that they *can* do this. Part of the function of the teacher is to assist in that. And that's where my own working-class background helped.

*The program builds their self-esteem.*

This is Chicago. We don't believe in "self-esteem." [*Laughs.*] But they do realize that they can do something that they were not sure they could do going in.

*Do you remember any jewels in particular?*

Yeah, and her name was Linda. She was a neighborhood activist before she came to us. She was a terrific writer. She had always written—poetry, stories, essays. She had been consistently abused by her father when she was growing up. She was a voracious reader; one of the ways she had coped with her childhood trauma was to read. For her senior thesis, she wrote about abuse. It was dynamite. Telling that kind of story . . . there was just this inspiring quality to it. And it wasn't just how terrible it was: all of that is there, but it seemed to me that she had a really healthy attitude toward it. There was big anger toward her father and also anger toward her mother. But also lots of love and understanding. She was just an incredible person. She went on to law school and wrote bills about women's and children's issues that became state laws.

*If you had to describe what your teaching did for her, is it like what Aristotle said about art? That it takes this trauma and brings about a catharsis in the person? Was education therapeutic for her?*
Education was *part* of what allowed her to become successful . . . but boy, I don't want to get anywhere near the term "therapeutic."

For the expressionists, art adds form to the chaos of reality. It was like that for her.

*But it can be internal chaos.*
Right, internal or external. So Truth and Beauty go hand in hand. Strong, clear form that brings unity to variety is both beautiful and satisfying because it is clear. You can call that therapeutic when it happens in a work of art or when it happens in life; that kind of clarity enables us to do things that we might not be able to do otherwise.

But someone like Linda, she was so strong-willed and so talented that if it hadn't been me, it would have been someone else. But she definitely needed education. She needed the credential, the support, the validation. She got that not only from me but from the rest of the faculty as well.

*Based on your account of your student Linda, would you say that education is teaching students to give form to reality? Is that what education is?*
I like that. I never thought of it that way myself.

I always have an agenda. I've always been political—in the broader sense. So whatever I do has a political aspect to it. But it never mattered that students agreed with me. It just didn't matter. On the one hand I wanted them to see the truth—which was my view. [*Laughs.*] But our whole thing in the program was independent, critical thinking. Over the years, what I tried to do was get into what a person was thinking and do "immanent critique." That means you're critiquing based on what they're doing . . . you're not bringing in external criteria. Of course, there are some external criteria: writing clarity, good grammar, and so on. But the aim is to get on the inside and help them clarify their own thinking. So a lot of the purpose of classroom discussion was to help them develop their own thinking. That was the important part of their education.

I don't know what it's like for young people, but for adults, they have this chaos of thoughts and ideas. If they seem rigid and simplifying, it's because they're holding back this chaos, so you have to show them ways to start with the forms they have, and then to open them to complexity, so that they can manage greater complexity without ever losing that sense that they have a framework for understanding things.

### *So in the beginning, it is your goal to make them more confused?*

Yes, and I actually say that in class. I'll say, "In this part of the class, my goal is to make you more confused. And then after that, I'll force you to decide, and it will be hard." And that's actually built into my method. You can confuse people just by presenting them two points of view that are equally compelling.

### *So your method is deeply Socratic?*

Yeah [*without enthusiasm*]. But I don't use that term either. It's like "therapeutic." Most people who advocate for the Socratic method mean, "I know the answer and you're supposed to guess it." I hate that. I've never done that.

But my method *is* based on the give and take of discussion, on building students' listening skills, and making sure they respond to what the other students actually said. This is not a given skill. A lot of faculty don't have it.

### *How did you learn to teach?*

Trial and error.

# 3 | Teaching the Healers

*"Treat the patient, not the disease."*

# Leslie Hilger

**TEACHER OF RESIDENTS
IN DERMATOLOGY**

*Dr. Leslie Hilger is a practicing dermatologist who also teaches at the University of California–San Francisco Medical School. He was educated at Stanford and the University of California Medical School. He receives extremely high ratings from his patients and from his medical students.*

The students have finished med school and an internship and they're undergoing specialty training in dermatology. Our job as the clinical faculty is to give them an idea of what it's like in the real world. It's an experience that they won't necessarily get in the university.

Let's say this is a patient with seborrheic dermatitis. We can tell the student, "Gee, you're going to see an awful lot of this in the outside world. It's often something the patient is going to mention after you've taken care of some other problem and he or she is heading for the door. You are going to need to have a lot of different ways to treat it. A patient might say, 'Oh, I'm allergic to that.' So you can't just have one way to treat it."

When I was a student, a wise attending physician said, "Learn a thousand different ways to treat stuff. Don't just learn one party line." I asked why, and he said, "Because you'll end up using all of them eventually."

When I went through UC Medical School, I had all of these attending physicians, each of them willing to teach me how he or she did it, each of them willing to give me the benefit of his or her experience in the outside world. So I learned a lot of ways to treat common things. I learned how different doctors approach different problems because I had different attending physicians all the time.

Now I am one of these attending physicians. So I can go over there and show them how I work, give them an extension of practical experience that they wouldn't get from the house faculty at the medical school.

You have to really know your stuff to go teach it because students ask difficult questions. And if you haven't prepared yourself, if you haven't done all the reading and kept ahead of them on the latest literature, then you're going to embarrass yourself and your teaching will have no credibility.

*How exactly do you work? Do they watch you treat the patient, or do you watch them?*

The classic way is for the resident to see the patient, take a history, perform a physical, and then say, "I'm going to bring my attending physician in here in a moment." Then the resident will step outside, and there I'll have other medical students who may not be seeing patients, maybe the chief resident if it's an interesting case, the other residents, the resident who's presenting the case, and myself—the attending faculty member. The resident will present to me the symptoms and physical findings. I'll say, "Well, it sounds like this, but let's go take a look." Our whole retinue will then go into the room. I'll introduce myself to the patient. I might say, "Your doctor has briefed me on this. I have a couple of questions myself. You mentioned it has been going on for this long—has it ever happened before?" It's a subtle way of filling out the history if the resident didn't ask some things. So I might say, "Gee, I can't remember whether So-and-So told me if this has happened before. Has it?"

I try to make it non-confrontational. Because I'm not trying to show up the resident, I'm trying to make him look good. So then I might say, "Well, this is an interesting case. It gives us a chance to talk about not only your case but also others like it, so we're gong to step outside and we'll be back in with some therapy for you." So we go outside and I'll ask the resident how he would handle it. He'll tell me, and I'll ask him why. I'll say, "That's a good idea, but have you thought about the possibility that it might be such and such?" If he hasn't, it's a good chance to teach something, to say, "Some cases present like this and they look like what you think they look like, but you can stub your toe by missing such and such."

I can inform residents whether or not they need to do a biopsy. I can tell them exactly how I would manage the case on the outside. The resident can take my example or reject it. And then I'll use it as a method of saying to the other residents—let's say it's a case of eczema—that they're going to see a lot of cases of eczema and this one is an eight on a ten-point scale. I can give them a little perspective on the range of severity and the range of treatments. Most of the cases are going to be less severe than that. We're using a high-potency steroid for this case because it's in the hands, but you can use a milder steroid for other cases. So it's a way of expanding and using that particular case as a way of focusing their mind on something. Then when they think of eczema, they'll think of that patient, and hopefully remember the discussion that we had around it.

*And if it's a minor surgical procedure?*

The resident will perform the procedure, but I'm right there. The nurse will set up the surgery, and I'll ask the resident, "Have you performed this before?" If he hasn't, we will go through it.

*If there could be one thing your students took from you, what would you have it be?*
Treat the patient and not the disease. Students' knowledge is more than adequate, and they should come out of there confident that they are going to be very well prepared scientifically. But how well they handle that in terms of dealing with patients is up to them. If I could make one other observation—in addition to "treat the patient, not the disease"—it would be, "learn from the patient." Because each patient adds to your own depth of knowledge.

I remember when I had been in practice for all of about a year and a half, and a patient came in with a dermatitis, and I looked, and took the history, and I really didn't have a clue what the heck was going on.

So I swallowed my pride—thankfully—and I went across the hall and asked my senior partner to come over and take a look. At that time he had forty-six years of experience practicing dermatology. He went in there, asked a few questions, and said, "Dr. Hilger and I will discuss this outside." I thought, "OK. Here comes the lecture: 'You blockhead, why didn't you learn this in medical school?'"

But he came out, he looked at me, and he said, "I haven't got a single clue as to what that is." And I felt much better. If he hadn't seen it in forty-six years of a busy dermatology practice, I knew it was pretty unusual and I didn't have to feel bad about not knowing the answer. But that's when I could use the knowledge that my teachers had imparted to me. How do you approach a condition when you don't know what it is? Well, you go with your worst-case scenario. Minimax loss theory. What is the worst possible thing that it could be, and let's rule that out first. And so you develop both a feeling for what's going on and an approach to solving problems.

*Are young doctors pretty much the same as when you were a student, or are they different?*
I think every generation of old farts like myself thinks that the younger generation is going to hell in a handbasket—but I don't.

However, I think they are not as well prepared for what the world demands of them besides medicine. I was blessed in that I had a lot of outside experience in the business world before I left my residency to enter private practice. I think many of them don't have the slightest clue what private practice is about, the economic and personnel and other decisions they'll have to make.

Conversely, I think the people coming through now are very well prepared scientifically. I think their scientific knowledge is as good or better than ours. They read the literature, and the literature is more accessible to them. They have at their hands greater access to information. They can tap their computer and have references that it would have taken me hours to find in the library—if I was willing to spend the time in the library to find them.

The question I can't answer is whether or not they're going into medicine for the right reasons. [*He pauses.*] I buried a brother, and later a sister. I grew up around sick people who had cystic fibrosis. I pretty much knew at age four that I wanted to be a doctor. I don't think everybody has to do that, but if you're going into medicine for the money or the prestige—the money's going down and the prestige is going down—then it's a real bad career choice. If you're going into it because it's a helping profession and you know you're going to do well enough to raise a family and have some comfort, then you're fine.

*What, in turn, do you feel that you learn from your students?*

I'm not a technical wizard. I'm smart enough to handle technology, I like to think, but the internet for me and modern technology is always a second language. Most of these people coming through now have never been alive when there wasn't an internet. If you said, "Go to the library," they would look at you like you had fallen off a turnip truck. Why would you do that? You have the library right there, at the computer. So the thing that I take from them is that there is much more data available, and if you don't know an answer, it isn't painful to go find the answer.

And of course they are getting the latest new technology at UC, because that is where it comes from; it develops in the universities and then diffuses out. So I can draw from their knowledge. If there's a new copper vapor laser, of which there are only six or seven in the country, and they are over there using it, then I can go over there and watch and see what it does that's better than the laser that I'm using.

And being around young, enthusiastic people sort of rekindles my own enthusiasm. Just as they can draw from my experience, I can draw from their enthusiasm. I think that if you're just going through the motions or watching the clock until retirement, then you should quit now.

*"I want them to take ownership."*

# Allan Friedman

## PROFESSOR, UNDERGRADUATES AND NEUROSURGERY RESIDENTS

*Allan Friedman is the Guy L. Odom Professor of Neurological Surgery; chief, Division of Neurosurgery in the Department of Surgery; co-director, Neuro-Oncology Program; and head of the Laboratory of Neurosurgical Oncology at the Duke University Medical Center in Durham, North Carolina. He received his BS from Purdue University and his MD from the University of Illinois. He is a world-renowned neurosurgeon, and he is widely published in his field. A month before we spoke, he had operated on Senator Edward Kennedy for a brain tumor.*

*Dr. Friedman is a fireball of energy and enthusiasm. We spoke on a Saturday morning in July. He had just come from giving a lecture, and he had an appointment with a student who was waiting outside his door when we finished.*

I lecture to undergraduate medical students; I give them an introductory lecture in their first year and in their second year. I lecture at the medical school. And I have my residents in neurosurgery. I have thirteen residents—people who have finished medical school and are looking to become neurosurgeons. They spend six years with me.

I also have an ad hoc course that we call "brain school." Duke has a unique curriculum. Ordinarily in medical school you spend two years studying the basic sciences and then two years doing clinical work. But at Duke they've taken all of the basic sciences and squished them into one year. This allows medical students to spend their third year doing research, so it's very much a research institution. But the cost is that because they go through the basic sciences so quickly, it's like trying to take a drink of water through a fire hose. So for people interested in neurology or psychiatry or any of the neurosciences, we have this impromptu seminar every Tuesday where we discuss various aspects of the brain. In part of it we're talking about basic anatomy, the sort of things you'd learn in a regular class, but in other classes we talk about advances in neuroscience, the science of how you move your arm when you see something, how you make choices, things of that nature.

Neuroscience is just moving in leaps and bounds, and it's fun because it keeps me up to date in the guise that I'm actually teaching somebody something.

**Given the tremendous amount of knowledge available, one of the challenges must be in deciding what to present and how to present it. How do you decide?**

Basically, when I'm lecturing to the medical students, I'm trying to do two things. I'm trying to open their eyes to the possibilities of the fields of neurosurgery, and then I'd like to leave them with something they can take home. So for instance, in this morning's lecture we talked a little bit about what neurosurgery is—an overview of the awake surgery I do on brain tumors (this is the gee-whiz stuff)—and then I spent the second part of the lecture talking about how you examine a comatose patient. You know, a patient comes into the emergency room unconscious; how do you figure out why he or she is unconscious?

Now in the brain school, these are students who are highly motivated, so I'm not teaching them a particular body of knowledge as such. What we're mostly doing there is exploring areas in which progress is being made, because these are really smart kids. You'd be surprised at how smart the kids are at the Duke medical school. And they're really motivated. So as I said, we do a little groundwork of this basic anatomy stuff, but the really fun stuff is a Socratic discussion where we pick some papers and we talk about what we've read in the papers and how it fits in with the other papers we've read over the years.

*And how do teach neurosurgery to your residents? It strikes me as an area of medical practice in which you need to combine the talents of Einstein and Michelangelo.*

Well, I don't know if it's quite at that level, but you're 100 percent correct about the two kinds of expertise. When I look at my residents, some of them have terrific hands and some of them just have a great surgical sense. So you're really teaching both. The manual skills, the basic anatomy, and the basic techniques—a lot of that I can teach before we even get to the operating room. The basic manual things you don't practice on someone with a beating heart. You can practice tying knots anyplace. Basic anatomy and basic techniques for surgery I can teach in a cadaver lab. The hard part, and the reason you spend so much time learning neurosurgery and doing the residency and participating, is to learn that surgical sense: When you look at a procedure, can you visualize every step in your mind? Can you see where the problems are going to be? Can you visualize strategies to avoid them? Do you have an idea of how to manage the problem when it comes up? And so on.

I'm there for every procedure, and the junior people are mostly watching. And the more senior people—I'm watching them. But it's always a team in the operating room. It's never "go do this operation and call me when you're finished."

*In that context, do you ever have an advanced student whom you realize is in the process of doing something wrong and you have to correct him or her?*

Yes, of course. You can see the student going in that direction, and you're talking about it. You're saying, as you get to this part of the operation, "What are you thinking? What might the problems be? What will you do if this happens?" More often than not, it's not that somebody did something wrong, it's that one of these anticipated detours occurs. For example, the artery is extremely fragile. Or you're operating through a tumor. So it's really fairly controlled. It's not, "Let's jump in and see what happens."

*Do you ever have a student who just has clumsy hands and you have to deal with that?*

Well, clumsy hands isn't so bad, because there are different levels of surgeries, as you can imagine. And so the people who just have clumsy hands—you can train them outside the operating room so that they can do some basic surgery. You have an understanding with them that they're going to work to a certain level. The hard part is the student who can't develop surgical sense. And those residents usually don't finish, to be quite frank with you. You try to identify them in the first year or two so it's not such a huge investment. It's that the person just can't anticipate the problems. In anatomy terms, these people have great temporal lobes—which is were your memory takes place—but they don't have good frontal lobes, which is judgment and decision making. And those people you try to steer away. You try to steer them into something they're more suited for.

*You no doubt teach your students not only surgery, but also patient care.*

Oh, yeah. And that's on multiple levels. First of all, there's the diagnosis of the patient. The patient doesn't come to you in the operating room and say, "I have this or that." There's a complaint. So you make what we call a differential diagnosis. You make a list of possibilities and sort through them.

Then there's determining the appropriate treatment. Frankly, the treatment of a thirty-year-old is not the same as an eighty-year-old with the same lesion. You tend to be more aggressive in a younger person, because you're looking for a cure; for an older person you might be looking for just palliation.

And then there's also the empathy, the compassion, and so forth. To be honest with you, if your mother didn't teach it to you, I can't supply it all. But you can direct students to a style of how they practice medicine and how they treat other people.

*In researching you for this interview, I was struck by your optimistic and positive attitude, in spite of the fact that you see many people who are very seriously ill. How do you try to transmit your positive attitude to your students?*

Well, I don't think you can. Part of that is just what your personality is. You didn't pick a profession that's all peaches and ice cream. These are people who need help. You might not be able to cure them, but you can give them the best care possible at this time, and hope that in the future we'll do better, and extend their quality of life as long as possible. And also help the patient cope with this terrible problem—or with just the mechanics of what happens when mom can't get out of bed. And you try to make those sorts of things easier for them. It's all part of what I do.

*Are there principles to the way you practice medicine that you want to pass on to your students?*

Yeah. One of the principles is, the patient comes to you with a problem, and it's your job to do your best—and that's all you can do—to solve the problem. The patient is an individual, and whether you like him or not, you have to show compassion and understanding.

I want them to do that, and I want them to take ownership, and know they're responsible: responsible for keeping up to date, for knowing what the latest treatments are, for keeping their skills set up, and for keeping their knowledge base up. Those are the principles I try to pass on.

The thing I'm most proud of now is the twenty-two practicing neurosurgeons I have out there. I could go to each and every one of them. They're just amazing individuals. They came to me with great skills, with great personal skills. A number of them were athletes and whatnot, and they've gone out and practiced medicine in a way that I'm just really proud of. I have my own three kids, but I have these twenty-two who are out there practicing, and I was the chief of neurosurgery when they finished, and I saw them all the way through.

*What are the things you try to do that make you most effective as a teacher, whether it's lecturing to undergrads or teaching your residents in neurosurgery?*

I think it's the fact that I connect, and I get a tremendous amount from working with these people. That's why I'm faculty advisor to the women's basketball team. Imagine this group of young women who not only can get through a university like Duke, but also carry the burden of practicing a high-level Division One sport. They practice, they're passionate, they're committed—plus they're going ahead and getting a university degree.

Another thing I do is have a program with another doctor, Henry Friedman (no relation), called the CAPE, the Collegiate Athlete Pre-Medical Experience program. I have a daughter who is now twenty-one, but I saw her at the age of five and I wondered and worried about how women would make out in the world. So four or five years ago we started this CAPE for women athletes who are interested in pre-medicine. We meet with them once a month. And they're just amazing individuals, and I learn a ton from them.

### Have you noticed changes in students over the years?

I think there are two changes. I'm just blown away by the people here compared to the people I went to college with. They're not just academic people; they're saving the world in a hundred different ways. They're really go-getters. They come up with their own projects. There was one fellow I dealt with—who was just a middling student academically—who went out and worked up an introductory program for incoming students to Duke. The week before classes, they go out sailing on the east coast of North Carolina in a communal group where they share and get adjusted to the folks they will deal with on a university level. This fellow had to find funding for the program, he had to find the boats, the meals, and so on. To me, that's just amazing. So at the undergraduate level, what I'm mostly blown away with is that these people are so community-minded, and do so much more than just study for courses.

On the medical-school level there's been a major shift. Among the medical students there's more attention to lifestyle. When I was a surgical resident, you were in the hospital every day and every other night. You were committed. My junior people are very interested in medicine, but they all have outside activities. Some are married and have kids, and their time with their family is very important to them. So even though people are very committed to neurosurgery, they're not doing it 100 percent of their waking hours.

### Do you think that's a healthy development?

I think it is, and I think we just have to figure out how to make sure we're turning out as good doctors. That's one of the real challenges of the present time.

### Why do you teach at all? Why not just do neurosurgery full time?

I honestly believe that I get as much out of teaching as I give. You're an older guy like myself, and you know that when you go out with people our age, they talk about what they have or what they've done. But what's really important is what you are and where you're going. I don't see the horizon yet, and I still see myself doing new and interesting things.

*"Teaching for me is very compelling."*

# Craig Campbell

## TEACHER, PSYCHIATRY RESIDENTS

*Craig Campbell is program director of Psychiatry Residency at the UCSF–Fresno Medical Education Program in Fresno, California. He received his medical training at the George Washington University School of Medicine and the University of Colorado Health Sciences Center. He was the 2004 recipient of the Henry J. Kaiser Award for Excellence in Teaching and the 2008 George Sarlo Prize for Excellence in Teaching.*

*He teaches courses for students doing their residency in psychiatry; he also teaches residents in supervision to discuss their work with patients in both group and individual settings.*

What I do in my course "Introduction to Psychotherapy" is attempt to bridge the theory students are learning to what they're doing when they sit in a room with their patients. The goal is to bring the theory to ground.

*Looking at it from a layperson's point of view, I sense that there are a variety of types of psychotherapy practiced. In your teaching, do you stress one of these over others?*
I am someone who believes that while, as you say, there are all these different types of psychotherapies, there are some fundamental commonalities, and that's "where the money is." It has been argued that the theory, what school you're working from as a therapist, is really more important to you than it is to the patient. If you were to watch a videotape of somebody doing good psychotherapy, and you turned the tape on halfway into the session, you wouldn't be able to tell what kind of therapy they were doing. Because what you're seeing is good therapy, and it is what is common among all the various techniques. That's the idea I use in my introductory course—trying to emphasize really basic principles that have to do with the relationship that's developing in the room.

*What are some of those commonalities to good therapy that you emphasize to your students?*

I believe that what actually promotes change and healing is grounded in the relationship between the patient and the therapist. I tell my residents, "The theories are for you; they keep you organized, keep you in your chair to sit still and be very present with this person who's in a lot of distress." A lot of times in therapy the task is to develop a relationship with somebody who doesn't do relationships—or has great difficulty in relationships. That would be the biggest overarching theme.

Any good therapy has what is called a "therapeutic frame." It's a mixture of ground rules and a treatment contract, a conceptualization of what it is that's being worked on and what the elements of that work are going to look like. That frame provides safety and some boundaries to the work. Any good therapy has a frame set up.

Another common element that residents are working on at that stage of their own development is starting to focus not just on the content of what's being said. When you start doing therapy, the process of the session becomes as important as content. It's really a different way of listening. There's a phrase from a famous book, "listening with a third ear." It's about listening in this way—not just listening to the content of what someone is saying, but everything else that goes with it—the timing, the non-verbal communication, the choice of words, all of that. And that's not something that comes easily to people.

Another commonality to good therapy is residents learning to attend to what's going on within themselves as they sit with a patient. Again, this is not something they're accustomed to doing. What feelings are coming up in me as I listen to this person? How am I feeling? The jargon would be "monitoring their counter-transference." It's important for all kinds of reasons. It's important for maintaining the frame. It's often diagnostic. It often helps the therapist understand what's going on in the room. It can guide the therapist in honing in on "where the money is." It helps to foster empathy.

Those are the main things that that particular course focuses on.

*What you're saying suggests that maybe therapy is more an art than a science, and that two therapists with the same knowledge base, both of whom made top marks in medical school, could really vary in their effectiveness as a therapist.*
That's absolutely right.

*And that takes us from the teaching of courses to your teaching in supervision. How do you develop that art of doing therapy in your residents? That must be tricky.*
It is. And not everybody gets there. Psychiatry is a big field and there's room for different types of people. Not everybody ends up being a psychotherapist. Not everybody's good at it; not everybody enjoys it. The key for me is that you have to know what you're working with. You have to know where somebody's starting. It's not helpful to teach in the abstract—you really have to find out where a resident is and meet him there and walk with him where you want him to go.

For example, one of the things I often think about is that there are two types of residents: those who tend to lead with their intellect, and at the other end of the spectrum, those who lead with their emotional selves. The latter type may feel their way along, get a sense of things, be much more intuitive, but may not be able to put in intellectual terms what they're doing and why. So if you've got two residents, each at the opposite ends of that spectrum, you've got two very different people you're working with, and two very different goals.

My bias would be that optimally you want to be someone in the middle, where you have access to both of these ways of working, where you can know your emotional and intuitive work with a patent with an intellectual and cognitive perspective. If you can bring those two together, you've really got something. So you've got very different tasks in teaching depending upon the type of resident you're working with. It's like working with a boxer who tends to lead with one hand or the other, and you're trying to get him to be more balanced.

*Having had friends in medical school, I remember their telling about walking around with an experienced physician doing hospital rounds and so on. Some of these techniques can't be used for psychiatry students. You can't do therapy with a patient while three residents sit there watching with their notebooks. What teaching techniques do you use in supervision to take the place of what other medical residents do?*

It depends upon what context you're in. If you're in an inpatient unit, you can absolutely have residents follow the doctor on rounds. We have a consultation service at the hospital here for patients in the medical and surgical services of the hospital who have some sort of psychiatric issue that the surgeon or the obstetrician has asked for our help with. And that's the typical five or six students traipsing around the wards, standing around the patient's bed. So there are contexts in which you can do the traditional medical-school kind of teaching.

In the clinic that I run, all of our rooms have video cameras in them, so whenever patients consent—which is most of the time—the sessions are being videotaped. That technology is so helpful, because you can sit and have a resident describe a patient to you week after week, and it can take you so long to get a feel for what's going on, whereas five minutes of videotape is very revealing.

*In the process of supervision, I assume you make criticisms, point out places where the resident therapist might have said something, that sort of thing?*

Partly. I try to create, much like therapy itself, a space and a relationship that's safe and structured and that facilitates a resident engaging in reflective work about what's going on—here's what I see, here's what I'm struggling with. A lot of times you're shining a spotlight on what you want the resident to pay attention to, both in him- or herself and in patients.

A principle of supervision, which we try really hard to teach in the program, is that supervision doesn't necessarily mean you're sitting with somebody who's senior to you, which is the traditional way that teaching medicine goes. You take your case, your work, to somebody who's ahead of you in training—and medicine tends to be very hierarchical—for consultation and critique.

So when people come into psychiatry, they've gone through medical school and usually done a year of internship, so they're quite socialized into the culture of medicine. And early on their expectation on their part is that psychiatric supervision will fit into that hierarchy: where you'll present a case to some superior, and the superior will tell you whether you did it right or wrong. As quickly as we can, we try to get them thinking differently about supervision. Sure, it may involve a faculty member who's your senior, but it doesn't have to. I tell my students all the time, "When you leave residency, where's supervision going to come from? When you get stuck or need to run a case by somebody, who's it going to be?"

It's probably not going to be some guru. It's probably going to be a peer, somebody you trained with. And you're going to say, "Hey, can I buy you lunch? I need to talk to you about a case." So we try to move to the point where they understand that supervision isn't about sitting with somebody who knows more than you; it's a process that has to do with discussing your case with somebody who's not part of that case, somebody who hasn't sat in the room with that patient and gotten sucked in to what's going on in the room. Supervision is about talking out loud, stopping to organize your thoughts.

*How much has psychotherapy and the teaching of psychotherapy been impacted by advances in psychoactive drugs developed in the past two decades?*
I think it's had a huge impact, some positive and some negative. There was a time not that long ago when the gold standard of treatment in psychotherapy was psychoanalysis. The best and the brightest residents went on to the psychoanalytic training. The best psychiatrists in the country were psychoanalysts. The irony about that, to my mind, is that the best people were treating the least sick individuals—treating the worried wealthy.

I was in residency between 1988 and 1992, and that was when the pendulum was in full swing toward medication. I trained at Denver, in a program that—at that time—retained a strong grounding in psychotherapy. But already there were programs in the country where virtually no psychotherapy training was happening, and there was a debate going on about whether psychiatric residents should be taught psychotherapy at all. The pendulum swung pretty hard in that direction, and I would say that we have a generation of psychiatrists in this country, trained in the past fifteen to twenty years, who don't know the first thing about psychotherapy.

What started to happen is that I think the promise of the biological age was somewhat blunted. Medications, no question, can be helpful. But the last time I looked, we haven't stamped out mental illness. They're effective, but not that effective. So there's a little bit of a backlash, because these medications by and large haven't lived up to the billing that they're going to eliminate psychiatric illness or psychic suffering.

*Earlier you spoke of the student who is far to the cognitive side, perhaps stiff and mechanical with patients. How do you get such a person to change? That could be like getting the leopard to change its spots.*

Yes, and not everybody can change. You're dealing with aspects of temperament, and not everything about us is plastic and changeable. If you work with somebody and they clearly are not going to have access to that other end of the spectrum, then you've got to help them maximize what they do have. It's like teaching a tennis player to run around his backhand; you're not going to have a good backhand, so you've to change how you play tennis. When you start to get into helping residents to know themselves, to know what their strengths and weaknesses are, then it becomes like career counseling—helping them to find practice contexts that are going to be a good fit for them. People usually want to do what they're good at and enjoy. Few of us enjoy things we're not good at. So if I see somebody who's very stiff and formal and über-cognitive, and they say I want to go into private practice and do a lot of therapy, I'll sort of say, "I don't know about that. You might want to think about that."

There are lots of different reasons why people might present at one end of the spectrum or another. Some people are just by nature temperamentally that way. Or some people might not have had the opportunity to explore that other end of the spectrum, or they might have come from a family where that just wasn't done, or—this sounds like a cliché—they may be repressed—and it might actually be pretty easy to get them to think about patients in other ways. Sometimes you'll see residents who seem pretty shut down emotionally early in training, and then by encouragement and good supervision they take off and blossom and end up really enjoying this other side of the spectrum.

I personally find it more difficult to go the other way. A few years ago we had a woman, a little older, and she had some previous experience doing therapy of some sort. As a resident, there wasn't a cognitive bone in her body. You'd sit and listen to her present a case and it was so frustrating because you couldn't make heads or tails of what she was saying. Her sentences sometimes weren't even complete. She was incredibly disorganized; she gave the impression of someone who was incompetent. And yet she had the most amazing ability to engage her patients. I don't think she ever had a patient who came to her that she didn't engage in ongoing treatment. And this is working with a lot of people from lower socioeconomic groups, who have a lot of problems with money and transportation and have all kinds of chaos in their lives—just all sorts of forces at work that undermine a commitment to ongoing psychiatric treatment—and yet she had amazing success. If you watched her on videotape with patients, it was almost like she could read people's minds. I mean, it was almost creepy. She had this empathic attunement to her patients, and they picked up on it, and she was extremely skilled in the room. I would say to her, "You could teach me about psychotherapy. You're very strong. But our task is to wed your skill set to the science of psychiatry. You need to be able to articulate what you're doing, communicate clearly with peers, think logically and rationally about psychopharmacology," and so on. And she was pretty resistant to it. She was someone who saw psychiatry as an art, and she was resistant to thinking about it as a science. I think I came into psychiatry more from the cognitive side, and for that reason, I think I'm more effective at helping residents follow that same path, and less effective at leading people the other way, from the intuitive to the cognitive.

*Trained as you are, you could practice full time. Why do you choose to teach?*

Well, it's just my nature. Both my parents were teachers. My father was a college professor and my mother was a kindergarten and first-grade teacher. I didn't grow up in a medical world. I think I came at medicine more from an educational perspective. I grew up in a family that believed you went to college not as preparation for a job—but that it was an end in itself to become educated. [*Laughing.*] I was someone who could have stayed at college my whole life because I loved it so much. I think I've always gravitated to teaching. Even in medical school, I was attracted to the faculty and to being a teacher. It's just always what I saw myself doing.

I really enjoy seeing patients, but I think half of that enjoyment for me lies in thinking of how this is a good illustration of such and such, and "I can tell the residents about this." I use a lot of my own experiences,—both good and bad—in teaching, so when something significant happens with one of my patients, either something that went badly or something that I thought was remarkable for one reason or another, I'm very often talking about it in class. I don't know, I just like to do it.

*Well that makes sense. It's something I hear a lot. I'm coming to believe there's a teaching gene.*

It's interesting, because I see a lot of parallels between teaching and psychotherapy, and a debate that you often hear around the teaching of psychotherapy is "Are good therapists born or made?" It's kind of the same thing you're wondering. Can you learn to be a good teacher or are you just born with a proclivity and then you can learn to refine that? In my mind, there are people born with the skills to be a good therapist or a good teacher and on top of that you can learn, but there are people who just don't seem to have that gene, as you said. But teaching for me is very compelling. It's very fun.

# 4 | *Teaching the Creators and Performers*

*"There is a magical change [in the students]."*

# Alexandre Sacha Pavlata

TEACHER, CIRCUS ARTS

*Sacha Pavlata is a fifth-generation circus artist. He grew up traveling Europe and North Africa with his family in a wooden circus wagon. His Hungarian-born mother came from a family of Risley act performers (the acrobatic foot juggling of people), and his Czech-born father descended from a long line of aerialists. Sacha himself became a master aerialist, and he has performed in a wide range of venues, including the Cirque Bouglione in France and the Big Apple Circus based in New York. In 1998, he joined the Flying Wallendas to help recreate their famous seven-person pyramid on the high wire, a feat for which they won the Silver Clown at the Monte Carlo Festival du Cirque in 2003.*

*Sacha has taught circus arts at the Conservatoire National du Cirque in Paris and the New York School of Circus Arts. He currently lives in Massachusetts, where he performs in his own circus company, Cirque Passion. When we spoke he had just returned from teaching a circus arts class to children at the Center for Creative Arts in St. Louis. He speaks with great exuberance in heavily accented English.*

**Can you tell me about the class you just finished teaching in St. Louis?**

It's a summer camp. The kids in the circus arts class are from eight years old to eleven or twelve. I set up a lot of circus equipment. We have a flying trapeze. There is a globe [*a large ball on which a person walks*]. They can walk on it, run on it, juggle on it, use the hula hoop on it. They do that for three or four days to learn balance, and they have a rope to hold on to so they don't fall down. Then I have a cloud swing that is my specialty—it's a soft rope in a V-shape. You swing on it and do all kinds of crazy tricks on it. Kids love it. Also we have a lyra, a round metal aerial hoop about a meter in diameter. Also the unicycle. The classes go for two weeks and at the end we put on a show. I have been teaching the children in summer in St. Louis for sixteen years.

*What effect does the two weeks have on the children?*

Oh, gosh. My classes have become so popular because it's challenging for the kids. They like to be challenged. They feel it's frightening, and I help them do it. Of course, safety ropes or my hands are always around them for safety. After one week, it's like they are my kids. They love me. When their parents come to pick them up, they want to stay. They are happy, and they have such confidence.

We have lunch, and sitting around me, they ask me questions: Where you come from? What have you done? And of course, I give them all the stories, how I grew up—because I'm five generations in the circus world. There is a magical change in them. There is a joy—it's just fantastic.

I see it is difficult with the children these days because they go to school, and it is a lot of pressure. From the moment we start our course, there is a magical change on them because it is fun. There is a joy to circus activities. It is just fantastic. I have a great time with them. I love to do it.

*What do you do if a child simply balks at something and feels too afraid to try?*

OK, that's a very simple thing. The children are different sizes. Some of them are a little bit heavy, some are skinny, some of them like to be in the air, some not. So after a few days I start to know them and I know which kids are good on this little thing and which are good on that little thing. Some of them don't like to be in the air, so I put them on juggling or on the unicycle or on the globe. It's divided so that everyone feels comfortable. There's also tumbling. We have a pyramid so the stronger kids can be on the bottom, the lighter kids on top. So everyone is pleased and nobody is left out. I find out in a few days who is good on what.

I teach also clowning. I have makeup, costumes. At the end we put on a show, and it's over an hour long. The parents come on the last day to see the show. It's a big hit and a lot of fun. The kids already cannot wait until next year when I come back.

*Is there a secret to your effectiveness with the children?*

Absolutely. It's very important to be very warm to the kids. Not every teacher has this. You see, I always have two helpers with me, and most times I use circus people. But sometimes those circus people are a little bit cold. Some don't really like to be teaching, but they do it because I pay them. So they just do it, but their heart isn't in it. And the kids feel it that they're not warm. So if I hear complaints, I talk to the teacher and fix this right away, and sometimes I have to change the people.

In teaching, and this is true in regular school, too, you have to give structure and not just beat them up. You can't just say do this and be always hard. You cannot push them past certain limits. You have to be kind with these kids. I always have a great time with those kids.

I remember when I was teaching about eight years ago at the Pickle Family Circus in San Francisco. There was a teacher just from China and he had a lot of little children six and seven years old. He was frustrated that they were progressing so slowly. He thought they were a little bit lazy. I just tell him, it is not China here or Russia where the teachers push very hard. In this country you have rich kids who cannot be pushed. So I help him to slow down, to moderate the training. Eventually, I saw him a few years later and he had had great success. He's a great teacher.

*It must have been very different teaching in Paris, where your students were older and training for a career in the circus.*

Exactly. They were very serious to have a career. They are very determined. They start at age sixteen, and most of them already have some physical basis, maybe gymnastics or other physical things. They have to be there at least three years. The first year they have to learn a little bit of everything, to find what element they like, whether they like trapeze or on the horse or juggling. Then the second year, they focus on that element and they start pushing themselves to build up, and they do that two years. Then they are tested before some juries to see if they're good or not good, and maybe they have to stay one more year to be perfect.

*What they do somehow looks both easy and impossible. How do you teach it?*

It is huge amount of practice. You start of course with the easiest things, then get harder and harder. Some of the tricks take great practice. It's like going to college—it takes four years. Or gymnastics, it takes seven years to be champion. With circus performers, it's the same thing.

The teachers all have been performers and they specialize in one thing, maybe flying trapeze or acrobatics. Everyone knows what they have done so there is great respect for the teachers.

When the students come out of there, they have great skill. Some of them even create their own show. The government there, if the students are really serious, will give them some funds to start their own circus. Sometimes I go back after a few years and see my old students are doing a great job and have their own circus. In this world today, it's not easy. You can be an engineer and the next day you have no job. But in my world, if you have the art form, you can also manage someplace to go and perform and make a living.

There are many great teachers all over the world. Some have great imaginations, so the students learn all kinds of new things. When you see the things they teach, you cannot believe it.

*Do you prefer performing or teaching?*

Well, if you can still perform, I mean, it's just such a joy. It's something magic to have the audience applauding you.

*"The more control the dancer has, the more freedom she has."*

# Suki Schorer

## BALLET TEACHER

*In article after article, Suki Schorer is named as one of the truly great ballet teachers of our time. She teaches at the School of American Ballet, the official training academy of the New York City Ballet, located in New York City's Lincoln Center. She has been a member of the permanent faculty there since 1972.*

*She began her career as a dancer with the San Francisco Ballet and joined the New York City Ballet in 1959, becoming a principal dancer in 1968.*

*She is also the author of two books,* Suki Schorer on Balanchine Technique *and* Put Your Best Foot Forward: A Young Dancer's Guide to Life.

*A few weeks after our interview, I had the pleasure of watching her teach a class. Though there were perhaps twenty-five young women in the room, Suki's discerning eyes seemed to see each one of them, and she would occasionally correct an individual dancer. Once she picked up a dancer's foot and repositioned it. "See," she said. "Here. Directly behind your spine. That's right." If a dancer's attention drifted for an instant, Suki knew it and called her back. I left with her corrections still sounding in my head— "Soften your arm. Your chest should be in front of your feet, not over your feet. Pull your butt up."*

*It's one thing to be a great dancer, but another to be able to teach dance. What's the difference? What are the ingredients of a great dance teacher?*

To be a great dancer, you have to focus on yourself. Obviously, you need a great deal of talent, musicality, hard work, dedication, passion, and all of that, but daily life is really concentrated on what is going to make your performance the best you can make it. When you teach, the focus is all on the students—how to make each student the best she can be, to help each one grow. It is the change in each student that the teacher looks for.

To be a good teacher, you put all the attention on your students. How can you best help them to grow? And then you have to figure out how to stimulate them so that they want to change, to do more, to take the risks and meet the challenges that come with development. You have to nurture their development and encourage them to work on their passion and love of dance.

*How do you encourage them? When it comes to performance teaching—piano, ballet, etc.—there seem to be two polarities, the encouraging teacher and then the drill-sergeant type, long on harsh criticism and short on praise.*

The teacher who influenced me the most, of course, was George Balanchine. He was demanding but in a very nurturing way. He did not correct in an impatient or angry way. He encouraged us by saying, "You can do a little bit more. I don't see it yet. Place your foot this way. Unfold your leg this way. No, that's not right. Yes! That's it. You've got it!"

So you have to nurture students, encourage them, and also ask for more. You have to make the student aware of the possibilities of more. You don't just tell them what you do; you have to insist, but in a gentle and not in a mean way. Dance should be fun. It should be fun in class. It should be a joyous occasion to take a class and to go on stage. And it can be, even if you're very focused and working to the limit.

As a teacher, you have to take joy in guiding students to change and grow. You have to be enthusiastic about the students' improvement. Or if they're not there yet, you have to be honest—because some things are going to take a long time. To become a dancer, it takes at least eight years of really serious training. You have to get strong and make the technique your own, and then make it automatic. The muscles have to know what they're doing without thinking, because when the dancer goes on stage, she can't think about how she's doing the steps—it just has to come out. It's muscle memory.

You have to look at each student individually because no one is the same, emotionally or physically. For example, a correction might be slightly different for each student, and when you make that correction, you have to see if the student understands it. Because sometimes the way you word something works for one student but not for another, so you have to keep changing until each gets it.

You have to make students aware of what they're doing. Often students aren't really aware that they have a hand, or they don't realize the lack of energy they're putting into the movement.

You have to teach the person who is in front of you. I try to make the dancers aware of how much more they can put into each exercise and just not do it by rote. Ballet classes are very repetitive—they have to be, because you have to train the muscles to move in a certain way to develop the technique, the clarity, and the articulation of the legs and feet. So you repeat and repeat. "Here we go again, another sixteen of these things." But if you could do each one like it's the last one you're ever going to do, it has a whole different dynamic. So I try to get that across, that there's so much more you can do. And that's how you're going to improve and change—by pushing your body beyond the comfortable, easy place.

You want them to dance bigger, to take a chance. You have to let them know it's OK to fall down. It's OK to look silly. Because in the end they will do fine.

As a teacher, you have to have a very good eye and know what you want each gesture, step, movement, and combination of movements to look like, and then be able to get that across to the students—through demonstrations, through imitation if there's a very advanced dancer in the class who's doing it well. Or imagery . . . any way you can convey the message of what you want to see.

*Can you give an example of the imagery you might use?*
Descend from the air—don't fall like Newton's apple. You take yourself from the air to the floor like the mother bird landing on her eggs.

*Those are nice. Over the years, you must add to your repertoire of little tricks like that?*
I do. I try to keep my class growing. I try to grow as a teacher. And I try to make it somewhat amusing. Balanchine would tell us wonderful stories related to the steps that we were doing. It kept me totally involved. His dancers really listened to him. I try to get my students totally focused for their hour and a half—whether it's making light jokes or puns or giving a difficult combination of jumps.

*Has your teaching been shaped by those who taught you?*
Yes, of course. I started dancing when I was very young. We did recitals, and right away, I learned the joy of performing when I was seven and eight. I try to teach that—the joy of showing and presenting yourself. Then my teacher said she had taught me everything she knew and suggested that I go to the San Francisco Ballet School. There I studied with Harold Christensen, the director of the school at that time. He taught me placement: how to stand up straight, how to turn out my legs from my hips—some of the basic technical elements of dance. Now I teach correct placement.

Then I came to New York, and the biggest impression ever was made by Mr. Balanchine. He gave me my life, so to speak. I became fascinated with what he had to say . . . about why we plié in a certain way. He would explain it all. It was so logical. And he was so musical.

That's the other thing that's so important in the classroom—the musicality of dance. Each step has its own look and its own accent and timing. It's not just even. It's put the foot out—and bring it in. [*Here her voice becomes musically precise and changes tempo.*] Or out and out, in and in. It's important for the students to feel the joy of dancing in the music, and to be on time—and in time—and yet phrased.

So that's all exciting. Balanchine always used to emphasize that dance is a performing art. He would say, "You have to want to show yourself." So a teacher has to get students to want to present themselves, their whole body participating in the movement. A teacher must bring that out—so they're feeling the tips of their fingers and the ends of their toes, and so their dancing becomes bigger and more expansive and more beautiful. A teacher must get them to feel the joy and the beauty in their movement. And when that happens, it's very rewarding to be the teacher that's encouraging it.

Balanchine didn't just teach how to dance; he also taught how to live.

*And how did he think one should live?*

He wanted us to participate fully in the moment, in the now. Your life is all those moments put together. It's the process that is your life. You may want to be a famous ballerina, but that's not your life. Your life is *becoming* that ballerina. You have to participate and enjoy the process, because you don't know what your life is going to be. You may become a ballerina, or you may not. But the moment you're in now is the moment you need to live in fully. So when it's time to cook a nice meal and have friends over, well, get a good meal on the table and enjoy your company. And if you want to see a show, focus on that.

*Do you in turn try to pass that same wisdom on to your students?*
I do. It starts with the focus and energy and concentration you begin class with. Because you are totally alive in your whole body, so you're alive in that moment, and that's what makes the dance interesting—the energy, focus, and expansiveness in the movement. And then relating that to the music, because the music of course is the floor of the dance. But you have to put everything you have into each moment.

*Do you teach differently when you move from the high intermediate to the advanced students?*
The combinations can be almost the same, or they could be harder. Instead of one turn, I might ask for three turns. I might change the tempo a little bit, slower or faster. By exaggerating the tempo, then the normal tempo becomes easier to do because you've pushed them to the extremes. Does that make sense?

*Yes it does.*
So maybe they do a very slow jump, and the landing has to be continuous, because you don't want to thud to the floor and stop. So that takes a lot of control. The more control the dancer has, the more freedom she has.

*Have you changed as a teacher since you first started?*
I think the combinations that I give are more interesting than when I first started teaching. I think the musicality I want within the steps is more precise, and I think I'm able to articulate it better. I have developed better ways to correct and ways to get the student to be involved and to change. I've developed better ways to get the whole class participating in the class even when I'm correcting one person. I think I look more at the whole dancer than when I started teaching and yet I still focus on the small details, too.

*Are there things in dance that can't be taught?*
[*Wistfully.*] There are.

*What are they?*
The intangible elements. Each dancer is special, and if you can bring that uniqueness out—some people just have a glow about them when they move. And some

dancers can have a very fine technique, but they don't make you look at them. I mean, there's nothing interesting about them, although everything's fine. It's that extra special thing that makes a star. Can you teach that? I don't know. You can try to nurture it if it's in there and bring it out. But if there's nothing there, it's hard to bring it out.

Performing on the stage isn't the same as sitting behind a computer or mopping the floor. You have to sell yourself and you have to enjoy selling yourself—projecting, putting out. Really, the vocabulary of ballet is very limited—with only x amount of steps—and somehow within those steps you have to create a beauty and an interest. That's the real talent. That's an innate quality.

*I assume a certain proportion of your students will not go on to perform but will do other things in life. Is there a value of ballet training apart from performing ballet?*

Yes—the concentration, the focus, the dedication that a student puts into learning how to dance. It takes tremendous effort. They can take that with them anywhere they decide to go. In fact, a lot of our students who decide to go to college, perhaps because they didn't get into a company, go to Harvard, Yale, Stanford—because they know how to study, even though they've been doing ballet up to four hours a day. When it's time to study, they know how to study. When it's time to dance, they know how to dance. When it's time to have a good time, they do that. I think training in ballet is a wonderful education.

And ballet gives you a certain bearing so that when you walk into a room you can walk standing tall—and proud of who you are.

*You started teaching while you were still a performer. How did you start?*

Balanchine looked at each of his dancers as individuals, and he knew more about us than we knew about ourselves. He could tell by the way I worked in class, how I listened to him, and how I liked to help people outside of class that I was a teacher. He asked if I would like to teach during my layoff, and I said sure. So I started teaching when I was very young, about twenty years old.

*And you must have liked it a lot?*

I love it. First of all, I so believe in what I teach. I'm passionate about dancing. I get very involved in teaching, and then when I see the students get involved, too, and grow and develop, it's very exciting and rewarding.

*Do you have moments when you wish you were still performing?*

Oh God, no. Not now. I think now, "How did I ever dance that?" But I did. But no, I don't miss it at all. I'm happy that I'm still walking and that I can still dance the Argentine tango.

*What are the moments of greatest joy as a teacher? Are they small moments when a student "gets it" in class, or larger moments of seeing a student perform on stage?*

All of it. [*She laughs with delight.*] Because six hours a day of my life is teaching, I have to take joy in the small changes. But when I see them do our annual workshop at the end of the year, it brings tears to my eyes.

I staged *Barocco* [Concerto Barocco *is a Balanchine masterpiece*] at the School of American Ballet's year-end workshop performance, and then our students also performed it at the Kennedy Center this year opposite the Bolshoi Ballet School, the Paris Opera Ballet School, and the Royal Ballet School, and my students were just wonderful, just magnificent. So that's very satisfying.

The School of American Ballet is a professional school, so almost all of the dancers at the New York City Ballet have come through the school. I start teaching girls when they're fourteen years old and work with them throughout their teenage years at SAB, culminating with our workshop, and then they join the company. So when I go to New York City Ballet performances—because I've taught now for thirty-six years—I've taught almost every female dancer in the company, so that's so exciting when a young dancer is going to do the Swan Queen, her first Swan Queen, and just three years ago she was a student at the school. So that's also wonderful. It's all rewarding. [*She laughs again.*]

*"Being a teacher has made me a better photographer."*

# Keith Carter

**PHOTOGRAPHY TEACHER**

*Keith Carter grew up in Beaumont, Texas, a small delta town near the Louisiana border. His mother was the local portrait photographer, and he became a self-taught fine-art photographer. Since the publication of his first book of photographs in 1988, Keith Carter has become recognized as one of America's top fine-art photographers. He has published nine books of photography, and his work has been acquired by the Art Institute of Chicago, the Smithsonian American Art Museum, the San Francisco Museum of Modern Art, and the J. Paul Getty Museum.*

*He still lives in Beaumont, and he teaches locally at Lamar University, where he holds the Walles Chair in the Visual and Performing Arts. He has received the university's two highest teaching honors, the University Professor Award and Distinguished Faculty Lecturer Prize. He also teaches workshops for photographers at such venues as the Santa Fe Photographic Workshops and the Center for Photography at Woodstock.*

At Lamar University, I teach beginning photography all the way up to graduate seminars. My classes are usually sixteen to eighteen students. Our lab classes are two and a half hours. I try to always give a lecture, forty-five minutes to an hour, looking at someone's work or a group of people's work. And then they either show me their work in progress and we do critiques, or they go work in the darkroom or to the digital lab.

My mission might be singular in that my school services for the most part about seven counties in a rural section of the eastern part of Texas, and my self-proclaimed mandate, aside from teaching the nuts and bolts of photography, is to introduce them to photography, art, and culture in a way that might not have been a part of the fabric of their lives up to that point. So I try to bring in a number of influences: the history of photography, and also film, film documentary work, art, just about anything I can think of that's germane to photography and the visual image.

I tell my students that they'll go into a profession of some sort and they'll work eight, twelve hours a day, but that's only a part of their lives, and art makes you more civilized, more humane. And I try to find ways to show them that it's a part of their daily existence, even in a rural culture. I throw in everything from Andy Goldsworthy to Henri Cartier-Bresson.

*And when you teach in the workshops like Santa Fe, your goals must be different?*
It's really a different mandate at a place like Santa Fe. The people have paid a reasonable amount of money and they're excited to be there, and often they're really hungry to hear what you have to say, or how you might open a window and help them to progress. And they're generally older. They're adults, and they've been through a number of things that an eighteen- or nineteen-year-old hasn't, so in a number of ways you're dealing with people who really want to learn, rather than students who are busy texting any chance they can get.

*Speaking of texting, in the twenty years you've been teaching, have you noticed changes in students? One might say that our culture has become ever more visual, but perhaps visual in a way that's less than aesthetic.*
Well, both of those things are correct. What I've noticed is—well, number one, never ever sell them short. For the generation I'm teaching now, the context of their lives and the context of information are different. When you and I matriculated, the heart of photography was the camera, film, and the darkroom, and now there are all kinds of ubiquitous picture-making systems from cell phones to satellites to ATMs.

I came in the other day to give a lecture on aspects of the history of photography, Fox Talbot and Daguerre [*two of the earliest pioneers of the photographic process*], and there was a young woman, a good student, with a box of Cracker Jack at her desk. She had pulled out the prize, and she was photographing the prize in her hand with her cell phone, and she was e-mailing it to her boyfriend. The whole idea of Talbot and Daguerre and what they went through and a young woman making a picture for fun to send to her boyfriend twenty-five miles away just struck me as one, beautiful, and two, completely ironic.

The other thing I'll tell you is that there used to be a handful of great photographers and you'd show students that work and show it to them in depth. I think to some extent their attention span is shorter than when I started, but on the other hand there are a number of great photographers who have evolved in those twenty years, so now I find myself not just teaching one photographer—not just teaching Sally Mann by herself, but putting Sally Mann with Nan Goldin and Julie Blackmon—three women photographing families in completely different ways. This holds the students' attention more, but also is probably more germane to contemporary photography.

The last part of this long-winded diatribe is you couldn't talk about photography in the eighties without bringing in Robert Mapplethorpe, no matter what your or my opinion of the work was, and now I find they couldn't care less about Mapplethorpe. That kind of homoerotic documentary just doesn't resonate with them. They find it pretty boring. That may just be my region, I don't know. They find Robert ParkeHarrison [*a contemporary photographer whose monochromatic images depict landscapes scarred by technology*] much more stimulating.

*It's one thing to be a great photographer and another to be a great photography teacher. What's the other ingredient required?*
That's a good question. I come from the secular world. I don't have an MFA degree and I just sort of fell into teaching, so I come more from the streets than straight out of a graduate program. I find teaching one of the most stimulating and interesting jobs, even after twenty years. I think the answer to your question is enthusiasm. I make photographs all the time, and I share that with them, but I love looking at other people's work and I love talking about other people's work. I don't feel beat down by the digital revolution. I find the whole world of photography, even in all of its changes right now, a thrilling journey to be on. So I guess the short answer is enthusiasm.

The other thing is, you know, even if I've got one or two sleeping in the back—I used to squirt them with a squirt gun or go bang on their desk. But if that happens now, I still love talking about photography, and I figure there are two or three, maybe more, who are really absorbing what we're talking about. In my program, if I get two or three who make art a part of the fabric of their lives and always remember it, and change a few things in the direction of their lives, I'm pleased. [*Laughs.*]

*What is the relationship for you between doing photography and teaching photography? Does each stimulate the other?*
There are much greater teachers than myself, and I've met a number of them, and I fancy myself as being pretty good. But a number of my colleagues really define their lives in large part by teaching, and I admire that greatly. But I'm not built that way, and part of it has to do with not coming out of the graduate school. I worked for a good while in the secular world as a professional photographer. So I don't define my life by teaching. It's just part of the patchwork of what I do.

Being a photographer hasn't made me a better teacher, but being a teacher has made me a better photographer. It has opened up a whole world of ideas. Trying to stay abreast of everything, and learning how to articulate the theory behind the work or the context of the work to younger people, has really helped me to grow and to derive a wide variety of pleasure from a wide variety of photographers.

In the fabric of my life, I don't want to *do* all kinds of work. There are certain things I focus on (no pun intended) but teaching has made me a better photographer by opening up a world of ideas instead of my just working in a solitary way in a rural area—which is what I had done for a long time.

Does that make sense?

*Yes, it does. You also teach at some of the best-known workshops, Santa Fe and so on. Why? Not for the money, I'm sure.*

No, you don't do that for the money. Part of it is for the stimulation. I really like to spend a week with mature people, who do a high level of work, and who are interested in discussing ideas. I find that stimulating. It's also like someone said, you feel at the end of the week like you've given blood. But for the most part, I find it stimulating. I find it fun.

*Are there particular students you've taught that you especially remember, maybe people whose lives you're turned around?*

Well, no and yes. I've had a number of interesting students. As for those I've turned around, that's probably a handful. I like to think I've influenced a number of them.

The thing about teachers is, teachers change people, but often teachers don't know they changed that person. Sometimes I'll get a letter ten years later and I don't even remember who it is, but they remember something, and they had the courtesy to write and thank me. It's not often, but it's happened a handful of times.

*I know what you mean. Sometimes I think teaching is like sealing a note in a bottle and casting the bottle into the sea. You never really know who reads it.*

That's true. I think teaching is a precious thing and . . . well, the word is "privilege," and it truly is. Particularly having come from the outside, I can't think of a better place to be. To me, the academic world—outside of the meetings—is a wonderful and pleasurable and stimulating world. It doesn't tire me out like some of my colleagues say. I find it stimulating rather than tiring.

*I love your phrase "outside of the meetings." Why do they do that to us?*

[*Laughs.*] I don't know. I think it was the West Coast photographer Jack Welpott who said he had cultivated a persona of being completely undependable and totally eccentric so he wouldn't be asked to do all those things. There's a certain bit of truth to that.

But anyway, the teaching part is a lovely part to me—because it's about art and it's about ideas. And I like talking to young people, and I like hearing what they have to say, too.

*"There's always something to be improved upon."*

# David Kelsey

## PIANO AND VOICE TEACHER

*David Kelsey has taught piano and coached voice for many years. He received his bachelor of music and master of music degrees in applied music from Ithaca College, where he served as staff accompanist, taught piano and accompanying, appeared as a soloist with the orchestra, and served as assistant director of the opera workshop. After graduating, he continued his studies with Jeanne-Marie Darré, the noted French concert pianist, and Cecile Genhart, professor emeritus of piano at the Eastman School of Music.*

*Mr. Kelsey has accompanied and coached regional winners of Metropolitan Opera competitions, a first-prize winner of the Eleanor McCollum Competition at the Houston Grand Opera, and a first-prize winner in the North Carolina Symphony Youth Concerto Competition, among others. He is currently a voice coach, performer, and accompanist in the Research Triangle area of North Carolina.*

I started teaching piano when I was an undergraduate many years ago, and then I continued in graduate school and beyond. The ages of my students ranged from children of six to a lady who was in her seventies. There was also a very wide range of abilities.

*As someone who doesn't play any musical instrument, I'm in awe of those who do, especially if they do it very well. And the piano always seemed to me especially difficult. How do you teach someone to play the piano?*

How do you teach someone to play the piano? [*Pauses.*] Well, first of all, they have to have an interest in it. I remember having battles with parents of children who really weren't interested but just acceded to the parents' wishes, and that never worked very well. So first of all, you have to have a real interest.

Second, it helps if you have some innate musical ability. If you don't, you can still learn to play, but it will likely be rather mechanical. If I were asked, "What is innate musical ability?" I would be hard pressed to answer, other than to say you know it when you see it—or hear it.

Then students have to learn how to translate what they see on a piece of paper into something that makes sense with regard to what their hands are able to do. Learning to play an instrument, whether it's piano or anything else, is partly a physical learning process, but it's far more a mental learning process. You have to develop strength in your fingers and your arms, but a monkey could do that. What you really have to do is develop the ability to translate what you see on the printed score into something that makes sense—in terms of mentally being able to hear it and then translate that into something your hands and fingers are able to do. That can be rather challenging. And it's more challenging for some than for others.

*Do you have teaching tricks? Do you do a lot of showing?*

As contrasted with a lot of music teachers, I generally refrain from showing them how to do something. To me, it is more important that they not copy but learn what it is they should do and then struggle with doing it themselves. Now physically, there are some simple things that students can be taught. Playing a scale, for example, you have to learn how to properly position your thumbs. That's a case in which you can certainly demonstrate to a student how and when you move the thumb. To be able to play a scale *legato* [*smoothly*], that's an aural thing as much as it is anything, and that's something that you have to train your ear to listen for. Playing a musical instrument is very dependent upon your ability to hear what you're doing. The better you get at that, the more progress you will make.

You have to have a knowledge of music in order to play any instrument. It's not enough that someone teaches you how to jump over a bar that's seven feet high. You have to learn how to approach it, how to raise the leg, and all of these other physical and mechanical things. But you have to have a mental image or concept of yourself actually going over the bar. The same thing is true with music. You have to have an understanding of rhythm, of tempo, of sound, of feedback, of the capabilities of the instrument, an overall appreciation for music—and it doesn't have to be classical. It can be country-western, popular, opera—any number of things. But at some level that music has to speak to you in a way that you have some inherent understanding of it. You bring that to a particular instrument of your choice before you even play the very first note.

I guess I could argue in contrast to that, what about a five-year-old child? Could he or she possibly have that kind of inherent appreciation? I guess my answer would be, yes, children probably do or they wouldn't be interested in taking an instrument in the first place. When a child starts taking lessons at an early age—and I was one of them; I started when I was five—they've probably already been exposed to some kind of music that on some level they have liked, appreciated. They have some inherent feeling for it, and then what you're doing by teaching them an instrument is helping them learn how to translate that into something they can do on an instrument of their choice.

You could be a great pianist and a lousy musician. I wouldn't want to name any people in particular, but I could probably come up with a few.

*In that case, would it be fair to say they might have the technical expertise, but what they're lacking is something emotional or even spiritual?*

Yes.

You have to have three things in order to be a fine musician. One, you have to have the technical ability to be able to do on the instrument what it is that you need to do. Two, you have to have an understanding of music on some level, whether it's that these are logical chord progressions and these are resolutions and these are dissonances or this is the structure of a particular work that suggests certain ways to interpret it, or whatever. And three, you have to have what some might call heart or soul, some emotional basis for identifying with the work. If you don't have those three things, if one of them is lacking, then in the performance—whether it's in your home or on stage at Carnegie Hall—it quickly becomes apparent to the audience.

Technical proficiency in this age—meaning the last fifty to sixty years—has always been there. There are lots of pianists who can play notes faster than you can imagine with close to 100 percent accuracy. But many of them, in my view, are rather dull and boring and they really don't have much to say.

*Does this suggest that some people might be able to play music that is light and happy, for example, but not something tragic because they didn't have that aspect to their soul? Or is that overdoing it?*

That's pushing it a little far, but it's possible.

*I guess I have in mind what Stanislavski said about acting, that you have to have an emotion within you in order to play a character who feels that emotion.*

I think that's absolutely true, and in fact, I can give you a recent example—in fact, she was here last night. I have a twenty-three-year-old lady and she was singing an aria from Carlisle Floyd's opera, *Susannah*. She's on stage alone, she's been abandoned by her boyfriend, she's pregnant with his child, and she has been ostracized by the town. She sings about that, but in order to do that aria successfully, you really have to identify with the character and her situation. The first few times Elyce sang it, technically it was good, but it was missing that part to it.

I worked with her on how to achieve that and she turned it around completely and it was much more effective. We performed it as a recital with some other singers two weeks ago and it was very well received. So she was able to step into the character, even though she has nothing in common with the character or her situation. So I had to keep working with her to put herself in that place and to be able to sing—and the aria is in English—words like "bleak" or "cold" in a way that the timbre in her voice actually suggested what those words mean. When she got to that point, the performance was really transformed.

For me, music is all about communication. When you can get up in front of an audience, whether it's one person or five thousand, and communicate on some level with them, then that's what it's all about.

*When you work with a six-year-old, you're teaching him or her how to play the piano. But with some of your students, you're trying to transform them from very good to excellent, or from excellent to superior. At that stage, are you still working on some technical things, or is it more the communication ability that you've been talking about?*

It's usually both. I don't think it matters whether it's piano, stringed instruments, or voice; there is always something that can be done better.

Let me use two examples. The singers, because of the internalized nature of their instrument, are not able to hear themselves as others hear them. So they especially need feedback from external sources. Pianists generally are lousy listeners. They get used to doing their own thing as soloists and they really don't develop a very good sense of listening until they do other things—like play chamber music or serve as accompanists. It's only then that they really start listening to what they're producing, and whom they're producing it with. Pianists generally need help with getting them to listen to what they're doing more carefully. So technically, it's more difficult to play a simple *legato* scale than most people realize and many pianists are sloppy with that. Getting them to come to the next level about communicating to an audience is another leap. So yes, both things are important—the technical and communication—even with people who are very good. There's always something to be improved upon, or there's always something you had never really thought of that someone comes along and points out to you. That's really the magic of teaching from the teacher's perspective, in that the better students you have, the more you are going to learn from them.

*So at that level, an important component of teaching is giving the best feedback, which depends upon the teacher's abilities as an expert listener.*
Yes. And it also is highly dependent upon the student. When I first started out teaching at the undergraduate level, one of the first mistakes I made—and I vowed never to do it again—was failing to learn the difference between two extreme kinds of students: the first is the kind who, the more things you find wrong, the more that student will like you as a teacher; at the opposite extreme is the person who, even if you gently suggest one thing he or she might improve upon, immediately breaks down into tears. So you have to develop a sense of who this person is you're trying to teach and what his or her needs are at the time. And that can be rather difficult.

It's important to know what the aspirations of a student are. If a student comes in and plays or sings for me and tells me that he or she wants to get a scholarship at Julliard, or wants to play the role of such and such at the Metropolitan Opera, then that is an invitation to find a thousand things wrong. Because if I don't, someone else will when the student gets there.

*You've been a teacher of piano and also a voice coach. You've suggested some similarities between the two, but are there also differences?*
Yes. Probably the biggest one is that if you're a singer, and you don't play any other instrument, then what you lack is the tactile sense that every other instrumentalist has. There's a correlation between playing an instrument that requires a tactile sense and a feel for rhythm and tempo. Singers who have not been trained on another instrument frequently have troubles with rhythms and tempi. So sometimes singers—and I have a couple currently—just need to be drilled with rhythm and

tempo. Sometimes I will tell singers who may be very good that they should take up piano or clarinet so they get a better sense of rhythm and tempo—and sometimes they even listen to me and actually do it. [*Laughs.*]

The other difference is what I've already mentioned—singers are not able to hear themselves as others hear them. It's like the rest of us—the first time we hear our recorded voices, we say, "Oh my God, do I really sound like that?"

*When you think back on your teaching, is there a student who especially comes to mind—either as a good memory or a bad one?*

Yes, I can think of two examples from the very first semester I ever taught. I had a student who had decided he wanted to be a pianist, and his ability was mediocre at best. One day there was a knock on my studio door and this boy's father introduced himself. He said he wanted to talk with me, and he proceeded to ask me point blank whether I thought his son was ever going to make it as a pianist. I was really unprepared for that, and after hemming and hawing for a while, I answered honestly that if he wanted to play professionally as a concert artist, no, he was not going to make it. But if he wanted to play for local choruses or for his own enjoyment, he should be encouraged to do that. Though I had no idea what kind of response I was going to get, the father sat back with this tremendous sense of relief and thanked me for my honesty, and said his son had significant other academic talents he could pursue.

So that's at one end, and at the other end, I had another student that semester whom I would have been happy to spend hours with and teach for free. She pushed me—unintentionally—to really rise to the occasion. She was very talented and very smart and very conscientious. At the end of that semester I suggested to her that she go to a better school—and that's exactly what she did. Those are the two students I remember best from those days—for very different reasons.

*For someone who is an expert like yourself, can musical talent be recognized with accuracy?*

Yes. [*Laughs.*] I'll answer that with an absolute *yes*; however, it constantly amazes me how some people can audition with a CD and one school will reject them and tell them to their face that they lack talent, and yet that same person with the same CD will be welcomed at another school with open arms.

*How do you explain that?*

I don't have an easy answer for that . . .

*Is it like Hegel said, "In the dark, all cows are black"? Are there simply people who can't recognize talent?*

I think there are a lot of bad teachers out there, to be blunt. And some people simply do not recognize talent. That's in contrast to how I answered your other question, that yes, I think talent can immediately be recognized. But I guess I would add to that, not everyone can recognize it.

*Is there anything else from your teaching career that comes to mind you want to tell about?*

Yes, there is. I'd add one story. It's one of these experiences that you don't forget.

One year, I volunteered to teach an economics sequence to ninth graders at a local high school. I had been in an MBA program at one point, and economics was always an interest of mine. The first day I walked into the class, there was one kid I knew was going to be trouble. I did the only thing I could think of. I said, "You come and sit here"—which was basically right in front of me. I had no classroom training, no teaching methods education, none of that crap. He still continued to have an attitude, but after a couple of classes, he and another kid that sat a couple of seats behind him began to participate in the class, and by the time this economics unit was over, the two of them were in the top four or five contributors in the class. I didn't think much of that until after the last class when the teacher whose class it was took me aside and told me that the one kid is mildly retarded, and the kid I had sit I front of me—his father was in prison and the kid was infamous as a troublemaker in the school. I said, "You know, if you had told me that before the first class, I probably would have treated them differently." But I didn't, and they became two of the more productive members of the class. And that was something that I really never forgot.

*"Determination is the key."*

# Lan Samantha Chang

## CREATIVE WRITING TEACHER

*Sam Chang teaches fiction writing in the University of Iowa Writers' Workshop, one of the nation's most prestigious and selective creative writing programs. She is also director of the program. Last year, the program received 850 applications for 25 slots. Previously she taught creative writing at Stanford and Harvard, where she was Briggs-Copeland Lecturer of Creative Writing. Her own work includes a collection of short fiction,* Hunger *(1998), and a novel,* Inheritance *(2004). In 2008, she received a Guggenheim Fellowship. She told me she does not like doing taped interviews.*

Over time, what I've discovered works best for me as a teacher is if every writer in the class gets a different workshop. I don't have a formula or a specific method for producing improvement in writers. It seems to me that everyone who comes into my class writes differently and has different strengths and a different set of concerns. As their workshop leader at this crucial stage in their development, I try to gauge what's best for everybody based upon their work and what I know of them as a writer—the stage they're in, what their personality type is.

For example, I will allow a workshop to be rigorous and even harsh if I believe that the writer can hear and learn from that kind of discussion. But I am very quick to step in and protect a writer if I feel he or she needs a different kind of discussion. Some people go into a fiction workshop wanting to get raked over the coals. If that's what they want, I often get a sense of that in my conversations with them before the workshop. Other people enter the workshop with some fear of group criticism, and as a result I try to make the workshop focused on constructive ways in which they can think about their writing, without taking it personally.

### How do you know what each student needs?

So much of it is intuitive that I find it difficult to describe in words. When I go into class, I get a feeling from the students. I get a feeling from their reactions to the things I say, and I'm able to understand them based on that.

At various points in my life I've been astonished to encounter how extremely talented emerging writers can be and yet feel enormously insecure despite their gifts. A writer like this has to be treated in a workshop situation with great care. Because some writers' insecurities work in such a way as to prevent them from continuing their writing. I can't control what people say in the workshop, but I try to frame the conversation in such a way that it takes the emphasis off of the writer herself, and puts it onto concerns that I think every writer in the room should be aware of when they're doing their writing. So I think of everybody's workshop as a lesson for the entire class.

[*She hesitates.*] I really want to talk about my teaching, but I don't think I have any big statements to make. And I think it puts the emphasis in the wrong place to talk about people's insecurities. This is why I hate being taped . . .

### Sam, I was lying. I'm not really taping the interview.

No, I know you're taping it.

What I'm trying to say . . . let me start again.

In a fiction-writing workshop in our program, a dozen or so people gather to discuss each other's work. So the work of the students constitutes the primary teaching text in the classroom. Because of this, our conversations can be extraordinarily passionate and personal. It's one of my responsibilities to make sure that what is said in class creates a learning environment that offers something to everyone and not just the writer who is being critiqued.

I often say to my students that they'll learn more from understanding their own comments and the comments of their peers than they will from having their own work critiqued. Because generally when people are having their own work discussed, they'll sort of shut down, and they don't always hear it objectively. So I try to create a conversation in which the entire group can learn something from every piece we discuss.

I don't have a set method for approaching the very diverse works by our extremely diverse group of students. For example, over the summer I taught a class in which there was an extremely confident, extremely prolific twenty-one-year-old writer, who I personally think will prove to be one of the most gifted writers of his generation if he continues to work at the level he's working at now, and if he continues to improve in the way that he's improving now. He is the kind of writer who takes enormous risks, and lives or dies by those risks. He attempts multiple formal inventions in one piece, and there's a huge amount going on in his work. If anything, the exuberance he shows in his work is so high that he loses focus.

When it came time for his work to be presented in the workshop, there was a kind of wonderful quality of bravado in the work, but it was out of control. He put it out for us with this deep excitement knowing that he was going to be critiqued by people who were extraordinarily smart. I could tell that he really wanted to hear what everybody had to say, regardless of whether it was polite. He really wanted to encourage honest feedback, and he would improve from the feedback. Everyone knew he could take it, and they also knew that they had on their hands someone who was extraordinary, and really deserved the most stringent critique that they could think of. That was the harshest critique that we gave in that class over the semester. But I felt that it was OK. I felt that he would continue writing, that the critique would fuel his desire for perfection, and that it would be fine.

On the other hand, I often have a student in class who, in spite of having truly marvelous gifts, has lost confidence to a tremendous degree. In situations like that, I try very hard to make sure that the student does not feel that our conversation is a personal attack. So I try very hard to make sure that everyone gets a very intelligent conversation about their work, but those conversations are not the same in nature.

I also follow the classroom work with one-on-one conversations with the student. Certain students have a tendency to stop writing because of lack of confidence. They may stop in the middle of a story and not finish it or they may stop revising a story so that it's not really completed. So I have to be really careful in class with this type of student to make sure that they feel supported—not only during the discussion but also afterward when I work with them one-on-one. It's my experience that in some of these cases having a supportive teacher can make the difference between continuing to write and giving up.

*Do you rely entirely on the critique of student writing, or do you sometimes do positive teaching where you try to give them certain fundamentals of writing?*
Is "positive teaching" some kind of pedagogical term of which I'm not aware?

*No, I just made it up.*
I don't know what it means.

*Well, suppose you were teaching beginning creative writing and students had no idea how to write a short story. So you might tell them about a common plot struc-*

*ture—action, background, development, climax, ending—that they might try. Do you ever supply that sort of thing, even if at a more advanced level?*

I never do that. What I do is to create a vocabulary that we share, and part of creating that vocabulary involves defining certain terms. Some of them are traditional terms—for example, the term "exposition." I try to talk about it in such a way that I don't simply define it, but uncover ways of thinking about it that the students haven't considered before. For example, one of the interesting things about exposition is that it generally has to end before the climax of the story. I don't think students are always aware of that as they're writing. Sometimes they can't see how information should be revealed and when. In an efficiently constructed story, by the time the climax takes place, we know everything we need to know. This kind of information is useful to somebody who has material in rough draft and is trying to figure out how to make it as strong as possible, but probably not useful to someone who is trying to learn to write his or her first story out of whole cloth.

My former teacher Marilynne Robinson once said to our class that a story is a pearl of mutually referring meditations. What does that mean on a practical level? It means that if you're trying to construct a story along these lines, you think about the idea of a pearl. A piece of sand violates the protective shell of that oyster and stays there inside the oyster until it is covered with the mutually referring meditations, the milky substance of the pearl. Most stories start with a sense that something is wrong, some sense of violation that gets under our skin and won't go away. Some students may find this a very useful way of thinking about a short story. So while one person may prefer writing a story with a traditional triangle model, another may prefer writing a story that is more like a pearl.

I believe in using different ways to describe literature and the creation of literature and then allowing students to work in the method that works best for them—that is probably my method of teaching.

Is that helpful?

*Yes. That makes great sense. Have you developed any tricks over the years for helping students with their writing?*

No, I can't think of anything I'd call a trick. The thing that I most wish for is that my students feel the confidence to complete a work of fiction. And I will do what I have to do in order for them to have that confidence. And at times I need to rein them in and explain that their work is lacking in formal control.

*Are there ways in which writing cannot be taught?*

Maybe the understanding that determination is the key. A teacher can't stand over them and make them keep trying. People still believe that what makes one writer better than another has something to do with innate talent. There is such a thing as talent, but ultimately the writers who succeed are those who come up with ways to keep approaching a work again and again, and they have a kind of stubbornness, and gosh, the qualities of a peasant, a relentless concentration . . . that can't be taught in a classroom. It can be discussed, but it can't be taught.

*So you don't put a lot of stock in creative genius or divine inspiration?*

In the teaching that I do, the students are at such a level that if any of them could simply clear their lives and minds of obstacles that keep them from working, and bear down and write what they can write best, and if they could see what that was or keep figuring out ways to approach it anew for a long enough period of time, then they would all achieve success in a conventional sense.

And the sad fact is that many of them do not. Life gets in the way.

*Do you like teaching?*

I take tremendous pleasure in teaching writing, and I find that it keeps me pondering the elements of fiction writing that are ultimately the most fascinating. I take it as an opportunity to study what interests me as well as what interests students. I think one of the reasons I'm able to do that is because the students I teach are so advanced. In any way that my mind moves, the students will move along with me. In that way, I'm very lucky.

I find teaching a deeply valuable activity, and it's one of the most regenerative, exciting, and solemn-producing activities that I have. And occasionally disappointing. But in general, the pleasure, excitement, and inspiration far outweigh the disappointment.

*"Use it, all of it."*

# Martin Landau

## ACTING TEACHER

*Martin Landau has had a distinguished career as an actor on stage, television, and film. In 1955, he applied for admission to the world-renowned Actors Studio in New York. Of two thousand applicants, he was one of two admitted. There followed a distinguished acting career spanning five decades.*

*In the sixties, he rose to fame among television viewers for his portrayal of Rollin Hand in the popular series* Mission: Impossible. *His acting in films included* North by Northwest *and* Cleopatra. *He was nominated for Academy Awards for his roles in Francis Ford Coppola's* Tucker: The Man and His Dream *and Woody Allen's* Crimes and Misdemeanors. *For his role in Tim Burton's* Ed Wood *(1994), he won an Academy Award, a Screen Actors Guild Award, and a Golden Globe Award.*

*First asked by Lee Strasberg to teach classes at the Actors Studio in New York, Martin Landau was one of several members instrumental in opening a West Coast branch in West Hollywood, where he also taught. He continues to teach there, and he is currently its co-executive director.We met over lunch at Jerry's Deli in West Hollywood, which turned out to be too noisy for an interview. He generously invited me to accompany him to a preview screening of his latest film,* Lovely, Still *(a beautiful film, acted with true mastery by him and Ellen Burstyn). Then we drove over to the Actors Studio for our interview. Throughout the afternoon, he was gregarious, warm, and generous. At seventy-seven, he has the energy of a twenty-year-old. I asked him one question and he talked almost without pause for two hours.*

### How do you teach acting?

That's a very interesting question because unlike medical school, where you teach anatomy, or a history teacher who teaches facts and dates, teaching acting is about what an actor *does.*

The approach I use is based on the Stanislavski "method." Of course, the term was badly translated—"system" is more accurate. So we're not method actors, we're system actors. That's a joke. It's hard to get a smile from you, Bill. [*But now I laugh.*]

The Stanislavski method changed the shape of acting in this country. Before, in theater, there was a kind of representational acting going on, with a lot of posturing, pontificating, a lot of vocal acting.

I started teaching because Lee Strasberg [*artistic director of the Actors Studio in New York*] asked me to teach. I got into the Actors Studio and Lee was really rough on me and very gentle with Steve [*Steve McQueen, the other actor accepted in the year that Martin was accepted*]. He made a mistake with Jimmy Dean by being very rough on Jimmy, and Jimmy stopped working at the studio. Jimmy still came to the sessions, but he didn't get up any more. Lee beat the shit out of me, but it was really good for me. It made me strong.

One day he said, "I want you to teach." It was like the hand of God telling me to teach. So I started to teach. I could help people. I understood it. I was in my twenties and I was teaching people in their thirties. I had a way of understanding what was happening, because it was happening to me, too, as an actor. I had solved the problem, and I found ways of helping them to solve the problem.

If I interviewed them, I would try to talk them out of coming to my class. And after what I said, if they still wanted to come, I felt that they were the right people. I liked people who had a sense of adventure, who also were complex . . . and nervous and worried and with a sense of humor . . . those were the things I looked for. And people who didn't take themselves too seriously, but took what they did very seriously, people who could laugh at themselves—which I think is essential.

What I teach is a conscious approach to free the unconscious and the imagination. Just stay in the moment. It should seem to the audience that what the actor is doing is happening for the first time ever. They don't want to see the rehearsals. A good performance is one that seems to be happening as we watch it, whether it be Shakespeare, Shaw, Ibsen, or Tennessee Williams. It's about living and breathing.

For example, if I tell you a joke and it's funny, you laugh. Now I tell you the same joke again. Uh-oh. But you as the actor know you have to laugh, to the point where it's real laughter. Because fake laughter is spotted in a second. How do you laugh again? If you can do that, you don't need my classes. Because that's what acting is: laughing at the same joke over and over as if you're hearing it for the first time. That's what I teach.

People often ask, "What is it you do?" Well, in a written script dialog, what people say to each other is what each character is *willing* to share. What the character is *not* willing to reveal is what I do for a living. Because everyone has a hidden agenda, and it's that element, the underbelly of a character, that is the basis on which modern plays are written. A Romeo will talk about his love for Juliet for pages and pages [*here he quotes from memory twenty or so lines of Romeo*]. But for a character in today's world to say I love you, it's like grabbing someone by the crotch and squeezing—hard. We live in an inarticulate world. We learn about a character not so much by what he or she *says* but by what he or she *does*. All this is a preamble to answering your question . . .

OK. How do you train an actor? The senses—our five senses: sight, touch, taste, hearing, smell—are what we use. Nothing on the stage is real. Tennessee Williams writes a play where it's a hundred degrees because it's New Orleans in the summer. He wants that. He wants the sensuality of that, he wants the sexuality of that, the slippery bodies in *A Streetcar Named Desire*. That element is virtually a character in the play. You're usually in an air-conditioned theater or a soundstage, so it's not really hot. So the actor has to create that.

When an actor's talking on the telephone, there's no voice on the other end. [*He puts his hand to his ear, as if he's talking on the phone.*]

Hello? Yeah. I can't talk now. What? I'm in the middle of an interview. [*He looks at me and mouths "sorry."*] I'll call—I'll call you back. Yeah. In about an hour. [*He continues with his imaginary call, his bare hand to his ear. At first I am amused—he's good. But then I am so utterly convinced by his acting that when he finishes, perhaps forty-five seconds later, I reach across the table and open his hand to see if there is a phone there. Later in our interview, he receives a real call on his cell phone, something about a meeting with Jennifer Lopez and "her people." His acted conversation was more compelling and convincing than his real conversation. He's not good; he's great.*]

*That was very convincing.*

Well, that's the bottom line. We create everything on the stage. Every object should feed us something.

The choices an actor makes are what governs his performance. A lot of people have said that a good actor doesn't have to be intelligent, he just has to be intuitive. Well, I don't know a good actor who isn't intelligent. He has to be able to read a script—which is just a bunch of words on a piece of paper—and it doesn't contain what a novel does, heavy description of what's going on. It's just the dialog. So what is going on underneath is what the actor has to discern.

Now in the theater you may have weeks of rehearsal to figure it out, but in film you're maybe meeting your wife of twenty years in makeup that morning. All of the scenes in your home will be shot that day. You don't even know the person. So how do you relate to that person as if you're incredibly familiar with her? You know when you're looking at her what's going on, and you know when not to look at her in order to avoid what you don't want to see—you're that familiar with her. Then you have a happy scene, you have the breakup scene, and then the making up scene and then you have the divorce scene—all shot on the same day with an actress you never saw before. To be able to touch that person with the familiarity you need, to be able to kiss that person . . . that's what the teaching of acting is about. I mean, if I can wake you up at three in the morning and you can do that, then I don't have to teach you that.

Some years back, Jack Nicholson said in an interview in the *New York Times Magazine,* "The reason I'm a good actor is because Martin Landau put me through a series of exercises for three years before I could do them." Those were exercises designed to make the actor aware of what goes on when the violin starts playing the violinist.

The exercise I'm talking about is a singing exercise. You sing a simple song like "Happy Birthday." I tell them to hold each note the same, long length of time. [*He demonstrates, each syllable is extended for several seconds. "Haaaaaa-peeeeee-biiiiiirth-daaaaaay," etc.*] Now what happens when the actor is trying to relax while he's doing this is that he's letting go of his thoracic tension, his vocal tension. And feelings that are there—some current, some not so current—start coming out. The only avenue of escape is the voice.

What happens during this exercise, if the actor is able to do it and relax, is that through the song, which is the only avenue of escape, they start to laugh, they start to cry. [*To my amazement, he tears up and his voice breaks.*] They become affected.

[*Martin notes my amazement.*] My own instrument is pretty much there; I can laugh or cry in a matter of seconds because I've trained myself. As a teacher, I never ask an actor to do anything I can't do.

It's very hard to do this exercise. It's almost impossible to do it the first time. What you're doing is breaking a pattern. What happens is, as soon as they feel a feeling that is unspecific, in seconds they'll go from laughter to tears to anger, because all of that is there. And most of it is held back because of years of arming themselves against rejection, pain—all of it: a boy doesn't cry, a gentleman doesn't do that, you don't say those things, you don't do this or do that. All of that stuff becomes a problem for the actor. The actor needs to be open.

The second part of the exercise is movement—vigorous movement. So that the voice comes out of the movement. It's very hard for a lot of actors to do that. Now these exercises are designed to get the instrument to respond, so that what's going on will affect you right there on the spot. That's why people watch Marlon Brando or Jimmy Dean or Al Pacino or Bobby De Niro or Kim Stanley or Jimmy Harris or Gene Hackman—because they all have craft. It's not mechanical.

Nicholson wanted to succeed in those exercises because he knew the value of them. And once he got it, he got rid of the strictures that plagued him. He learned how to consciously relax musculature, to breathe.

*These exercises, are they something one can do four or five times and find them helpful, or is it more like learning a backhand in tennis, that you have to do them hundreds of times?*

It's learning a backhand in tennis, until it becomes organic and part and parcel of his instrument, until he begins to trust it as something that will be there for him.

One of the things I look for when someone auditions for the studio is tension. I've learned over the years that the more talented an actor is, the more tension they have and the most susceptibility they have to tension. Tension is basically feelings that are not coming out.

The thing we call talent is the ability to feel a great deal. Actors who are more talented have more acting problems than actors who are less talented. The more representational kind of stock actor is not prone to the stuff that inhibits and squelches the kind of expression that is necessary. In a well-trained actor the voice, the body, the emotions are all connected. When the tension occurs, the senses shut down.

You don't give someone talent, but you help them to use their talent. You recognize that they have talent. And you encourage them to let go of all the strictures that society has laid on them. An actor wants to cry. No one wants to cry, really. To cry means to be sad, to be miserable, to be hungry, to be cold, to be hopeless. No one wants to go there. There's an inordinate amount of damage done before they want to be an actor. What's keeping them from being great actors is all the training they had by society to be polite.

I used to have students do an exercise I call the primitive man exercise. They have all of their senses, but they don't know anything. They're a blob with feelings. When I clap my hands, they take their first breath. They open their eyes. They make their first noise. It's a very difficult exercise because their knowledge gets in the way. They start discovering each other. Eventually they touch each other.

I admire talent—a lot. But a talented actor who can only use 25 percent of that talent is not as good an actor as an untalented actor who can use 100 percent of his talent. My job as an acting teacher is to help that first actor find that other 75 percent and learn how to apply it so that he can repeat a scene again and again and again.

Actors tend to go toward the thing they're most comfortable with. The thing they're least comfortable with is probably the most important part of their talent. Most people deny negative feelings, things that are upsetting. We armor ourselves. We learn not to go there. But the actor *has* to go there because he draws on that very stuff. We're basically a vessel of everything we've ever experienced. It's still there, right now. How do we bring it out? Showing what one feels is not acting. Many people are afraid of their own feelings. And one of the things I do—as a teacher of actors—is get them to team up with their feelings and not be afraid of their feelings. They're not going to die if they touch those feelings.

A character with pain . . . I always try to inject a degree of that in anything I do. It's universal. Everyone—no matter how happy he or she may appear—has had some pain in his or her life. Whether it's emotional pain or physical pain—it's very recognizable by an audience. Most people in life run away from pain: that's why Bayer is a multi-millionaire.

Actors are continually subjected to emotional pain by being rejected. Auditioning is not like selling Fuller brushes, where if the customer doesn't buy he's saying I don't like your brushes. Actors armor themselves against that, so the very seeking of work creates problems for the actor, because it's very painful. Actors are saying, buy *me*, and sometimes the person says, sorry, I don't want you. Whoa! Well, that "whoa" doesn't help their training. It's very tricky stuff, and a good teacher of acting is sensitive, having been there and overcome a lot of it, and is capable of doing everything that he preaches.

*It strikes me that one thing especially difficult about acting is that you can't see yourself. You may think you appear afraid, but maybe to the audience you do not.*

That's why we have the Actors Studio. Did you succeed or fail? We will tell you. How are your colleagues seeing you? Our criticism will be on the basis of what you chose to do today. The start of the criticism will begin with, "This is what I saw." And then from that we go to, "This is what you left out, this is what you should work on next time."

*In addition to doing your exercises, will an actor sometimes bring in material he or she is working on at that time?*

Yes. Or sometimes they're in an off-Broadway play and they want to work on a scene they're having trouble with. Also, we have a session here called "How to Rehearse." And we have sensory sessions—they're about getting the senses to respond to an imaginary stimulus.

I always say, a great pianist practices, and there's this section that gives him trouble. Well, don't ignore that. Do that part over and over and over again. That's what I would do. I would get them to a point where they'd embrace something that they dreaded before. People have a lot of fears. If they really embrace them, then they realize it's not so bad. It's like going to the dentist. You dread it, and then after you've gone, you see it wasn't so bad. The fear of it is worse than the expression of it.

I've never had an affair with any actress I've ever taught. Mainly because it's very personal work, and it's about trust. They need to trust me, because I'm not going to hurt them and they're not going to hurt themselves. But it is getting into areas that they tend to ignore.

Teaching acting is being able to understand that person, to see what his or her fears are, being able to say, "This is what you're not using." So I'll suggest a scene to students that will *demand* they use that part of themselves. I'll choose a scene knowing that it's loaded with stuff this actor is not doing, not going toward. There's no avoiding it. That person is struggling like hell, and I'll help with it. And then they say, this is not so bad. And then they'll be brave enough to use it in their work. It will be part of their kit bag, as I call it, their vessel.

It's all there, who you are, everything you've experienced, everything you know. Use it, all of it. Some of it you deny. Some of it you're not going near. But it's all you. Join up with yourself.

I hang out with wonderful people—a lot of kids these days. I've worked with Johnny Depp, Jim Carrey, Matt Damon, Edward Norton, Johnny Cusack, Matthew McConaughey, Woody Harrelson . . . as far as I'm concerned, they're my contemporaries. It keeps me young. It continues to challenge me in the same way that acting challenges me. What can I do to help this person? I recognize a lot of stuff because I've been through it and dealt with it. What I'm basically saying is that helping an actor take what's written on a page and turn it into a living, breathing, multi-layered human being is what one teaches.

I've tried to answer your first question, and I'm stumbling through this, but it's only because it's manifold, it's huge, and it's complicated.

# 5 | *Teaching the Fixers and Makers*

*"I try to instill pride."*

# Kina McAfee

### INSTRUCTOR, APPRENTICE
### CARPENTER PROGRAM

*Kina McAfee is a journeyman carpenter who teaches carpentry in the Chicago Regional Council of Carpenters Apprentice and Training Program. A native of Chicago, she graduated from Northwestern University with a BA in political science and urban studies. She is a member of the United Brotherhood of Carpenters and Joiners of America, Local 1. She has been a carpenter for twenty years.*

*I had an uncle, a German immigrant, who was a carpenter, a real Old World craftsman. He once built me a doghouse. I watched him build it and it was a great doghouse. Has carpentry changed since my Uncle Fritz did it?*

Actually, we lament the changes in our trade quite a lot. The general trend in industry toward breaking jobs down to their simplest components for speed and profit—and not necessarily for quality—has really affected our trade a lot. You can still see quality work here and there, but a lot of our work is done in shops now. So they'll build a wall in a shop, ship it to the construction site, and then erect it on the site. It's all about speed. The hurry to get things done to minimize cost and maximize profit works to break tasks down to their simplest components. So carpenters are not as well rounded as they used to be.

Our students are not Old World craftsmen—they are builders. They put walls together. They've lost the sense of pride in the job—not all of them, obviously, but many of them. The ability to learn all aspects of the trade and apply that on the job—that's been taken away. I think that we as carpenters don't have the appreciation for our trade that carpenters used to. People do, though, work on their own, they build things for themselves, and they get to try to do that Old World craftsmanship for themselves. But we simply do not do it on the job site. And that's a pity. It's a shame. It's a rare thing when you really get to do quality work on a job site.

*How does one become a carpenter these days? What if someone says, "I want to be a carpenter." What does he or she do?*

Most people come through our apprenticeship school. We take people straight out of high school, or sometimes it's later and the person is starting a second career. They start with a nine-week preapprenticeship course—that's before they ever go out on a job site. That course teaches a lot of safety, print reading, the use of hand tools and power tools. We actually build a small house in the shop.

Then they go out as a first-year apprentice carpenter. They go to work for a contractor. Then every three months they come back to school for a week. The first time they come back they learn how to do labor management, how to do layout for walls, things like that. Then they go back out to work, and three months later they come back to school and they learn how to rig scaffolding and they get certified in that. Then they go out and the next time back they do metal stud framing. Next time it's grid ceilings. So they do something different every time they come back to school.

The training is just an introduction—to grid ceilings, for example—so hopefully they get to work for a contractor where they can put their skills to good use, but sometimes they don't. The total apprenticeship is four years.

### What exact courses do you teach?

I teach metal stud framing, low wall framing, grid ceilings, concrete, heavy gauge framing . . . so I teach mostly commercial building classes.

### How do you actually do the teaching?

Typically, we start with a classroom portion. There is math associated with everything we do. For instance, this week I'm teaching concrete, and the math associated with that is estimating concrete. They will learn to build from just a print, but since some of them have never done concrete, I have photographs of various stages that I show to them. Then we go out into the shop and I take them around and show them where everything is. As they start to build it, I hang around and give them pointers, let them make a couple of mistakes.

So for this week, we probably spend a quarter of our time in the classroom doing the math and learning some background about concrete, and three-quarters of the time in the shop building concrete projects. We are doing two projects this week, two different types of form work: one mostly plywood and the other with metal framing. That is not even 5 percent of the concrete that's out there, but if they went out on a concrete project, they would recognize the hardware. If they had never been on a concrete project, they would start at the bottom, but then they could quickly work their way up since they understand the basic concepts involved.

In the school, I can expose them to a lot of construction, but they really learn this sort of trade by getting used to it and doing it over and over again. If you have carpenters who have done only one kind for thing on a job site, that's going to limit what they know. They can also come back and take more night classes. So if a carpenter is mostly doing drywall on a job, he or she might come back and take some additional night classes on trim work to learn more and get up to speed.

*I hear you're a really good teacher. What do you think makes you good?*
[*She hesitates.*]

*I mean, whether it's kindergarten or anything else, some teachers are more effective than others . . .*
I understand what you're asking.

I think I make an effort to appeal to different methods of learning. That's why I use pictures of stages of construction to go along with the reading. A lot of carpenters are very visual, and so I spend a lot of time trying to get them to visualize a project before they actually get out into the shop for the hands-on part.

I think I have a lot of patience. Sometimes we instructors—because we're all carpenters—get a little impatient with our apprentices, and so we skip over things. Or maybe we assume that they know things. I make no assumptions. I start from the bottom and work my way up each time. I try to do it a lot of different ways. I go over it on paper, I show them pictures, and then I do a lot of correction when we're out in the shop, a lot of walking around and monitoring. So I'm a real hands-on teacher. But the main thing is I never take for granted what they know. And the young men—they bluff a lot about what they know. "You got it?" "I got it." Well, I don't believe it. [*Laughs.*]

I break everything down. I figure the first time I go through something, I've got maybe 25 percent of the students in the class. So I've got to hone and re-hit some points until I've got the other 75 percent. And I don't believe I've got them all until we've done it out in the shop and then we go back into the classroom and review it. So when we get back into the classroom, I'll have them all sit there and I'll say, "OK, without looking at your notes, just from memory, what's the first thing we did?" It's amazing how many can't come up with it and are stumbling around—and they just did this out in the shop. A lot of our learning is about repetition, so I try to get to them to report it, at least in their minds, after we've done it out in the shop. I want them to work it through in their heads a couple of times so they can see the logic of the steps.

A lot of these kids are fresh out of high school, and they pretty much think they know everything. So we get all of that attitude. You really have to have a lot of patience. I tell them that they want to be able to look back on the jobs they do as something they take pride in. I think it sinks in. Sometimes when they first get into the program, they're like high-school knuckleheads. But after four years, they see the importance of doing something they're proud of. I try to instill pride.

*I was recently told that even now there are still problems with gender issues in terms of how women carpenters are treated. Is that true?*
Oh, it's unbelievable. I can't understand how that kind of sexual harassment and discrimination has persisted for so long. It's partly the nature of the work—it's very physical work, and a lot of guys just don't want to accept women doing it. So that's

one thing. A lot of guys, after they've worked with a woman or two, will loosen up from that. But that doesn't explain the constant and pervasive atmosphere at the job site where there are pictures, things drawn on the walls, writing—it's like no one was ever involved in a lawsuit before.

A lot of women know about that. We train women to expect it and how to deal with it. Of course, it's not all the men. I would say 50 percent of the men I've worked with have respected me and respected what I did.

But even worse than that, in this really depressed economy, a lot of women are not working. It's a lot worse for the women than it is for the guys. When it's a contractor's market and they can pick and choose, they never hire women. It's really bad. I know some women who are really good, hard workers and they can't buy a job. That "last hired, first fired" practice—it's still going on.

Some of the trades are better, more fair. Like the pipe fitters—it's more like hiring halls where there's a list of people out of work and they pull off the top of that list. The electricians are better, too.

*Are there still Old World craftsmen like my Uncle Fritz?*
Absolutely. We see them, but they're all old.

*And when they're gone? What about the future?*
There will always be that carpenter who wants to be the absolute top of the line and wants to learn everything. I think our society is changing a lot. And I can't just point the finger at those kids, because whatever high skills they learn they are never going to put to use on a job. They're not appreciated for it. But it won't disappear. People do it on their own, and they do it for relatives and friends and achieve that level of quality they want. There are always going to be those who love the trade, who love the work they're doing. Our instructors are like that.

I went to college and I had some college instructors who really inspired me, people who just really knew to the depth their field. I remember a couple of instructors—in African literature and psychology. You could ask them anything and they'd go on and on in a very interesting way.

My first carpentry instructor was a woman. She had been non-union forever and finally broke into the union and started teaching. She was the first woman teacher in our regional council. Her hands-on style is what got me involved in carpentry. I had been volunteering for a community organization and we were fixing homes for poor people. I thought I was doing construction, but of course it was just cosmetic stuff—patching up holes and things like that. She gave me appreciation for what is a shoddy job and what is a good job.

I love being a carpenter, and I also like the teaching. Every now and then, you get real appreciation from your students. Not always. But they'll tell you they liked your class. Often, it's years later.

*"I go to work every day with a smile."*

# Ralph Salemme

### HIGH-SCHOOL TEACHER, HEATING AND PLUMBING

*Ralph Salemme teaches heating and plumbing at Platt Technical High School in Milford, Connecticut, a public high school whose mission is to combine a technical and academic education. He has taught there for twenty-two years, and he has been on the curriculum-writing committee for his trade area. Students attend Platt Technical by choice. The students are in session 182 days a year, and they alternate between half of the time learning a trade and the other half taking traditional high-school academic classes. As freshmen, students are exposed to each of the fourteen trades offered in an exploratory program, and then they choose a trade area to pursue for the next three years. The school reports a very high success rate at finding students jobs when they graduate.*

We have a huge and rich tradition in this state of training people to join the work-force. The state does a pretty good job of funding this program, though of course we could always use more. I myself am a graduate of this system.

*Could you describe the way you teach?*

The kids are with me from 7:30 in the morning until 2:20 in the afternoon. From 7:30 until 9:30 or 10:00, we'll do theory classes—the theory that actually backs up the hands-on work. Then I'll release them out into the shop and they'll have specific tasks that they have to complete. I'll usually do it on a demonstration basis, and the kids get to work at their own speed, and they essentially have to do the same thing that I've done. Then I grade them on it and we go on from there.

Right now I have about sixty projects in the shop, so the kids are always busy. There's never any down time. They keep a work-based journal every day that I tell them is akin to how it will be when you work in a trade. You'll need to be able to complete the paperwork and be specific so that you can have accurate billing and be successful in the career.

*Is critique a big part of it, showing them what they did wrong when they try something and don't do it right?*

Yeah, as a matter of course, that's part and parcel of teaching—without making anyone feel strange. There are times when I'll stop everyone and say, "Listen, I notice that several of you are having trouble with this . . . widget, if you will, and here's how you can attack the problem."

Sometimes it's pretty interesting to watch, because things you didn't think would be a problem are, and things you thought might be a problem aren't. Sometimes I'll stop people in the middle of things and say, "OK, we need to reassess how we're doing this."

*Are there qualities other than technical knowledge that you're trying to teach?*
We call them soft skills. And yes, there's a huge percentage of time that we spend on just that. You know, how to be respectful, how to act in people's homes, how to act with one another. It's interwoven with the other lessons, and it is considered to be very important. It's generally not a block of time that I set aside and say, "OK, we're going to talk about how to approach Mr. and Mrs. Smith."

*How do you teach that—talking about it, demonstrating it, critiquing them when they slip up?*
All of those are part of it. A large percentage of what we try to do—and by "we" I mean myself and the other instructor I work with—is that we work very hard to be professional with the kids. When they're in the shop, they have to have their uniform on and it has to be tucked in. There are very specific things that we require of them every day. And if they don't do it, they can lose points. The language they use in the shop—they can lose points for that. And just by modeling those skills in the way that we talk to them, in the way that we act, the way that we dress— everything. We try to maintain everything as professionally as possible and still work with kids.

*Do they respond and catch on pretty well, or is teaching those soft skills a difficult task?*
In the early years it was difficult. By now we have a tremendous amount of phenomenal kids, and sometimes I'm actually very surprised at how good the kids are. Especially the group I'm working with right now—they're just phenomenal. They really catch on quickly. As long as you reinforce what you say you're going to do, they know you mean business.

*What are the things that make you a good teacher?*
[*He grunts.*]

*I mean, whether it's baseball or plumbing, there's a difference between doing something well and being able to teach it well to others.*
Yeah. Uh, it's a difficult question to answer. But if I have to . . . I think the kids realize that I genuinely care about them. I think once they realize that you're really there for them and you're really there to help them, they respond. And you have to be effec-

tive at explaining to them the opportunities. A kid can leave there and never go to college and probably make more than quite a few college graduates. So they know that we care about them and that we're offering them something.

*Do you have many failures in the school, kids who drop out?*

We have a very small dropout rate, but there are a few who do drop out. And there are times when people decide it's not a fit. My oldest son graduated here, and he came through my shop and he's a very successful plumber today. My youngest son came to the program but he decided it wasn't for him, and he's in college today. So it's not for everyone. One size doesn't fit all.

I think a lot of them walk in not knowing what to expect, but once they do see it, most of them are intrigued. And when we talk about the opportunities that await them, most of them pick up on it.

When they're in my shop, under state guidelines they are pre-apprentices. When they graduate and get their job, they are registered through their employer as apprentice plumbers, and then in three to five years, they can take the state test to become journeyman plumbers.

*Do you get any girls in the plumbing class?*

We usually get some. I think the most we've ever had was four girls in a class of eighteen, and some years there aren't any. It takes a special kind of person, because the plumbing and heating trade is a heavy trade, it's a dirty trade, and I'm very up front with the kids as to what they're getting into before they actually choose the shop. It's no different with the girls; I let them know that it's a tough trade and a dirty trade, but it's certainly a trade that needs women, and if you're interested in doing it, there are wonderful opportunities there for you.

*What's the racial balance at your school?*

I think we have about 40 percent African American, a smaller population of Latino, and then the rest Caucasian.

*Do you have any of the racial tensions among students that plague some public schools?*

We really do not have those problems.

*What's your secret?*

I think the kids really have the sense of the school as a family. In fact, here's an interesting statistic: our attendance is very high on a daily basis, somewhere between 95 and 98 percent.

The students like to be there, they're happy to be there, and they're there every day. And I tell them that they need to be there because we cover so much ground every day that you don't want to miss anything. They take it as gospel and they're there.

*Are the skilled tradespeople you graduate more immune to job loss and the out-sourcing of jobs overseas that have shrunk the working class and union jobs so much in recent years?*

Yeah. It seems to me that there's a place for every student, and I think it is a good hedge against the shrinking workforce. I work in a licensed trade that you really can't take overseas. In the school where I teach, we have fourteen trade choices for students. I think my trade in particular is wonderful because they can't outsource it, but quite frankly, unfortunately, as the workforce shrinks there are more and more people who can't afford to call the plumber.

*Am I correct in thinking plumbing probably hasn't changed as much as other trades over the years?*

I think you're incorrect. I would say it was maybe stagnated for a long time, but the amazing thing to me is that I can bring a lot of zest to the classroom because there have been so many changes, and I'll give you some examples.

With the rising energy prices these days, people are always looking for alternatives. So one of the things I'm going to concentrate on this year—that I think is a wonderful opportunity for the kids—is geothermal heating. It's been around for years, but it will probably become more commonplace as time goes on because energy costs have risen so much. About ten or twelve years back we did all the radiant floor heating in a nature center with the kids. We looked at it as a new process, but in fact that process has been around in Europe for many years. So there's always something new. We now have indirect water heaters, and we have tankless water heaters. Technology has given us quite a boost in terms of the things you can offer people today.

*Have you changed much as a teacher in your twenty-two years?*

I think patience comes to each of us with age, so I believe I'm more patient than I've ever been. When I started, I thought teaching was a good thing to do and I liked working with the kids, but I think that as you grow older, you realize just how important your work is, especially with the way that there are many families these days that don't have a male figure in their household. So my partner and I sometimes become almost surrogate parents. We are very conscious of the fact that we need to be good male role models because there's a shortage of that, I feel, in this country.

*What led you into teaching instead of working full time as a plumber?*

I had a high-school teacher who was very influential. I had remained close with him after I graduated, and he was the one who suggested that my personality was such that I should probably think about teaching. I also had a friend who did the same exact thing. He was influenced by a teacher as well, and he went back and did the same thing.

*And since you've stayed with teaching, I assume you like it.*

I don't believe that there is a more noble profession than teaching—I really don't. When you stop and think about what it is that a teacher does, and the influence that he or she can have on your life, you realize it's one of the most important jobs that a society has.

*I imagine that you must know a lot of your former students, and that many of them still live around there.*

That's true, yes. I actually keep in touch with quite a few of them, and that's a rich tapestry as well. You get to keep in touch with these younger people—though some of them are actually getting older. [*Laughs.*] It's great to see them be successful. Some of them have their own businesses, most have stayed in the trade, and the ones who haven't stayed in the trade still keep in touch, and it's good to see them doing well for themselves. You like to think that maybe some influence you had on them has been a positive force in their life.

*It sounds like the country could use another ten thousand of you.*

I go to work every day with a smile. It's very important work. Plumbing is a very old trade, and it's really the key to some of the greater civilizations. I don't think a lot of people really realize that. They even think that the downfall of some of the greater civilizations might have had something to do with poor plumbing. I try to explain to the kids how important it is. I don't consider that a licensed plumber is any less important than a doctor, because the bottom line is we both affect health in ways that are huge.

*"When the student is better than the teacher, it is the biggest reward."*

# Dieter Schorner

## PROFESSOR OF BAKING AND PASTRY ARTS

*Chef Schorner received his training in Switzerland and Germany. He has had a distinguished career as a chef and teacher. He was pastry chef at several of the world's finest restaurants, among them Le Cirque, Le Chantilly, La Côte Basque, and L'Etoile in New York; the Savoy Hotel in London; and Caféhaus Konig in Baden-Baden, Germany. He opened his own Washington, D.C., restaurant, Patisserie-Café Didier, which was named by Condé Nast Traveller as the third-best restaurant in America. In 1988, Time magazine named him the best pastry chef in America.*

*He was chairman of pastry arts at the French Culinary Institute in New York City. For the past ten years he has taught at the Culinary Institute of America in Hyde*

*Park, New York. He has taught many of the world's best pastry chefs. He speaks English with the heavy accent of his native Bavaria.*

You see, I believe teaching is like being a farmer. If you tend to your crops, sometimes you get something out of it. I'm seeding the ground with knowledge, and I hope it sprouts not only great craftsmen but also good human beings. Of course, it's like with the weather—sometimes if you're lucky you have a wonderful crop; sometimes you're not, and nothing comes up. So it is also with students—you try very hard to educate them, not only that they learn the craft, but I also believe a craft doesn't mean anything if they are not good human beings.

I tell them in the beginning, you see here, if you use a half a roll of paper just to take up a little spill of water, the more papers you waste, the more trees we will cut down. You may think we have enough trees, but in the end they will be gone. So I like to teach them also to be stewards of the earth, of the future.

So it is not only that they need to learn how to make a beautiful cake or beautiful chocolates, but also to be wise about how to make it. When I go into shops, everything is over-colored, everything saturated with chemicals. I tell them, if you want something pink, you can easily take pomegranate seeds that make beautiful pink. So I try to help them go away from all the chemicals, but this is probably the hardest thing, because people love dark colors. They want the reddest red: it doesn't matter if there's a half bottle of chemicals inside. And when I tell them, they look at me like I'm coming from a different world. You see here, there are so many illnesses in the world and we don't know from where they come. Why not use Mother Nature first, before you use the chemicals? That's how I try to help them be good stewards of the earth as well as good craftsmen.

I tell them to make a wedding cake, and I say, "Do not overuse color and the chemicals." Then, the next day you should see what they do. They take so much color. It's doesn't matter if it's brown color, blue color, orange color—they love it. I can't explain these things. And to talk them out of it . . . it's like Galileo, who said the world is round and nobody believed him.

*I am surprised at the resistance you're describing. I would think that young people these days would be very receptive to messages about healthy eating, natural ingredients, and ecological concerns. But they are not?*

No. Not at all. It takes, I think, another ten years or so until we reach the view that less is more, stay away from all this artificial stuff. It is not there yet.

We are known around the world as the country where everything has to be big. I tell them, it's much better to make it small, make it first class, make it beautiful and good. You live longer, you live healthier, and you enjoy it much more than eating until your belly bursts. But sometimes it's like talking against a wall. It takes a long time. Most people grow up in the way they call it, "Get my money's worth." The plate has to be so full it runs over. I see something like that, I don't even want to eat. It has to be beautiful, simple, and natural. My teaching is to help them to be healthy people. You see always students come in to the program and they are thin, but when they leave this place we have to roll them out.

[*I burst out laughing.*]

You laugh, but it is true! It is so much food and it is good, and when there is no control, they just eat it all. We have three thousand students, and we have a swimming pool, tennis courts—but once they start overeating, they feel sluggish and they do not even use these facilities. It is usually the people who look fit who you see in the gym, not the ones who most need it. So it's part of my teaching to help them be healthy. I tell them, "If you overfeed your customer, the only one who will make money is the doctor. If your customer once in a while complains, 'That was very good, but couldn't you give me a bigger piece?' then I assure you, your customer will come back. But if the doctor has to tell him he has high cholesterol, then he can't come back and you lose your customer."

*It seems to me that of all the areas of cooking, pastry might be the most difficult. What do you emphasize to your students? How do you try to make them great pastry chefs, not just OK pastry chefs?*

I tell my students the first thing is you need to love what you're doing. For example, most of the time what we do is copy. But if you copy, you can make it better. The people who worked before, they were not dumb. But still you can try to do it better.

Just to give you one example, when I came to the States, the owner of Le Cirque told me, "I went to Spain and I had a beautiful custard, crema catalana. Can you make this for me?" I said yes, I had made this at the Savoy Hotel in London. It was done in a big cup, so the outside was usually overcooked and the inside was too soft. So I chose a very thin, flat mold and put the custard in there, so it baked more even. In London they used a cream that was too rich, 45–50 percent fat. And they used too much sugar. They used sugar on the inside, but also sugar on the top. So I reduced the sugar. And I changed the way we baked it. Instead of baking it in a water bath, I turned the temperature down to 200 in a convection oven, and it was the most silky custard in the world. In the end it was actually a big success, and it's the way everybody in America makes it now—my way.

The first time I went to a bank for a loan to start a restaurant, they said, "Why did you go to one place, two places, three, four, ten places in your life? Can't you stay in one place?" And I said no, because I went to this one and that one to learn, this place because it had the best chef in this, and the other place because that chef was a master in something else. So I got my experience going from one good place to another good place. But the gentleman at the bank couldn't understand. I did not go to all those places for money; it was to get knowledge, to be a better craftsman.

It's one of the things we still don't understand here in the States—to learn takes time. To learn is to see other craftsmen and how they work. I tell my students that you have to put knowledge in your head, then you can draw from that.

*How do you actually teach? Do you give lectures, demonstrations, have the students cook, and then critique the results?*

Yes, it's like that. For example, I tell them what we do tomorrow. For example, the day before I tell them, "Tomorrow, we're making six or seven custards: from rice pudding to crème brûlée to crème caramel. So study these."

When they come in the next day they have the recipes already, and then I make teams—two make this one and two make that. I tell them about custard, where it comes from. Then I explain how to do it, then I say let's start and I watch them do it. Then I help them bake. After baking, I evaluate. For example, if it's overbaked, they'll have some little air bubbles. So it goes—lecture, demonstration, making, then evaluating.

*You've been at the Culinary Institute ten years now?*

Yes, and before I was at the French Culinary in New York City, and I also did teaching eight years at New York City Technical College as an adjunct professor. Teaching was fun and what I do with my knowledge.

In one of the places where I worked, I wanted to learn how to blow and pull sugar, and every time I came close to the chef and he was working the sugar, he would say, "You have nothing to do? Go do this or that." He didn't want me to be close to see what he's doing. He wouldn't have lost anything if he had told me, but he didn't want to tell me. He wanted to be special.

En-Ming Hsu, one of the great pastry chefs, worked for me when I had my restaurant in Washington. When Queen Elizabeth came to Washington, the British Embassy asked us to make the dessert for the luncheon at the Library of Congress. They asked for dessert in the shape of a book by Thomas Jefferson. En-Ming Hsu helped me to make this book. Without her, I probably could not have done it. She was so good and her work was so beautiful. It made me so, so happy that she helped me—the chef with thirty years experience—to make these beautiful cakes. It's so wonderful. When they are better than we are, when the student is better than the teacher, it is the biggest reward.

I tell students, "You come to see me whenever you want because I want you one day to be better than I am." They say, "Oh no, no, impossible, you're the best." But I say, "No, you will better than I am." That's the greatest thing I can think of.

*You have a great generosity as a teacher.*

You have to, because so many people have so much talent, and there is no progress in the world if you don't help the young people to be good. I really believe that good is not enough. You have to be better than good.

I know certain top chefs in the world, and they may be great craftsmen, but as human beings they have certain things that aren't very beautiful. It is my philosophy that you need to be a good person and a great craftsman.

I am seventy-one now, but I can give my knowledge. I'm like the farmer. You need fertilizer, you need to give water, you need to take care of it. Suddenly, out of this comes a beautiful tree. With teaching, it's the same. I tell them I have an open door. At the school, they say you have office hours from twelve to two. I say, I don't want this. I have an open door, they can come any time. If you want help, I stay an hour longer or two hours longer. Your success is my success.

I still love what I'm doing. One day maybe, when my brain doesn't work so fast anymore, I will stop. [*He laughs.*] But as long as I have fun, as long as I can teach properly, I will go on.

> *"If you create an atmosphere of excellence, those who want to be excellent will rise to it."*

# Doug Butler

## TEACHER OF FARRIERY

*Doug Butler is an internationally renowned farrier who has been teaching the craft of farriery for forty-five years. He holds a Certified Journeyman Farrier (CJF) classification and a PhD in equine nutrition from Cornell. He was the first American to achieve designation as a Fellow of the Worshipful Company of Farriers (FWCF), of which there have been only 155 since the fourteenth century. He is author of* The Principles of Horseshoeing (P3), *the most widely used farriery textbook in the world. He has been inducted into the International Horseshoeing Hall of Fame at the Kentucky Derby Museum in Louisville, Kentucky. He teaches at the school he founded, Butler Professional Farrier School, near Chadron, Nebraska.*

*How did you first become a farrier yourself?*

My family always had horses, and for generations our family has had blacksmiths in it. Every person, I suppose, has to find his or her own way, and as a boy I watched the blacksmith come to our place, and it was something that was very interesting to me, so I began to want to do my own horses. Then my father, who was from Arizona, took me to Arizona on a cattle roundup when I was thirteen or fourteen, and it just ruined me. [*He chuckles.*] After that I just wanted to be a cowboy. I wanted to learn that job, and one part of it is that you have to shoe your own horses. So I had to learn that as well as roping and riding and all those other things that you do as a cowboy. I became particularly interested in the shoeing aspect.

Then in my freshman year at college, I had to write a paper about something that interested me, and so I wrote about the craft of farriery, and I got really interested in it and decided to apply to farrier school. At that time there was only one school in the country, and it had a two-year waiting list. I applied in 1961 and went in 1963. From there I got really interested in it and I became an assistant to the teacher, and he sent me to different places to teach two-week schools. Then I went back east to school and got a master's degree and eventually a PhD.

But the way it all started out was that I thought horseshoeing was part of what I needed to know as a skill in being a cowboy, and as I began to get into it deeper, I found that there wasn't any bottom. And I just kept wanting to get better and better and better at it.

I guess the capstone of this drive was that in 1980, I won the national horseshoeing competition, and then in 1986, along with my partner, I won the international competition.

*From practicing horseshoeing, how did you then get interested in teaching it?*

I believe in the statement that's been made by a number of people that in order to really know something, you've got to teach it. And if you're going to teach it to someone, you've got to be good at it. So teaching horseshoeing forced me to do that. Ralph Hoover, who was my mentor when I first studied horseshoeing in California in 1963, was asked to teach a course at Montana State University in the spring of 1964; he didn't want to go, so he told me that if I would go, he would teach me how to do it. I had just three months to get ready, so he taught me the principles I needed to know.

I taught that course at Montana State, and then I went back and did it three more times. Then I taught at Penn State and various other places for him, and eventually it became something I did myself.

*One thing that strikes me about your teaching is that you teach it all—horse anatomy, the blacksmith skills of working with the iron, the skills of working on the hoof. You're like the old-time cobbler, making the whole shoe and teaching the making of the whole shoe.*

That's right. And I designed the curriculum back in 1964 at Montana State when we started doing the short courses. I did it that time as part of my assistance to Mr. Hoover, but eventually it became accepted as *the* way to do it, and it's been copied now by all of the other schools. I became the pioneer of how to do it in this modern age.

Back then, this was a craft that was dying out—because horses were dying out. In 1916, there were twenty-six million horses in the country, but then automobiles and tractors and trucks came in, and the number of horses kept going down. In 1960, when the USDA stopped counting horses, there were only two and a half million.

So when I was getting interested in this as a young man in 1963, horseshoeing was a dying craft. The older people were dying out and they were discouraging their children and others from going into it. But as the work horses died out, the pleasure horses and show horses and racehorses increased, and there was growth in that sector. Today, we have over nine million horses in the country.

The curriculum of our school is based on the textbook that my son Jacob and I wrote. It's 990 pages and it's called *The Principles of Horseshoeing (P3)*. The first six weeks of our course is based on the first half of the book, and the second six weeks is based on the second half. It's a very structured system. We know exactly what we're going to do each day. We assign students homework where they do a lot of reading, writing, and drawing in the evenings. During the day they forge horseshoes and work on horses. It's quite intense.

They have homework sets and they write answers to the questions and then illustrate those answers with drawings—so they're developing both the left and the right sides of the brain. We believe that to be a good farrier, to be a good craftsman, you have to be able to use both the left and right sides of the brain.

Most people who go into this are very right-brained. It's the same with a carpenter—he sees spatial relationships very well. But to be a good businessman, you've got to be left-brained, so we try to develop that. Or sometimes I get students who are more left-brained, and I get them to be more right-brained by having them do the drawing. I learned this when I was in England.

The hands-on part is a lot of trial and error. I've tried it other ways, where I just say to them, "Do it this way," but they don't get it. What they have to do is do it, make a mistake, then I correct the mistake, then they do it again and again and again.

My son who works with me here at the school said he wanted to be good at this and asked what he needed to do. I said, "Get a hundred pieces of steel and turn them into a toe bend and then bring them back to me." He did that, and it took him several days. Then I told him, "On each of the ends, make a heel,"—so that's two hundred heels. So he did that. By the time he got to number 195, he could make a good heel.

It's no different than any other craft. One of the Renaissance painters is said to have ripped up the first fifty paintings that he did—and of course they'd be worth millions today—because he wasn't satisfied with them. That's the way you have to be if you're going to be a craftsman. Anybody who is satisfied with whatever he or she produces the first time, I know that person's not going to be any good. The ones who are going to be really good say, "Tell me how I can fix this so I can go back and get it right," and then they work on it again and again and again.

When I first started teaching, it was show and do, show and do, show and do. But I made quite a study of learning and eventually wrote a book on visualization called *Shoeing in Your Right Mind*. In that book I try to outline the principles I learned while studying how artists learn. If you just use the left side of the brain, as I had been doing all of my life, you won't develop into a good craftsman. The man who won the Nobel Prize for his right brain research said that if you go past a bachelor's degree and go on to graduate school, you kill off the right side of your brain. So at our school, we try to balance those two. Because you've got to practice the right side stuff if you're going to get good at it.

*So you made a deliberate study of artists and craftsmen in order to see how to best teach the art of horseshoeing?*
Absolutely.

*How did you get the idea to do that?*

I realized that I didn't have it. It wasn't in my eye. I was around people who were trying to teach me things and I couldn't see it. I thought there was something wrong with me. I finally figured out that I wasn't seeing the spatial relationships, and that comes from the right side of the brain.

I was really affected greatly by a book I read called *Drawing on the Right Side of the Brain*, by Betty Edwards. I tried to take what was in that book and apply it to horseshoeing. It was amazing.

Some people interested in horseshoeing have a natural talent for it, but to take somebody who doesn't—that's the real challenge for the teacher. If people have the desire, they can learn it, but they have to learn the right techniques.

For example, I have a brother who had a natural knack for working with horses, but he chose to do something else with his life. Yet when we were kids, he was always better than I. But eventually I got better because I had more of a drive and desire, even though I didn't have as much natural talent.

The first twenty years I practiced horseshoeing, I didn't understand any of this stuff; I was just trying to do it the best I could. Whatever talent I had didn't get developed very much until I hit on some of these principles, and then I took off. Even now that I'm sixty-six, I learn more each time I work at the forge than I did in the first ten or fifteen years I did it. I think any craftsman would tell you that—the more background you have and the more images you have in your mind of what's correct, the faster you can progress.

*A few months ago, I interviewed a teacher of carpenters who lamented the decline of true craftsmanship in her trade. But I assume horseshoeing by its very nature is immune from that.*

Well, it *was*. But I'm afraid it may be becoming more like carpentry, unfortunately. We are getting companies that produce pre-made horseshoes, the kind the farrier used to have to fashion on the job. Now you can buy almost any type of shoe pre-made, so you don't have to be as good at the skill. It used to be that you made a shoe out of a straight piece of iron.

*Are the manufactured shoes as good as the ones custom made by a farrier?*

We could say that the manufactured shoe was not as good, and that would be true if the farrier was extremely skilled. However, what we find is that a lot of people go through a short course of a few days or a few weeks and they begin to practice. They don't have the skill, so then they buy the machine-made shoes because they can get by with them. But the skill that's necessary to apply them properly develops along with the skill to make the shoe. So if they don't have the skill to make the shoe, we find that they also lack the skill to fit the shoe correctly to the horse.

*Your students speak very highly of you and your school. What are your keys to success as a teacher?*

Wow. That's a hard question.

I think a lot of it is the desire I have for them to learn it, and they pick up on that.

Another thing is that I've had a lot of experience. I started teaching this stuff in 1964, and I've learned that there are ways to teach and ways not to teach. Not everyone who can shoe horses really well can teach it. I think that's true in other crafts as well. There are people who are outstanding craftsmen, but they couldn't teach you how to do any part of the job. They're more interested in the thing than the person. To be good at teaching, you have to be interested in teaching that person as much as you're interested in the craft.

It's one thing to teach the skill and another to motivate the student. Some students come to me already very motivated, but others get it while they're here. They catch it. I know that happened to me.

### How do you motivate your students?

If you create an atmosphere of excellence, those who want to be excellent will rise to it. If you set a standard and they reach for that, they will get good.

There is a great man who was a mentor to me. He's now in a rest home in Scotland, and his name is Edward Martin. He was a master blacksmith, and once he was going to judge a competition that I went to in Colorado. He was an old fellow then, in his seventies or better.

When the competition organizers told us what shoes we had to make, Edward said, "I'll make them up now."

And they said, "You don't have to make the shoes. You're the judge. We flew you over here from Scotland, and we don't expect you to make the horse shoes."

I'll never forget what he said. He said, "If you can't make the shoes, you've got no right to judge." So he made them, in a lot less time than it took us, and they were better than any that we made. So we had great respect for anything he would say to us. There was no murmuring about his judging.

We just had a kid here from Iceland, and that happened with him. He knew how to make a horseshoe when he came, but it wasn't very good, and he knew it wasn't. I'd lay one of mine next to his and I'd say, "I want to see yours look like this." He'd ask what he had to do and I'd tell him, and he'd go practice and practice. Toward the end, we'd lay his next to mine and I could say of his, "Now that's real skill."

I tell my students that it's so important whom you select for a teacher because that will determine how you look at life from then on and how you look at your work from then on.

Not too long ago there was a fellow who gave a talk about this, and he said that there are three important choices you make when you're learning. The most important one is the choice of the teacher. The second is your choice of what you're going to learn. The third is how hard you're going to work to learn it.

In our craft, you're no better than the guy you're learning from.

ſ

# 6 | *Teaching the Athletes*

*"My best teachers never judged me."*

# Tom Nordland

## TEACHER OF BASKETBALL SHOOTING

*Tom Nordland grew up in Minnesota, where he led his high-school team to two straight state basketball championships. The team was built around his extraordinary shooting ability, and his name became a household word throughout the state. In one championship game, he hit nineteen out of twenty free throws, a record that still stands. He was recruited to play basketball at Stanford, where his first day in practice delivered a shock to his confidence from which he never recovered. He was a sub for his entire Stanford career. After college he became a computer programmer, became interested in tennis and golf, and one day, at age fifty, during a lunch break at Apple Computer, he stepped onto a basketball court and after a few minutes, he began to swish every shot. He realized what had made him a great shooter in high school, and he began his career as a basketball shooting teacher.*

*He teaches workshops, holds summer basketball camps for kids, and coaches individual college and professional basketball players, including NBA players. He has made two instructional videos. He is something of an evangelist for good shooting, and he is disappointed over the decline of shooting in the game. He speaks with passion and enthusiasm.*

My life seemed without purpose for a long time. In high school I was such a star that I didn't develop a personality to go with it. I thought I was somebody, but if you think you're somebody, then you're not open to *becoming* somebody. I never had the personality to go out and create who I am.

At Stanford, I never made the starting team. I was a failure. I had this "catch and shoot" shot—not off the dribble, just catch and shoot. At Stanford, in the first practice—I think it was in the first hour—I started getting my shots blocked, which had never happened before in high school.

I had been famous in high school. I remember when I went to get my driver's license, they said, "Oh! You're Tom Nordland!" You know, I got all sorts of little favors and so forth. So I felt good about myself. But it all came crashing down in college when I had to work off the dribble, and when I tried to do that, I lost my confidence, and then I lost my shot. Here I am, a one-dimensional player, recruited by Stanford on a basketball scholarship, and my one thing I could do well I couldn't do any more. And the coach didn't have the time or the interest to train me. He didn't talk to me about who I am. He didn't know what was going on, and I was too shy to ask. So I spent three years on the bench wondering what had happened.

By great fortune, one day in 1976, a great friend of mine, a golf professional, said, "Get the book *The Inner Game of Tennis*." And so I got it, and I read it the night before the state amateur golf tournament, which I had qualified for. The book said, "Let go," and I didn't know what that meant. So I let go right and left [*chuckles*] . . . I played very badly. But it started me thinking about the inner game, the mental side of life. About a year and a half later I moved from Minneapolis to Los Angeles to be near the author, Tim Gallwey. I spent five years with him as part of his staff. He opened my eyes to the mental side, the inner game. He was my first major mentor. Then years later I met Fred Shoemaker, an incredible golf master.

So now I'm a coach of this little thing called basketball shooting. I look at shooting and I see everything at once, but it's just a small thing. Fred looks at golfers and sees the whole golf swing—much more complicated than shooting a basketball.

We have this mind that's crazy. Everybody has this ego—you're you and I'm me and we're separate, and I'm better than you or you're better than me . . . the ego is just driving us nuts all the time. I learned that by being around Tim and Fred. I had a decade of training, of thinking I knew something and then realizing how little I knew, and when you realize you know nothing, then you're open to everything. It took me a long time to figure that out—maybe twenty years from meeting Tim Gallwey.

*And then came the day in 1989 when you stepped onto the court during your lunch hour . . .*

Yes, I discovered my high-school shot, and basketball opened up for me. So now for eighteen years I've been studying shooting, seeing more and more what's going on.

So what I have to offer the world is a great technique of shooting that can be proven to be the way the great shooters have always shot. They didn't get it from me, and I didn't get it from them. It's just the way things work.

*So how does one shoot a basketball?*

You want to shoot from big muscles, not small muscles, in an upward motion. You want to shoot high. You want a consistent release that's repeatable. You want the ball, eye, and basket aligned. This is the language I speak, and nobody else is speaking it. They're all saying, "You must do this, and the elbow should be here." Some say you have to line up hand, elbow, knee, foot. [*He gestures in demonstration during all of this.*] I say, "Why?" I come along with the audacity to say the emperor has no clothes. It's BS, what's being taught. It's not that effective. Check it out.

John Wooden [*legendary UCLA coach*] said that the hand should be over the elbow over the knee over the foot before they go to shoot—which means he doesn't understand shooting at all. The line that matters is eye-hand-ball-target. That's the line you want to get right, not this line going this way [*imitates shooting motion with elbow over knee*] . . . that has nothing to do with anything. You want to relax the wrist and hand. Most coaches and players think you have to flip the wrist. But that's small muscles. But I say make it all one constant. From the shoulder up, make it all constant. And so you vary the angle but not the release. Most people vary the release and wonder why they can't shoot.

*So what you teach is not so much what we might call rules, but principles.*
Yeah. One morning I was shooting baskets at a friend's house outside, and a thought came into my head—an object in motion tends to stay in motion. I hadn't thought of that in thirty years, since high-school physics. I remembered the terms, but I didn't know what it was. I had to Google it. It's Newton's first law of motion. An object in motion and in line tends to stay in motion and in line unless acted on by an outside force. I realized, "My God, I was doing this all along and I had never noticed it."

*So you discovered consciously what you had been doing unconsciously as a high-school basketball player?*
Yeah. I had lost it for thirty-two years—from the first day of practice at Stanford in 1957 until 1989. I hadn't touched a ball in six years. The three principles were constant release, vary the arc, shoot from the legs. So for sixteen years those were my three key principles. Then two years ago I added the fourth one: align the ball with the eye and basket as long as possible before the release. So now those are my four principles. There are other subtleties, but if you do those four things, your shooting will start to soar.

*What's the difference between teaching a twelve-year-old and an NBA player?*
The twelve-year-old will be more open to coaching. The NBA players think they know. It's the ego that's protecting them from all the outside influences, but also blocking them from real learning. So they're kind of uncoachable. But those few who are coachable can learn like that [*he snaps his fingers*]. My stuff is so simple. I can see what anybody needs. I can look at anybody in the NBA and tell you right away how he could improve his shooting.

*So part of your skill as a teacher is having a good eye, being able to look at somebody's shot and see where he could improve.*
Yeah, that's the starting point. I learned from Tim Gallwey that if you teach awareness, you can teach anything. You don't have to understand the skill to be a good coach, maybe even a great coach. Of course, if you understand the skill, you can be a little better, because then you can go right to the source of the problem.

For example, I can teach a twelve-year-old to coach a violinist—by simply asking questions. Let's imagine you're a world-class violinist but you're having trouble with your vibrato. Something isn't quite right. So you come to me as a coach. Here's how I would coach you. I say, "What's the problem?" And you say, "My vibrato isn't quite there like it used to be." And I say, "What's vibrato?" And you say, "It's that movement of the finger that doesn't change the tone but gives you a kind of coloration." I might say, or even the twelve-year-old could say, "Play me a piece, and on a scale of one to ten, tell me how good your vibrato was." So the violinist would play and then say, "That was about a four." I don't know what a four means, but he does. So I'd say, "Play it again." He might say, "That was about a six that time." I say, "OK, do it again." He does and says, "Wow, that was about a nine. That was almost perfect." Then, "That was a four again." So he would teach himself what was wrong and what needed to be fixed. The violinist might say, "You're a great coach. Here's a hundred bucks."

*So if we were on the basketball court, and I were a twelve-year-old, or a college freshman, or even an NBA professional, where would you start? Would you just have me shoot and then ask, "How does that feel?"*

I would *not* say, "How does it feel?" Because the answer could be, "Great." [*Laughs.*] A lot of coaches say that—"How did that feel?" And the player can give any phony answer. The perfect question to ask as a coach is *what?* If you say, "What happened?" then the person gets into the awareness mode and is open to learning all kinds of things. What you want is for people to discover what happened and what works and how to get there on their own. Self-discovery. Self-exploration. What I teach is self-coaching. The ultimate goal is that they can coach themselves.

*When you teach, do you articulate the four principles for your students or do you wait until they discover them on their own?*

I don't want to tell them what to do. So I might say, "How do you stand?" And once they're aware, then I might say, "Try a little more open stance. Is alignment easier that way? Does it feel more natural?" So it's a little bit of leading, but mostly it's discovery. So mostly you want to create an environment, not say, "I know something that you don't know."

Another thing that's important is being non-judgmental. We all judge our students and our coaches and ourselves. My best teachers never judged me. It was always, "What happened?" and "What was the effect?"

*What if you say, "What happened?" and they don't know?*

The temptation is to tell them, but that sabotages the learning. So you keep at it until they start to feel something. Find something that they can be aware of. Maybe something specific—how high was the hand on that shot? But you have to avoid telling. You have to keep working with awareness, and the more you see, the more the focus of the awareness can be directed. That's how knowing a sport well helps. I go down and shoot outdoors a lot. I'm always working on distinctions, and I get new insights sometimes. I just love it.

What sabotages learning is to give answers. Sometimes it makes teachers feel important to say, "Your hand was not aligned with the basket." In my coaching, I've made the mistake over the years of saying too much. What you want to do is say very little and make everything experiential. If you're talking about alignment, have them try a few shots, and then you ask, "Was the hand aligned with the eye? Now do it on purpose off line." If you can get them to be aware of their own alignment, then learning happens. Awareness is the master skill. In performance, the master skill is concentration. But in learning, the master skill is awareness.

Sometimes I have kids shoot back and forth and tell their partner what their alignment was. The shooter speaks first. Was the ball aligned with the eye or the nose or the shoulder? They have to say or show what their alignment was. Then the partner says, "Oh, yeah?" Then they try again, becoming aware of what their alignment is. The awareness teaches them. Feedback has to come first from the performer, then from the observer. They start to awaken. I've had some great success having them give feedback. The shooter's experience is the main teacher.

If your main intention is to increase awareness, you can't mess it up. Awareness is how we learn. If you're telling them what they should do, or judging or criticizing, then definitely you can screw it up.

If the student is aware, and developing awareness, then you're doing your job. Just get out of the way. If you're masterful at a skill (a physical skill, in my example), then you have the chance to see better where to highlight and spotlight the most significant areas for learning.

I've been trained to realize and know that the student is the genius in this learning stuff, not me and my good ideas. Once you know that, it colors everything you say and do. Coaching becomes easier—student focused instead of coach focused. It makes a lesson sort of a "holy encounter."

*"Speed is your enemy in learning."*

# Arthur Lane

### FENCING TEACHER

*Arthur Lane retired from a lifetime of teaching fencing at ninety. At the time of our interview, he was ninety-two. He is a slim man whose dignified posture—chin up, shoulders back, head erect, back straight and yet relaxed—makes him appear taller and much younger than he is. We spoke in his room on a sunny spring afternoon. He frequently had me hold a fencing foil so he could demonstrate physically what he was saying.*

The very first thing I do with beginning students is put a weapon in their hand, and then I show them how it is held and how it is maneuvered. You have to teach them tactilely.

Then I teach them the background, how fencing developed as a sport. It did not derive from battlefield combat but from an individual, one-on-one form of combat. It derives from an aristocratic class and its traditions.

So the best way to do it is to put a weapon in your hand, so you can feel it and draw your own conclusions. [*He walks to his bed and picks up a fencing foil and hands it to me.*] OK, hold it any way you like. OK, now wrap your thumb around it . . . that's it.

*He has me hold the foil up, and by knocking it first one way and then another, he shows me which grip is the most advantageous. He shows me how to defend, aim, lunge. His demonstrations are effectively convincing. I get it. When he places his hand on mine, with his firm but gentle touch, I feel knowledge passing from his hand into mine.*

Fencing is constantly developing, but every time it overdevelops in one direction or another, then it returns to its classical roots, and it's stronger. I teach classical fencing. What do I mean by classical fencing? Nothing more than high efficiency.

Fencing is an elitist sport. If you're a fencer, you don't do anything else. More often than not the fencer—the real fencer—is a loner. He's always overcoming personal obstacles. The fighting is individual.

I was never a top-notch fencer, but I've always been a damn good teacher—I think largely because I've gone back to the roots of fencing.

*And how did you instruct? Did you pause to give them feedback?*
Yes. I might say, "What was your feeling of balance when I hit you just now?"

*You correct them by asking questions rather than giving them the answer in the form of a critique?*
Oh, yes. You don't just arbitrarily say, "Do it this way." You need to give them a reason. And the reason would be in the question.

For example:

"Why do you drop your hand when you lunge?"

"I didn't know I dropped it."

"Well, move your hand forward like it's on the top of a table that is so high." And that rings a bell.

As for doing a point movement with their fingers only, I'd say, "Imagine putting a screwdriver in your hand. Put your hand down a fairly large pipe. Now move the point of the screwdriver around in a circle. You can't move your hand inside that pipe. That's the way you should move your point. So there we have the circular motion as you're going forward."

*So part of being a good teacher is asking right questions that, as you say, "ring a bell." Because one could ask questions that don't ring a bell at all.*

Teaching individually, you get to know them very well. That's why I never liked to teach groups.

*Since so much of it, as you explain, goes against instinct, there must be a process of unlearning . . .*

What you do is not really unlearning, but learning new patterns. Let's take an instinctive reaction. Don't try to bury it. Take control of it. Practice it, slowly, deliberately, with a high level of consciousness, then practice a different action that is the one you want to do and have command of. Both are effective. The instinctive is effective in its own context. The non-instinctive is equally effective—in its context.

*An important element in learning fencing must be practice.*

An immense amount of practice. Very boring.

*So in teaching, did you find it important to break things down into stages for your students?*

Oh my God, yes. Speed is your enemy in learning.

They must know what they're doing and not try to know everything.

Too often one who learns too quickly, too easily, will be a flash in the pan. He'll be around for one or two years, get bored, and move on to something else. So you want someone who really works. But really good people are rare.

*When you teach, you often fence with your students . . .*

[*Emphatically.*] Oh, yes.

*Did you find that there were key ideas—expressed in phrases, perhaps—that you often repeated to your students, the way a tennis coach might say, "Watch the ball and bend your knees"?*

Yes, but not until about ten or twelve years ago did I see enough of a whole picture to emphasize it. And it was, "Front foot, always, directly forward!" That keeps you from landing on your toe. It also keeps you from having your knees inside. Every time you move—elbows outside, knees inside. [*He picks up a foil and demonstrates—convincingly.*]

*So like many forms of athletic activity, even though you're holding this foil in your hand, the key is footwork.*

Oh yes, you're like a flatcar carrying a big load. The load is top-heavy.

I learned that from a particular fencing master. He was Jewish—a refugee from Nazi Germany. I went to see him, and the first thing he asked was to see my lunge. Well, I thought I had a pretty good lunge. He said, "Good, but slow." He said, "It lacks acceleration. Let me see it again." I showed him again, and he said, "Ah. You are pushing with your toe." I was using only my calf muscle. He taught me to use my thighs. So I started pushing with my knee. And using my butt muscles, too. [*He demonstrates both ways, and he shows me that pushing with his thighs, he can acceler-ate better but also stop more effectively, having better control of his movements.*]

In fencing, the legwork is quite different than what's natural. You play side-ways—like a fiddler crab. And that is not an instinctive way of fighting—this is. [*He mimics a charging, front-on attack.*] The Tarzan leap—a total commitment when you leap forward. But in fencing, oh no. You want to get in there and out. A man jumping cannot plan beyond his jump, especially if something goes wrong. [*He demonstrates the proper fencing footwork, moving back and forth across the room like a nimble twenty-five-year-old.*]

Of course, this is very different than the Hollywood stuff. There you do things for an audience. If you were to fight that way against an experienced fencer, you'd be dead—immediately. You don't attack your opponent with your weight already committed. You'll land like this. [*He demonstrates lunging forward, leaning too far forward and thus off balance. Next he demonstrates a lightning-fast thrust, but his body stays erect, balanced, ready for what may come next.*] You do it with a push from your rear leg, not the toe.

I remember one parents' day at a private high school where I was teaching. Two parents, both lawyers, had a son who was built just like them. Here's father talking to me. [*Arthur stands and demonstrates the father's bodily posture: shoulders rounded, head jutting forward.*] The mother stood the same way, as did the son when I first got him. They asked, "What is our son getting from fencing?"

I said, "Well, he's getting something that's coming from his feet." They looked puzzled. Then I said, "I want you both to freeze exactly as you are. Now I want you to change your balance and throw your weight off of your toes and onto the outside edges of each foot." [*Arthur now demonstrates the change in his feet, and as a result, his shoulders roll back, his posture becomes more erect. He laughs.*]

*Those parents asked a good question: What did their son get from fencing? What do you feel your students got from fencing—apart from the ability to fence?*
The ability to lose their shyness. To speak directly, with authority, to someone. One of my students had to write a college admissions essay on the topic of someone who had greatly influenced her life. She wrote about me.

When she was a freshman, she had started lessons with me. I told her after one of our lessons, "You are a fighter." And that's what she learned through fencing. She learned that about herself—that she was a fighter. Not in the sense of being combative or vicious, but in the sense of standing up for what she believes. So fencing taught her that she was a fighter, and it encouraged her in that direction. She wrote that she want-ed to stand up and fight for things in which she believed. That was her purpose in life.

*Did you find there were differences between teaching boys and girls?*
The girls are more willing to deal with personalities.
The guys are far more arrogant. And far more stupid. Much more juvenile.

*Did your teaching methods get set pretty early in your career or did you find that you were constantly evolving?*

I did not feel any evolution in my teaching methods until I was rather advanced, and that was when I started to teach preparations. Preparation is simply any movement done before an attack. This is an attack. [*Arthur stands and lunges with his foil.*] This is not. [*Here he offers some fancy handwork that makes circular patterns with the tip of the foil.*] It is a threat, but not an attack.

In my first teaching, I was a simple mechanic. My first master gave me lessons and let me repeat the lessons to beginners. Then during the war [*World War II*], I had four years of no fencing at all. But at one place where I finally found a gym with a boxing ring, I could practice by myself. I began to practice combinations. These were combinations I had never used myself, but I found them in a book. So after the war, I began teaching these combinations in classes at UC–Berkeley. And it made an enormously effective way of teaching—not right away, or course, but after some months. And the students had never seen anything like it. For two or three years, my fencers dominated the local intercollegiates.

*It seems that your knowledge goes beyond fencing itself and you end up talking about the personality of each student . . .*

Yes, because fencing is a whole world. When I was young, I never had a group lesson—only individual lessons. You can't really teach fencing in group lessons, though at times I had to do it. You have to work one on one.

"*If you make a mistake, you get bit.*"

# Mike Hileman

## ALLIGATOR WRESTLING TRAINER

*Mike Hileman has worked at Gatorland in Orlando, Florida, for sixteen years, where is now head trainer of the alligator wrestlers and also director of entertainment. He is thirty-five, and he started wrestling alligators when he was nineteen.*

I first learned alligator wrestling from a guy that's been doing this a long time named Tim Williams, and he had learned from another guy. Alligator wrestling has a lineage. It just gets passed on. It goes all the way back to the Seminole Indians in Florida. They've been doing it for many generations.

It's an interesting job. It's a lot of fun if you do it right. It takes a certain kind of individual to want to do it. You certainly don't do it because of the money. You do it because you like working with the animals.

### How do you teach your trainees how to wrestle alligators?

Basically, you teach it step-by-step. First, you learn the anatomy of the animals, then the behaviors. Then when you start handling the animals, you try to apply what you know about the anatomy and the behavior in order to stay out of harm's way.

Alligators try to tell you what they're going to do before they do it. They open their mouths up, they'll kind of flap their ear flaps at you, they'll hiss, their muscles will tense up . . . they'll kind of let you know when they're getting ready to do something. You try to predict what the animal's going to do, but you can't always fully predict the actions or reactions of the alligator. So there's a little bit of a surprise element to it.

They have a striking range. Once you learn that striking range, you try to do your best to stay out of it.

In the training, we do a watching-type program at first. They go down and they observe. We use a lot of videos for the anatomy part. I take a lot of videos and show them the things that alligators are capable of—spinning, jumping, lurching forward. If you've never seen that, you don't know what they're capable of. If you show it to people who are visual learners, they're going to remember that. They might say, "Man, I didn't know that thing could jump four feet." Well, now they know.

We jump into a moat with eight-foot alligators, and the first day you might just grab the tail and start pulling on it and see how strong they are, or see what they do when you try to do that. And then you pull them up on the ground and try to jump on them. It's a step-by-step, day-by-day process.

Our shows take about fifteen minutes to do, and it takes at least two months to train somebody to do that fifteen-minute show.

I've trained people fairly quickly, and I've had people who took seven months to do it. We move at their speed. We don't try to force anything because confidence is a huge part. If you hesitate or you're not sure of what you're doing, you're going to make a mistake. And if you make a mistake, you get bit.

### When they've finished the watching stage and move to hands-on work, do you give them critiques to improve their practice?

Oh yeah. I'm there at every training session. I tell them which animals to grab, what I want them to do with the animals and why, and if something goes not according to plan or they need to do something better, I point that out to them.

### What would be an example of something you might point out to them?

Sometimes when we pull them up out of the water and we go to jump on their backs, somebody might take too much time—they're not doing it fast enough. Or their hand position is in a wrong place, or they're landing wrong in a compromising position where the animal can get them. So I'll stop right there and demonstrate the correct way of doing it and then make them do it over and over again until they get it. Then we'll move on to the next step.

*What makes a good candidate for training to wrestle alligators?*

First of all, the people have to be somewhat athletic. There are movements involved where you can't be sluggish. You can't be extremely overweight. You have to be flexible. So an athletic build is something we're looking for.

But attitude has a lot to do with it. You don't want people coming in here thinking that they're superman and alligators can't hurt them. You want them to have a respect for alligators, but you don't want them to be scared to death. So it's kind of a fine line.

Usually the ones that come in with a healthy respect for the animal, who pay attention while you're talking, and who do what you tell them—those are the ones that work out. It's the ones who come in with preconceived ideas of what they want to do and how to do it that tend to be the problem. So if they're like that, or they've got experience elsewhere, you have to untrain them. Or sometimes they've watched *The Crocodile Hunter* on television for seven years and they think they know. Those are the ones that you try to weed out.

*You train both men and women?*

Yes. We have several female alligator wrestlers, and we have one that's in training right now. She's doing fine. Because of the size of the animals, you've got to have hand strength and be able to get leverage, so it might take a little longer for the females to build up those specific muscles. But once they have those muscles, it's no different than a guy.

*And the show you put on is both for entertainment and education?*

Absolutely.

We demonstrate the jaws by pulling the mouth open if the alligator lets us, and we show the inside of the mouth. We also demonstrate that most of the jaw strength is in closing, not in opening. So we can hold the jaws shut with just one hand. We'll roll the alligator over onto its back and induce anatomic immobility where it's kind of confused and just lies there upside down. And while we do these things, we explain the educational points behind them.

*Have any of your trainees ever had accidents and been bit?*

Oh yeah. One of the first things I tell them is that if you're going to handle animals—it doesn't matter if it's a dog or a cat—the law of averages is going to catch up with you and you will get bit eventually. It might take two months or it might take six years, but if enough time passes, you will make a mistake because we're human.

*And what happens then?*

We have different scenarios. A lot of times the alligators are biting out of anger, like a dog snapping. They'll bite, hang on for a couple of seconds, and then they'll usually let go. Sometimes they'll bite and hold on and shake. And then sometimes they'll bite and hold on and start rolling—which is our worst-case scenario. There are steps we can take with the backup people we keep around. Any time we handle an alligator of at least four feet, there are always two people there. That way, if something goes wrong, we have help.

After they learn to do the wrestling shows and they've been doing them for a little bit, they develop an ego and a big head, thinking they can do whatever they want with the animals—until they get bit or have a close call and then that brings them back to reality. If you wrestle an alligator a hundred times, you tend to get a confidence level that says, "Hey, I'm good at this. Nothing can happen to me." And then you blink, or look at somebody who's walking by, and—bang—you're nailed.

*If you've been wrestling alligators for sixteen years, I assume you've been bit?*
Twice.

*And I assume it wasn't too awfully bad, or you wouldn't be here to talk to me.*
Nah, it wasn't too bad. I got a couple of holes the first time, and a bruise and a cut on the second one. I can't say that it was too awful. If you're going to get bit by an alligator, I did it right both times.

*Have you progressed as a teacher since you started?*
Oh yeah. I've trained nineteen people, and I learn something off of each one of them. It's not just the animals we're dealing with. People learn differently. I may have to tell somebody the same thing six different ways until they comprehend it. I learned something once from a guy named Brian. He was bitten during a show. The alligator grabbed him on the knee and we had just been working on his technique of jumping on the alligator not more than a week before he got bit. He reverted back to his old way of doing it, and that's what caused him to get bitten. He left his left knee hanging too far out to the side of the alligator instead of putting his knee down into the sand where the alligator wasn't able to reach him. The alligator swung his head around and grabbed the knee. I always look back on that as a lesson—that I need to trust myself more and be more assertive when I know I'm right and make sure to get the point across. I probably could have prevented that. I should have been more forceful or even taken him off the shows until he got that down right. That accident could have been prevented.

I've also learned that I need to communicate a lot better. I was always brought up to believe you don't ask too many questions—whatever you're told, you just do it. That doesn't work with today's generation. They're brought up to question authority, to question the way of doing things. So I've had to learn how to communicate to the younger generation, and it was a difficult task for me. Every time I train somebody I'm forced to learn a different way of communicating what I need done. So I still learn even to this day.

*"Getting people to feel what you have felt."*

# Mark Wolocatiuk

### RACECAR DRIVING INSTRUCTOR

*Mark Wolocatiuk is chief instructor at the Jim Russell racing school located at the Infineon Raceway in northern California. Drivers were preparing for a major race coming up that weekend. I had never been to a racetrack before, and walking past the track, I was struck by the speed and earsplitting noise of the cars screaming past. We talked in his office, which overlooks the track.*

We take people right off the streets, and we put them into racecars and teach them how to drive. We teach them how to race, and we teach them how to compete.

Some people do it just as their weekend getaway—almost as a hobby, instead of a golf tournament. And then we have people who want to race professionally. There are people out there in Formula One, in NASCAR, in IndyCar, that started with us.

Most people are here for the thrill, for something challenging.

*Everybody who comes to you knows how to drive . . .*

Most people, when they drive their cars, don't drive them anywhere near their capabilities or limits.

*Nor should they!*

Right. Nor should they. Nor can you really do that. But we do it here.

So we introduce them to the car. They learn to shift better than they do in their own car. So we do some drills, get them out in the cars, watch them, pull them over, talk to them about what we see, talk to them as a group, talk to them as individuals. Then they go do it again. Then we introduce them to the corners on the track, get them driving around the track. We introduce some theory.

It's a three-day course. It starts with a lot of group stuff, but by the second half you're working pretty much with one person.

We break habits as much as teach from scratch. Most people have gotten used to driving one way—you know, around town.

*That's a theme that's come up a lot in these interviews—that teaching is not just adding; it's also subtracting. What is an example of a habit you want to subtract?*

Most people don't drive onto the highway full throttle, full revs. And that's something we try to get people into the habit of pretty quick. We want them to drive full throttle, shifting at specific points, accelerating aggressively—because that's one limit of the car, and that's the easiest one to learn.

Then we turn it around, and after a little while, we get them slowing the car down with the brakes, but at the car's limit—not like most people do, which is tap the brakes and coast. Most people don't appreciate how quickly a racecar can stop.

Then it's blending it—maximize acceleration and maximum braking. Then the hardest part is maximum cornering speeds. It's figuring it out and also learning to teach yourself, because you have to be able to decipher what you did. Good golfers know why they hooked a shot. A driver has to be able to do that on a track. He has to be able to recognize a mistake he made on a turn, fix it, and not do it again. On slow corners, drivers tend to go in too fast; on fast corners, they tend to go in too slow. The fast corners are the ones where the best drivers make up a lot of time. And a slow corner is one where the best drivers don't throw away a lot of time.

This corner right here [he points out his window at the track] is a thirty-five- or forty-mile-per-hour corner for most cars. Even the fastest, most sophisticated car in the world can't get around this hairpin better than forty. But the mistake the drivers make is that they come in a little too fast, a little off line, don't get back to the power as soon as they should, and so they lose time.

Then there are mistakes that make them lose control or go off the track and crash. So managing your mistakes is something that drivers have to learn. That's part of a three-day class. We get into mistakes that you will make, what to do when you make those mistakes. And how to recognize them soon enough so that you don't go flying off the track.

People crash. These are pictures of the cars we use right now. [He points to photographs on his wall.] And then we take them and put them back on the horse, and basically we don't let somebody who has crashed get away without getting back in. We get them to do at least a few laps, even if it's the last time they'll ever sit in a racecar.

### How fast do those cars go?

On this track, about 120. On a longer track, about 140. But on this curve [he points out his window again], 42 is fast. On the curve before, 120 is fast, but 115 is not.

You have to be confident, but you can't be arrogant. You've got to recognize where you're good, and you have to recognize when you make mistakes. The mental aspect of racing is a huge challenge for people.

### How do you teach that?

It's so individualized. Because people have different personalities. We get everything from the "A" personalities who think they know everything to people who make us wonder, "What in the world ever got him to come out and try a racecar?" You know, he's timid and shy and he won't even give it gas, and he has no mechanical linkage from the shifter to the clutch.

But most people you can work with individually and help them improve. We work with our instructors about recognizing types of people.

We have a curriculum that's evolved over the fifty years that the school has been here, and I've been at the school half that long. But you still meet new personalities, and so you try to make them feel like they're in control to a degree, but at the same time, you're trying to get them to do something different.

You don't just want to say to them, "That's wrong, that's wrong, that's wrong." We instructors talk about how you've got to pump them up a little bit. The things that they did well, that's great. But if they really need to change something, you've got to get it in there in a way that would benefit them.

For those who go on with it, and the few that reach the highest levels, I don't think we have as much input into building their ultimate skill. It's more their desire. This particular sport doesn't necessarily drag talent along with it all the time. There are a lot of drivers that have been super talented and not gotten to the highest levels. And at the same time—and that's the frustrating side of this sport—there are drivers that you know should not be there, who are running at Indianapolis, for example.

*How did they do it?*

Sponsors. You can buy your way to the highest levels of the sport. You can't buy your way into the Masters golf tournament, but if you have a certain level of skill, you can buy your way into the Indy 500. Outside the sport, and in the mainstream media, people don't recognize that too much.

*What makes for the greatest drivers?*

Confidence. That's something that you have to have behind the wheel. You have to believe that you are one of the best out there. If you have some doubts, you're not going to be as quick behind the wheel. Of course, that can go the other way, and you can drive over-aggressively and crash a lot.

You've got to have a lot of self-discipline. You've got to be smart enough to know the limits without going over them.

And you've got to be a pretty calm, cool individual under pressure. There are guys in front, behind, beside you, and they're trying to get around you, and you're trying to race them at high speeds, and you're dealing with that lap after lap. Cars crash, spin out in front of you . . . so you've got to be unflappable. Most of the guys who have made it to a certain level, you'd recognize them as pretty laid back, pretty low key. They're not the kind to jump around the end zone spiking the ball.

*It seems like a lot of what you're trying to teach is a certain feeling for the moving car.*

There's feeling to it. But some are very analytic about learning to drive. Others are more emotional. One will say, "I think I can go faster. I'm going to go try." The other will say, "I took that a corner at sixty-two miles per hour. Tell me if I can do it at sixty-three." Again, it's different personalities.

*Does one of those approaches tend to be more effective, or is it just that each suits different people?*

Probably each just suits different people.

A teacher needs to listen. That's a good start. I've seen instructors—maybe they are new or maybe they're trying to impress people with what they know—and they give them too much information and it's overloading to the student. I'm always trying to remind instructors, just give them one thing—two at the most—to work on. And try to make that thing what's most important. They don't need sixteen things to work on.

*What is the satisfaction in teaching racing?*

Getting people to feel what you have felt. Getting somebody to respond to what you're trying to tell them. They get on the track and they understand what you've been trying to tell them for a day and a half. They get it. And most people do, even if it's just one corner they hit. And they know when they get it really well because they can feel it. And they say, "Wow. Now I understand." You watch them on the track and think, "He's really going good. He's figured that out." That's cool.

And they want to be here. Some of them have been dreaming about it for years.

*"I do everything close up. Close up gives you the feel."*

# Ron Washington

## MAJOR LEAGUE BASEBALL MANAGER

*When Eric Chavez won a Gold Glove, major league baseball's highest award for fielding, he gave it to Ron Washington in appreciation for Washington's teaching him how to field. In his ten years as a coach for the Oakland Athletics, Ron Washington distinguished himself as the game's best teacher of the art of playing the infield.*

*Born in New Orleans, Washington played major league baseball from 1977 to 1989. After retiring from playing, he became a coach in the New York Mets organization and then coached for the Oakland A's from 1997 to 2006. In 2007, he became manager of the Texas Rangers. Though he hasn't played in eighteen years, he looks fit and powerfully lean. We spoke in the clubhouse before a game.*

*How do you teach somebody to play the infield?*

The one thing I personally try to do is see their base. Their base starts with their feet. I always believed that if you have good feet placement, the hands work. Everything works from the center of your body, which is where your balance is. So that's where I start. I always look at a kid from his feet up. Then from that point it's easy to correct what needs to be corrected. It's very simple.

I can look at you make a mistake, and I can tell why you made that mistake because I looked at how your feet were, or how your balance point—which is your lower half—was. So with Eric [*Eric Chavez of the Oakland A's*], that's all I've ever done. I showed him how to use his feet. Once I showed him how to use his feet and he trusted me, the rest was simple.

*When you say you showed him, you mean literally—that you stood there and showed him how?*

Well, what I do is I draw a triangle in the dirt. That is the perfect fielding position: you've got good width with your feet, and the point of the triangle is where you want to receive the ball. So your eyes, glove—it all lines up. And once that lines up and you play everything out of the center of your body, with good width, which is your strength, then your hands work.

And then from that point, we talk about angles. Any time you can cut a baseball off by going at the angle, you make your own hops. You see a lot of guys, they'll move left and right and they'll sit and let the ball come to them—and that's when you get eaten up. But if you cut off the path of the ball at an angle, then you've got an opportunity to pick your hops. Why? Because your feet are in motion, and if your feet are in motion, and you recognize that you can get to a certain hop, then you attack that hop. But if your feet are not in motion, that's when you hear the saying, "The ball played him." And you always want to play the ball, because if you play the ball, then every time there's a mistake, it's easy to correct that mistake. But when the ball plays you, how can you correct it? And you get played by the ball when you sit there and your feet stop moving.

That's my simple philosophy. That's the way I taught it to Eric, to Miguel Tejada, to Jason Giambi, Mark Ellis, Bob Crosby . . . that's what I basically teach. And it's a repetitive thing, repetitive thing, repetitive thing. And once you get it down, then you become self-sufficient, where you can correct yourself.

*What has made you such a good teacher?*

I think what helped me to become a good teacher is I do it through the person that I'm teaching. I let you have your say. I let you have your feelings. I never try to take what I want to give you and just put it in you. I give what I have to give, and then I get your opinion on it. And because I have the most knowledge at this, I can put holes in what you're saying. And by putting holes in what you're saying, you begin to see what is right and what is wrong.

You know what they say: "People don't care how much you know until they know how much you care." Well, I let you know I care. I'm willing to let you have your say, which is something that the best teachers do. I've got all the knowledge in this, but I'm still going to let you say what you feel, because there's no way I can help you if I don't know how you're feeling.

So for me to come out and say, "Do this!" and, "This is the way it's supposed to be done!" ... Well, that's not the way I do it. I go through the process of showing you that this is the best way it can work, and then I give you all the points: balance, the center piece, and the vision. If you've got balance, you play the ball center, and you've got vision, you've got to have success.

And that's the reason why I think I've been a good teacher, because I go out there and I don't just cram it down your throat. I give it to you, and you begin to see the difference because I can also do it. And because I can do it—I'm way older than you—and you've got all this athletic ability, then you should be able to do it.

And I haven't had anyone—to be honest with you—that has had one day good defensively in the game of baseball that I couldn't make have many days good defensively.

### Did you have model teachers who influenced you?

Chico Fernández [*Washington's infield coach when he played for the Dodgers*] had the biggest influence on me as an infielder. Because what I'm doing, he taught me. He didn't break it down the way I broke it down, and as I got older in the game, I started seeing what makes you consistent. But what I did, he taught me. He gave it to me, and then I figured out a way I can explain it to other people.

I've always been able to give what I got in a very simple fashion. As a ballplayer in all the years I've been in the game, I just never believed in the difficulties of things. I look at things and I see what I can eliminate. If something takes five steps, I try to see if I can get it done in less. And that's what I did with infielding.

### So simplicity is key?

Simplicity. Exactly. In everything.

As a manager, I'm simple. I look at all of this stuff. [*He points to a thick statistics binder on his desk.*] I register what I think is important, but I'm not going to spend all of my time looking at that stuff. Most of the time I'm reacting to what I see and the knowledge I have and what my gut tells me.

### You're known for your great teaching of fielding, but do you also teach batting?

No, I don't mess with hitting. It's a very difficult business. Infield play—I've got maybe six guys I have to deal with. In spring training, I might have eighteen guys. But I have a system where I break them down to two or three at a time.

Everything that I'm trying to get them to do, they've got a chance to do. And if they've got any questions, we can talk. And then some days we just sit around and we talk about it. Because I've got to know what you're feeling, and I've got to make you a part of it for me to give what I want to give. It's hard for me to give it if I can't get you to receive it. In order for me to get you to receive it, I've got to make you a part of it. And then once I've made you a part of it, I'm like E. F. Hutton—I speak, you listen. Because you are going to see the results.

I do everything close up. Close up gives you the feel. You get the feeling of what it's like to pick up that last hop. You get the feeling of the position you should be in. So now when I get far away from you and start hitting balls at you, all you've got to do is work to that position and get that feeling. And you start to get that feeling, and it becomes routine.

So if you can do what's supposed to happen last close up—when I'm away from you, and we start doing the work, I don't have to scream at you, and I don't have to stop the work and come up and try to correct anything, because we corrected everything before I got started. Most guys, they get started and then they correct. I correct first and then get started. Does that make any sense?

*Yes, it does. It makes a lot of sense.*
That's the way I do it.

*You must love teaching.*
Well, after the first two months [*as manager of the Rangers*], I got back to it. Because I'm not one of those guys that can oversee. That's not me. I do my best work when I'm in the trenches. I do my best work when I'm out there hands on, so I can feel, so I can touch, so I can know, so I can have an idea of what you're thinking. So we can ease those demons that are inside of you. That's what we want to ease.

*What are the demons? Fear of failure?*
That's the main one. And the thing about the game of baseball is, you fail more than you succeed.

*No one bats a thousand . . .*
Why worry about the failing part? Let's worry about the 30 percent that you can be good. That's the part we want to focus on. Not the 70 percent that you're bad. And like I said, anybody that ever had one day in the game of baseball defensively where they went to the locker room and was proud of what they did, I can help them to do that more consistently.

You see a guy out there make a mistake—watch his feet. Because that's where the mistake was. A lot of guys look at video and come out with the wrong idea of what they saw. They see the symptom. I see the cause. They might say, "He led with his elbow." Well, something caused the elbow to lead. What caused it? The balance point—which is your feet. The stride was too short, or the stride was too long. If your balance is correct, your arm will stay where it's supposed to stay. [*As he talks, he demonstrates balance and off balance while sitting in his chair.*] Your feet make your hands. Hands don't make feet. It can't get any simpler than that.

You talk to anybody that's been through me, and they'll tell you—feet make hands.

*Were there influences outside of baseball that helped make you a good teacher?*
My brothers. I used to go with them and play with older guys, and a lot of the time I used to complain. And they would tell me if I can't handle it, go home. Well, what are you going to do? You're going to prove to your older brothers that you can handle it. That was a big influence in dealing with adversity.

*There must be people you've had who are not easy to teach . . .*

Scutaro was one. [*Marco Scutaro was an Oakland A's infielder when Washington coached there.*] Because of his style, you know. [*He speaks reflectively here, perhaps sadly.*] But he incorporated some of it.

But I learned quick that I can't change him. He is what he is. That's just his style. And if you take that from him, then he's not Marco Scutaro. And you've got to recognize that. Some people you just can't change.

Most people go try to teach with the ego, that, "I got all the answers. It's got to be my way or you've got to hit the highway." Well, that's not the way I do it. I look at what you've got to offer, and sometimes what I can do is subtracting. Everybody always wants to add. But sometimes all you've got to do is subtract.

And I've been able to recognize that. It's just a blessing. I can't explain it.

Being out there on the ball field teaching is the best thing the Lord could have ever done for me. Because that's when I'm at my best.

*Do you like it better than playing?*

No! [*We both laugh.*] No, no way. I loved playing. I never liked teaching better than playing. But once my playing days were over, I had something to offer.

# 7 | Growing the Body and Spirit

*"What we're actually teaching here is who we are."*

# Lokita Carter

## TANTRA TEACHER

*Lokita Carter was born and raised in Germany, studied in India, lived for a time in Australia, and then moved to northern California, where she teaches classes and workshops in Tantra. Most of the classes she co-teaches with her husband.*

*An attractive woman with lively, deep-blue eyes, she speaks with a trace of a German accent in a voice that occasionally lilts with excitement. We met at an outdoor café near her home.*

I began with Tantra when I was fifteen, and I came across a book that talked about Tantra being the integration of spirituality and sexuality. I was still a virgin, but the concept fascinated me, so I started on this path really young. I started reading, and then I found a boyfriend who was interested in the same subject, so we played around and explored. Then I found my spiritual teacher, who had a community in India where I lived for a number of years. I did a variety of different trainings there and read and meditated. My main inspiring teacher is Margot Anand, who is an author and teacher.

**Some readers of this book may not know what Tantra is.**

It came out of a variety of ancient traditions. There was a Hindu Tantric movement, a Buddhist Tantric movement. It's over two thousand years old. I'm not sure anybody really knows its exact origin. For me it is a spiritual path that includes our body and our sexuality as a way to transform our lives. So instead of negating the body, we are celebrating the body. We are using the life-force energy of the body to become better people: to enjoy life, to relate to others, to make love, to be more ecstatic. Some of the spiritual paths—they don't really like the body. They say the body is bad, or the body is something down there. . . .

Without the body we wouldn't be here, or we would be here in some ungraspable form! [*Laughs.*] In Tantra we are experiencing life through the body. In a nutshell, that's what Tantra is to me—a spiritual path that celebrates the body.

*How do you teach it? It must be different than teaching the causes of World War I or photosynthesis—something purely intellectual.*

Tantra is a form of spiritual expression that is experiential. You can read fifteen million books about Tantra and never really get the essence of it unless you experience something physically: sitting in meditation or relating to another person. So the way it has always been taught is experientially. There are different processes you do—things you do with another person, or you meditate by yourself, or in a couple you have communication—but basically it's experiential.

In the workshops I teach we don't talk much about the theory, we just give people a series of experiments and then we guide them through—let's say a breathing practice—and then they experience something and they talk about it afterward. They say, "I felt something," or "I felt my heart open," or "I felt closer to my partner," or "I felt nothing," or whatever it was. And then they have some kind of an "aha," but the "aha" experience is in the body rather than mentally. That's the way we teach Tantra.

*So the teaching is a way to guide people into experience. But I suppose one could find a description of these exercises in a book. But what's the role of the teacher? Couldn't one just read a book?*

Most people read it but never really do it. I don't know about you, but when I read about an exercise in a book, I think, "That sounds like a great exercise, I should try that some day," and then I forget about it. With the real-life experience of having a teacher there, it actually gives permission to try it. And we guide . . . we guide the participants through these exercises, some quite complex. We guide them through, we remind them of things—we're facilitating. We're creating a space—I know that's a "New Agey" kind of term—but we're creating an environment where they can just relax and experience something. And if they were to forget what to do next, we can tell them what it is. Or if somebody has an experience that's unpleasant, we're there to coach him or her.

Also in that environment, the teacher serves as an example, as a living example. What we're actually teaching here is who we are. I'm sitting there and I'm saying, "Communicate like this to your wife of thirty-seven years," but I'm actually embodying that because that's how I talk with my husband of ten years. And so they see the example. They're learning through the experiments we've proposed to them, but at the same time they're also learning from watching what it is I might do as a teacher. Because it embodies the reality of what I'm teaching . . . if you follow my drift.

*Yes. It like's that old saying, "You don't just teach your subject matter; you also teach yourself."*

Oh, yeah. Exactly. One of my wise teachers once said that teaching is like a pyramid. The top of the pyramid is *what* it is you teach. You've got to know what you teach, whether it's accounting or Tantra or whatever it is. The next level of the pyramid is *how*—how do you teach that. How do you present it, logistically and intellectually, so that others can grasp it? But the bottom of the pyramid is the *who,* because that's who you are. And so if I know what I'm teaching and how, that's all very well, but if I don't live it, if I'm not what I say I believe in, then the whole pyramid falls down. So it really comes down to who I am.

*It seems that teaching Tantra is an interactive process. The student may react to an exercise in any number of ways, and then based on that, you in turn react in a certain way. How do you know how to react? I would think that the difference between a very good Tantra teacher and one who's not so good is that the really good teacher often reacts in just the right way in leading the student to the next step.*

I think there's an art to it. Of course, I've had training in how to be with people in those situations. I'm a trained body worker and a rebirthing therapist. That background of how to facilitate growth or transformation in people helps. But in terms of the teaching, one just has to be really perceptive of where they are and talk with them. Sometimes we have to employ tools like confrontation, or sometimes we have to employ tools where the whole group helps them go through the process, or sometimes they just have to leave. Like if a couple is talking about something to do with their sex life and suddenly they have a really hard time and all this unresolved material arises—which can happen—I might talk with them and suggest they do certain things, and we always bring it back to how they feel now. So instead of confronting a problem, we like to say, "OK, here was a big problem for the past twenty-five years, but what is it now? Do you still love each other?"

But I guess it's an intuitive thing. But I've been doing it nine years now and I've taught over thirteen thousand people, so one gets kind of an experienced eye.

*Do you feel you're better as a teacher than you were two or five years ago?*

Yes, I think so. The wealth of experience is important. But also I've learned to trust. You know, I'm from Germany, so there was a time when I was very rigid in my teaching. I would always come to a workshop with a schedule: from nine to ten we will do this, and from ten to eleven we will do this, and so on. If anything changed, I would feel kind of nervous. But one day my computer hard drive crashed and I had to go to this workshop without a written curriculum for a whole weekend. So I taught the whole workshop without an agenda. I realized that I had integrated everything, and that I could still be with the situation. So instead of being so rigid with my teaching, there started to be a certain flow. Then I realized that I could do anything. A certain trust developed.

On another occasion I was teaching the women's workshop and made up this wonderful program, but the day before, I realized I hated it. I didn't want to teach that at all. So I walked into this room where there were thirty expectant ladies waiting for the presentation. I realized I didn't know what I was going to do. But the beautiful thing is there's a certain freedom in this kind of work—it's not like teaching math. Then some woman said something about her relationship with her daughter, and suddenly the whole material evolved. So all this material presented itself so the whole workshop ended up being about beautiful, amazing things that I never could have conceived of beforehand.

*Can you give an example of something you might do in one of your introductory workshops?*

We might say for a couple to just sit down across from each other—in chairs or on the floor, wherever they feel comfortable—and decide consciously, "Now we are going to enter into sacred time together." Sacred time means time that is just for me and my partner. To create the sacred time, we are going to take some elements out of our space. They might use their hands and they pick up a resentment, and they say, "I take out these resentments." [*She gestures, pretending to pick up an object with both hands and then toss it aside.*] And the other one will say, "I take out this anger." Whatever doesn't serve them, they can just take it out. Because if you want to give a massage to your wife, it would help if there wasn't any anger or resentment or stress from work.

And then we say, "OK, now take in things that you want to have for your sacred time together." So then they bring in love, connection, relaxation, positive communication, whatever. Now there's a space where they've taken out negative stuff and brought in positive stuff.

Mind you, they do it for themselves, not for their partner. So let's say, if I had PMS and was moody, my partner could not say, I take out your PMS. I wouldn't appreciate that. [*Laughs.*] Then they might honor each other. One might say, "I might honor you for being such a beautiful man, and your eyes are shining bright today." One might give a compliment or a gift, something for real or something we make up, like "here's a key to my heart." Then they would start talking about their desires, fears, and boundaries. By that, I mean . . . let's say here they are, husband and wife, and the wife wants a foot massage. The wife wants a massage that's two hours long, but the husband has only half an hour. So my desire, she says, is "I want a two-hour foot massage, and my fear is that you only have fifteen minutes, and my boundary is that you can't go higher up than my knee." Then the husband might say, "My desire is I give you a foot massage for half an hour, my fear is that I'll start thinking about work, and my boundary is that I don't want you to touch me back." So then they may negotiate and reach a compromise, then they give the foot massage and then they thank each other. But all this time, they have pledged to just be with each other during this sacred time. If the phone rings or the dog barks, it's completely irrelevant because this is it. So basically they've made the commitment to be fully present with each other. That sounds kind of simple, and it is simple, but at the same time, in simplicity often lies the greatest key. This ritual is *the* most powerful one, in all the workshops.

*Really?*

We've taught countless people, and that is the major thing that they take away—that they create this environment just to be with their partner, to be together undisturbed for a period of time, and to do something together that they both enjoy and have it as a ritual. People really, really, really like it a lot. I like it and that's why I teach it. [*Laughs.*]

*That sounds fairly talk oriented . . .*

Yes, that's the example I chose. There are many other things that are not so talk oriented. But they're more difficult to describe.

It's fairly rare that someone doesn't take to this. Although it sounds like Tantra is some great big eastern mysterious religion about rituals and sex and orgies—you know what you read about—really it isn't. Tantra is really a way of life. It's about relating, it's about being, it's about being with yourself and being with others, it's about your energy and your life. Everybody wants that. Everybody wants to have a good life and a good relationship and an open heart and have love and make good love with each other. I would imagine that 99 percent of all people would love that.

*Can you describe one other exercise you use in teaching?*

You might just sit across from your partner. You put your hand on her heart and she puts her hand on your heart, and you just gaze into each other's eyes for five minutes and breathe together. It's a simple exercise, very powerful.

*And when it works, what is the power of it?*

When it works, all these layers of the normal kinds of behavior we exhibit just disappear. I don't know how it is with you, but I can be very engaged with my work and I'm sitting at my computer, and my husband walks in and I look at him, and then I have something to eat and then the telephone rings, there are veils in front of what's really truly him and what's really truly me. Not that my work isn't truly me, but when we're *really* together, it takes away the veils when we look into each other's eyes. We become present. There's so much multi-tasking going on in today's culture. All these gadgets are beeping and ringing and demanding our attention. But when it works, we are really present with each other, right now. And usually it opens the heart—feeling love, feeling good, feeling positive, feeling connection.

*As a teacher, are you ever aware that some past teacher of yours has shaped the way you teach? Do you ever hear an old teacher's voice in your own?*

I actually do. [*Laughs.*] I know it's a little bit absurd, but there's one particular teacher, I think he was my fifth-grade teacher . . .

*He probably wasn't teaching Tantra to fifth graders . . .*

No. [*Laughs.*] He wasn't teaching Tantra. But he used to just mutter these things to himself about how to be with a classroom. He would say, "Oh, I have to remind myself to look left and right because there's no attention coming from the left of the room. Maybe I have to look there more!" It's something so bizarre. Often when I sit in front of groups, his sentences will come to me in German. It's really very odd. It's quite sweet. He was a wonderful man.

I've also had teachers where I didn't like their style or way of teaching, so I learned what not to do. [*Laughs.*]

*Are there things about contemporary American culture that make it especially challenging to teach Tantra?*

I don't personally think it's that challenging. Mind you, I do teach this in California and maybe that's a different culture than the middle of the country. But the thing is, I think that Tantra is especially important now that a big generation of people is coming to the point where they're beginning to retire—the whole baby boomer generation who have money, who have done the children, who might have grandchildren, who find themselves with this beautiful partner of thirty years and they're going, "Now what do we do?" In that way, it's a wonderful thing and really necessary. And in the next few years, there's more and more of them coming. Most of them want to have more spirituality in their lives.

So for me, I think Tantra is needed and it's very well received. But because Tantra has been misrepresented in the media as this sex-type thing, I have thought for a while we should rephrase the language so it's a little bit easier for people to take and not to think it's this sexual-cult-from-the-East thing. Instead, it's a spiritual path about ecstatic living—which is the name of our organization, the Institute for Ecstatic Living.

*Often a particular student will come to mind for a teacher, one who was special in some way. Does anyone like that come to mind for you?*

Oh, yes. For sure. Many.

*Can you tell the story of one?*

Well, let's see . . . which of my lovely students can I choose?

There's one particular couple who came to a workshop. They were very nice people, but they were very skeptical about this workshop, sitting in the background. They were very reserved—even when the workshop was over, they were still reserved, so I didn't think we made any impact on them. They hadn't seemed very receptive to the work.

Time went by and then a few months later they called and registered for another workshop. And I thought, "Really? That's very interesting." So they came to the second workshop, and in the middle of that event, the man had this amazing experience, a spiritual experience in which he saw something about his life and the meaning of life, and his relationship. He just had a huge spiritual revelation, and he told the group about the revelation, and I'll never forget that because he used the identical words as the words I had used for a very similar revelation I had years and years before. It was beautiful. And he's gone through a huge transformation ever since. He and his wife have been married for a long, long time, and they had brought up a beautiful family. They are very different people than this reserved couple who had come to us at first. They are very open with each other. They have a beautiful relationship.

*It's so interesting. In talking with a lot of teachers, I'm finding that sometimes it's the students they don't think they're reaching that turn out to be the most affected.*

Exactly. It's completely out of my control. I sometimes leave a teaching assignment, and I think it's maybe not that good. And then six months later I get this e-mail from Frank, and he says, "You have no idea how much you affected me." My husband, he reminds me—we don't really know how we're affecting those people. As time goes by, I'm trusting more and more that whatever I'm presenting, they will take that with them in whichever way.

*"When the line is busy, God can't call in."*

# Jan Chozen Bays

## ZEN TEACHER

*Jan Chozen Bays teaches at the Great Vow Zen Monastery in Oregon, which she helped to found, and where she is co-abbot. She received Tokudo, priest's ordination, in 1979. She finished formal koan study in 1983, and she was given Dharma transmission, authorization to teach, the same year. She is the author of* Jizo Bodhisattva: Modern Healing and Traditional Buddhist Practice. *She is also a pediatrician.*

I went to medical school and became a pediatrician, but after about seven years of practicing, I became dissatisfied. It just didn't feel correct in terms of alignment with my life purpose. When we moved to Oregon, I got a job teaching at a hospital. It involved supervising residents and medical students. So I realized that this is what I am. I'm a teacher.

It was wonderful that I had eight years of practice under my belt, because I was an informed teacher who could speak to people who were taking care of patients on a daily basis, especially poor patients who have no resources. So then I tried to clarify what it was I loved about teaching.

There are two aspects of teaching that I like. One is that I dislike intensely people being confused. It even irritates me when people give bad directions about how to get from one place to another. I feel the same way about learning. Learning is so much fun. But all of the fun, excitement, and curiosity can be drained out of it by bad teaching, or confusing teaching. So that's the first thing I love about teaching—trying to take a mass of information and clarify the essence, and then the stages of learning, and then lay those out so people can be guided from an early understanding to a much more sophisticated understanding. And it's important to teach beginners without condescension.

The second part of teaching that I really love is the "aha" moment, when someone is really puzzled or confused about something, and you clarify it for him or her and the person gets it. You can see the light dawning in people's eyes, and it doesn't matter if it's a five-year-old learning to tie his or her shoes or a Zen student or a medical student. That wonderful moment when people really understand something is the reward for teaching.

*How did you move from teaching medicine to teaching Zen?*

I had two parallel careers. At the same time that I was doing my pediatric training I was also studying Zen. I learned to meditate when I was an intern, and then after my internship we did a sabbatical year to Australia, and that's when I began to meditate on a regular basis and to read books about Zen. When we came back I found a teacher, Maezumi Roshi, and I began my training under him. Years later when we moved to Oregon, we bought a property to become a Zen center. Eventually as the demands of Zen teaching have increased, I've eased out of my medical practice.

There's something very satisfying about teaching people who come to you saying, I know I need a change, I know I'm the problem, I know my suffering originates with me, and I know I need help in figuring out how to reduce that suffering and increase that happiness from within.

A lot of people aren't really interested in changing. For example, most of the health measures are very simple: don't smoke, don't eat junk food, don't eat a lot of sweets, exercise, get enough rest. But most people aren't willing to do that. [*Laughs.*] Then they get upset because they're unhealthy. So the feeling for me about Zen teaching is that you're going directly to the heart of the problem, which is the human mind.

*Some readers of this book may not have a clear idea of what Zen is and what you teach when you teach Zen. Could you explain?*

Sure. Buddhism fundamentally is a system of education. The Buddha did not propose a religion. He designed a system of education about the nature of the mind and the mind's role in creating happiness or suffering in our lives and the lives of people around us.

Everyone is going to have ordinary forms of pain and discomfort—getting old, getting sick, and dying. That's a given. But how your mind treats that can turn it into what we call suffering, or can use it as a source of investigation and education and deepening spiritual awareness of universal truths of life and death. In Buddhism you are the research subject and you are also the scientist; so you are doing investigation into yourself, and the primary tool is meditation. So through meditation you quiet the mind and the ceaseless flow of thoughts in the mind enough to look beyond those thoughts, and see deeper into what's really going on in the mind and the self.

That's exactly what the Buddha did. The Buddha's primary question was, "Why do people suffer? What causes suffering?" And he looked into his own mind to see how suffering originates within. That's exactly what we do when we teach Zen. We help people to look directly into their own hearts and their own minds.

*How do you do that with your students?*

We have many pathways into this practice. Some people like to read and go to classes, so we have classes where we present material and discuss it. Some people are more interested in the direct experience—and Zen in particular is focused on the direct experience, accessible through meditation. So when people come to the Zen center, many come seeking instruction in meditation. We teach them how to sit—the various kinds of posture—so they can see which is most comfortable for them. We also help them learn how to use various kinds of meditation aids, like different kinds of cushions and benches. There are many different kinds of meditation: meditation on the body, meditation on the breath, meditation on sound, loving kindness meditation. We teach the different kinds of meditation and how to apply them. We also do meditation retreats. We also teach classes on relationships as spiritual practice, to help people with difficulties in their relationships. We have a class on difficult emotions—anger and jealousy. There are specific Buddhist tools for working with emotions within ourselves that cause suffering, such as the inner critic. We have classes on sexuality and its relationship to spiritual practice: What is sexual energy and how can it be used well? We have a very popular class on preparing for your own death.

*Maybe you can talk specifically about one of these—for example, working on the inner critic.*

Sure. The inner critic is a voice in us that develops early in life to protect us from harm. It criticizes us to get us to shape up so that we won't get into trouble. Its motive is that if we criticize ourselves from the inside and shape up, then we'll avoid criticism from the outside. It's usually modeled on somebody in our life, usually a parent, who is critical of us. So it has phrases that it picks up from early childhood, but also phrases that it picks up from later on. Some people are aware of this voice and how powerful it is, and some aren't aware of it until they meditate on it and quiet the mind down. Once you have learned about the inner critic, it is easy to detect it.

So if someone gets up to give a speech in public and they say, "I'm sorry, but I didn't have time to prepare this speech," that's a thinly disguised form of the inner critic trying to win the audience over—when the inner critic is saying that the talk is not going to be very good. But what it does is alienate the audience, because the audience will think, "Why did I bother to come if you didn't prepare?"

Or let's suppose that someone compliments you on your pie. Instead of just saying, "Thank you," you say, "Well, it's not as good as I usually make." So the inner critic can become this neurotic, overblown voice that takes control and leaks out in all aspects of life.

What we do first is try to get people to hear the voice of the inner critic. So we point out flagrant examples of it—in a lighthearted way, because if you take the inner critic too seriously you can end up spiraling down into a very bad depression. Actually, there's a group that has a psychological scale now that says you can measure the risk of suicide by measuring the strength of the inner critic. There's even something we call the killer critic, which says things like, "You should never have been born" or "The world would be better off without you." We take this seriously, because the inner critic really saps people's energy and takes the joy out of their life. It's the source of writer's block.

So we first get people acquainted with the inner critic. Then through many forms of exercises, we try to hone the inner critic down to its primary essence, which is a certain kind of discerning wisdom. If you take out the sting of the inner critic, it becomes discernment. It would say something like, "Well, John is quite a bit taller than me," but it doesn't draw any conclusions from that in terms of self-worth, such as, "I'm so short that I'm worthless," or "I'm so short there are many things I can't do." Discernment would say, "Here I am on the podium, and though I'm not as prepared for this speech as I'd like to be, I'm going to do my very best job." But you don't tell people that. The energy of the inner critic is contagious.

*And you said there were also exercises.*

Here's a very common exercise we do. Look around the room, and let the inner critic speak about the room. So people will say, "The rug is ugly and it has stains on it, and I hate fluorescent lights, and you can hear a weird sound from the air conditioning ..." So you bring the inner critic out full force, and people start laughing. Then you switch to the opposite voice, the voice that says everything is OK just as it is. Then people say, "The rug has character and the stains just tell me that the room has been well used, and the sound of the air conditioning is conducive to meditation," and so on. So you switch back and forth between the voices and learn to balance. You can't go around saying everything is perfect as it is when the economy is collapsing. If we keep our minds clear and our hearts open, we can work our way through this.

*Your website says that you do koan practice. What is that?*

Koans are historical accounts of people facing an existential crisis. The usual format is that a monk in all earnestness asks a teacher a question. "In all earnestness" means that that monk has been struggling with that question for a long time. So the famous one is a monk who asks the master, "Does a dog have Buddha nature?" What that means is that this monk has heard that everything has Buddha nature: everything in its essence is whole and complete and perfect as it is. Or in Christian terms, one would say, "Everything is a creation of God." And the monk looks at the mangy, flea-bitten, smelly dog and thinks, "How could this creature have the nature of perfection?" He ponders this for a long time, and finally he asks the teacher. The teacher responds with what are called turning words, some succinct phrase that opens the monk's mind to a deeper reality.

Almost everybody who has spiritual life has a koan that they're carrying around with them. For example, I had a Catholic woman who came to a retreat, and I asked her, "What is the question that you carry around with you all of the time?" She said,

"My question is, 'Is there anything outside of God?'" For example, how could there be children caught in bombings in Iraq? How could God allow this? So we melted it down into this: "Is there anything outside of God?" So she spent the weekend pondering that question and looking around her. Is your computer outside of God? Is your hand outside of God? Is that homeless person at the side of the road with a sign asking for a handout outside of God? So the koan is a way to dig down through layers of confusion to have insight into a deep truth. If you read about them, they seem nonsensical. People often read about the koan, "What is the sound of one hand clapping?"

*Yes, that's the common one.*

But that's actually a very deep inquiry into sound, first of all—to deep listening. With all koans, you have to parse them of the extra words. So it's, "What is the sound of one hand?" or "What is the sound of one?" or "What is the sound?" So the teacher will help the student refine the essence of what this question is and then guide him or her into listening. So you begin to listen to all of the sounds of the world without listening to them—listen to them as if you've never heard them before. It leads people to some very interesting insights.

So in Christian terms, you could say, "What is the sound of God? Listen. Are any of these sounds outside of God? Listen. What is the sound of God's voice?" So when we teach people meditation, if they're coming from a Christian context, we're teaching them to be still and listen, to be completely receptive. The catchphrase is, "When the line is busy, God can't call in." If you're thinking all the time, then you're not going to get to hear the voice that tells you about reality or what you should do in life.

*What makes you a good teacher?*

I'm naturally curious and I love to learn myself. There's an excitement to me about continually learning. It could be learning things with the body—so it could be learning yoga or learning how to use your non-dominant hand to brush your teeth. Or it could be exercising your mind in a way that you didn't before—so you learn a new meditation technique or you learn a new language. Or when I was forty, I decided I wanted to learn to play a new musical instrument, so I took a class and learned to play a recorder and some other medieval instruments, and now I'm learning to play the piano. I just think that one of the fundamental reasons we humans are here on earth is to learn and to grow, and when we do that, it makes us happy. It's an innate source of happiness.

My parents were both teachers, and my grandmother was a teacher. I think they were very good teachers, and they communicated their love of learning and creating to me, and I'm just passing it on. My Zen teacher was very good, too, and he loved what he was teaching. When you have those kinds of examples, then it's natural to do it, and it's fun to do it.

There's nothing worse than young people turned off to learning. I was talking to a school superintendent a few years ago and he said that one of the problems he's seeing in schools is that young people expect to be entertained. He said they've lost the point of education for the sake of education.

The body feels good when it's exercised. The body likes to be exercised. And the same is true of the mind. When we develop our innate capacity for learning it feels good, and we feel competent and capable, and empowered in the world. It's sad to me when education is made to be rote or turns kids off. If we can start early and instill enthusiasm for pure learning—for exercising the mind and the body—we can really turn the educational system around, I think.

*"I teach by pastoring."*

# Robert Smith

### PROFESSOR, DIVINITY SCHOOL

*Robert Smith is a professor at the Beeson Divinity School of Samford University in Birmingham, Alabama. An ordained Baptist minister, he was minister of the New Mission Missionary Baptist Church for twenty years before returning to the seminary to complete his PhD. He taught at the Southern Baptist Theological Seminary in Louisville, Kentucky, where he received the 1996 Findley B. Edge Award for Teaching Excellence. He has been teaching at Beeson since 1997. At Beeson he received the Teacher of the Year Award in 2005. He is the author of* Doctrine That Dances: Bringing Doctrinal Preaching and Teaching to Life.

My discipline is homiletics, which is a fancy word for preaching—the art and preparation of the delivery of sermons. I teach two courses: a basic course in the fall, and the practicum in the spring. And then I teach advanced electives in homiletics.

*How do you teach someone to preach?*
I believe that I can teach a system and the method to prepare and deliver sermons. The rest I depend upon the Holy Spirit to do. A person has to be called to preach.

*Can you describe your system?*
I use Sidney Greidanus's books, especially *Preaching Christ from the Old Testament*. He has what he calls a Christocentric method, and I take students through that. It starts off with the principle "select a text with an eye toward congregational needs." So I want my students to look at a text and through the lens of the text see what the congregational need is. We call it exegeting the text and exegeting the audience.

Suppose you're preaching a text like, "Take no thought for tomorrow, for to-morrow will take care of itself," from Matthew 6. Well, if you're teaching that text to rich people, to well-to-do people who have plenty of money, that's one thing. To preach it to people who live on the streets and come to the rescue mission to get their meals, that's another thing. That's what I mean by selecting a text with an eye toward congregational needs. That the first principle of his Christocentric method.

The second one is "read the text in its literary context"—whether it's a parable, a gospel, an epistle, history, or prophesy. Each biblical literary genre is different, and they have to be respected and preached according to the literary form. You have to outline the structure of the text and formulate the theme and goal of the text. You have to ask what the text is trying to do in terms of a behavioral response—to pray more, to repent, to rejoice, to think, to serve? The sermon has to be written in oral style, meaning to write the sermon in the way you talk, so the sermon is written for the ear. And so on. . . . So these are the kinds of things we teach.

*Is there a point at which your students give a sermon and then you judge it?*

Exactly. Much of the first semester is devoted to lecture. I meet with my students four times a semester. I have thirty-two students, sixteen in each of my two classes. When I meet with them the first time, for about an hour, I am mostly reinforcing what I taught in the class. They will come to my conference with a sermon skeleton worksheet that they have been working on. They will have been pre-assigned a text, and I will have studied it too—so even before they show me their worksheet, I will offer them comments on the passage that I think will be helpful. We'll talk about what they give me.

In the second conference with me, which is about an hour and a half, they give me an expanded and revised sermon skeleton. The third meeting will be just before they preach, and I meet with them about two hours. Then after they preach, I critique them and fellow students critique them. We use an evaluation form, and the forms are given to them. In this meeting with them, we'll watch their sermon on DVD and spend another two to three hours. I try to challenge and stretch them.

*And is this sermon in a mock service, or is it at an actual Sunday morning service?*

I call it church. This service is just as important to God as if you were preaching in a cathedral. This is not a trial sermon or a mock sermon: this is a real sermon and you're preaching to real people, and all of us have spiritual needs that the word of God will address. Sometimes their relatives will attend—or their parents, fellow students, and fellow professors. It's real worship.

*It strikes me that preaching is more an art than a science, and that might make it more challenging to teach. Have you developed any techniques over the years for helping people develop at this art?*

It *is* an art. I begin with the premise that every person has to find his or her own voice. I don't want them to give themselves to imitation, but rather to assimilation—

where they gather approaches and techniques from different people, from different cultures and different ethnicities, and they take the best of that and make it their own.

Many of these students have never preached a sermon, and they come frightened and intimidated. I say to them, "Find your voice. Read, study, listen to others, and eventually you'll start finding your voice and appreciating the gift that God has given you."

So that is very important. We'll listen to different preachers by videotape and by reading, men and women with different styles. I will always be very inclusive when it comes to different models. I want them to appreciate the best in all cultures. I expose them to what I think are excellent techniques and artistic devices from all cultures.

We have international students, white students, African American students, international students, male and female students, new Christians, PKs and MKs [*preachers' kids and missionaries' kids*]. So I throw it all out like a big smorgasbord dinner, and they feast on what they like and what they can relate to and what they can handle. My desire is that they will undergo a metamorphosis, so that when the semester is over, they are wowed and amazed by how they've grown, and how confident they have become.

Some students are more left-brained and some are more right-brained, and what I want to do is get the two hemispheres of the brain to be merged, so that the analytical people become more imaginative and the imaginative people become more analytical. So I'm about variety, and somehow in that process a person finds his or her voice.

### *What do you think are the things that have made you a good teacher?*

Well, I've been blessed by being around in the African American tradition what is known as fathers in the ministry or fathers in the faith. These are elderly men—elderly preachers and pastors—who in different seasons of my life have helped to shape not only the way I preach and pastor, but also the way I teach. So that's one of the things—models: great teachers who I've sat under either formally in seminary . . . and informally at their feet as they pastored me or made themselves available to teach me outside of the classroom.

Another thing is that preaching for me is fun—what I call holy hilarity. It's fun. I don't go to work; I go to the playground of the spirit. It's not laborious. Yes, I have to do my work; yes, preparation stretches me and all of that. But I have a great deal of fun. I love what I'm doing.

Another thing—if I am a good teacher, I am that because I love my students. I spend time in student's homes, I go to eat dinner with them, and I hold their babies, I go to the hospital when they're sick—those kinds of things. I say to them the first day of class, "First, I want to be your pastor, then I want to be your friend, and then perhaps I can be your professor." I teach by pastoring. I form relationships. If I am effective at all, it is because I've been their pastor-teacher. That has been the strength of my teaching.

*Do you ever have students who are having a crisis of faith or who once felt the call-ing and now aren't sure they still do?*
Sure.

*How do you deal with that?*
Well, it happens to the best. It happened to Jeremiah. He begins that verse with "I will not speak" and he ends it with "I cannot help but speak." So Jeremiah went through it. The best preachers have gone through a crisis of faith, and I personally think it's good. Because what it does is to get you to doubt your calling until you keep searching and reach a point where you can't doubt any longer. You move from illusion, which is not good, to disillusionment, which is breaking up illusion—and that is the crisis of faith.

I had a crisis of faith. As a twenty-year-old preacher I decided that I wasn't going to preach anymore. I had started preaching at seventeen. And I was going through struggles that caused me to doubt. There were a couple of elders who got with me after I gave my pastor my resignation, and they talked with me and shared with me and prayed with me—until I moved from illusion to being disillusioned and eventually to enlightenment.

So it's good to come to the fork in the road, and you decide that it is true that you are called to be what you are. It puts steel in your bones. It strengthens you to overcome the next crisis of faith, whatever that may be.

*I wonder if you think preaching is harder now than in the past. What I have in mind is that people, children included, used to learn to sit and listen, but now there are so many things that seem to cultivate short attention spans and a desire for visual stimulation—TV, computers, computer games, DVDs. Can people listen to a preacher as well as they once could?*
Well, I think you're right on. We live in a visually oriented society, with commercials and sound bites, and it does affect the attention span of people.

But I don't think preaching is passé. As Paul says, I become all things to all people . . . I can be a Greek to Greeks and a Jew to Jews. In other words, I can adopt the necessary approach to make myself effective to whatever audience I'm preaching.

There is a proverb—I believe it's an African proverb—that says the wise teacher is one who turns ears into eyes: a person who can take a word and then create an image for the word.

Clarence Jordan, who wrote the *Cotton Patch Gospel*, paraphrases a text in Second Corinthians 5:21, "God was in Christ reconciling the world back to Himself." He takes the concept of "reconcile" and uses in its place "hugging." So, he paraphrases it, "God was in Christ hugging the world back to Himself."

So I believe that we need to change our approach and be in tune with where people are. How do you speak to people when they've been so bombarded with words they don't necessarily speak to us anymore? You use images. Jesus did that: "The kingdom of heaven is like a field that is sown with wheat and tears."

"Is like" . . . images, metaphors. We really need to move toward that. As a preacher, say what you see, because it's important for people to see what you're saying, not just hear what you're saying. The images make the difference.

*"This is nothing outside of you. This is inside of you."*

# Catherine Rose

### EXOTIC DANCE TEACHER

*Catherine Rose has been teaching classes in exotic dancing in the San Francisco Bay Area for almost nine years. A native of Canada, she originally became an exotic dancer to pay for her education.*

I teach exotic dancing, primarily to women and occasionally to couples. It's all styles of exotic dancing; it focuses a lot on pole dancing because that's very popular right now—a sexy, X-rated, aerial dance form. And it also includes stage dancing, floor work (which is crawling around like sexy yoga), and lap dancing, which is another popular form of entertainment/dance. They're all great for fitness, and they're geared toward women who want a fun, sexy way to get fit: to feel sexy, to feel stronger, to feel more attractive, to feel more connected to their sexuality.

*And the way you teach it is to demonstrate it?*
Generally I do a demonstration, they watch, and then they copy. In some of my workshops I've created experiential exercises to help them drop into their own sense of movement and their own connection to their bodies. So in those instances I'm not demonstrating anything; I'm just creating an exercise where they can find movement within themselves. But for most of the material I teach, it's a verbal breakdown, so it's not just a visual copying as if they were watching a DVD. I break the material down piece by piece, pointing out all the places where it's easy to do it wrong. And then I give feedback. So it goes back and forth. I might have them work in pairs or in groups, so sometimes they're giving each other feedback as well.

*Would it be true to say that the method is not that different than if you were teaching ballet or the tango?*
Pretty much. I used to teach graphic software in art school, and I broke down the material in the same way—broke it down piece by piece and explained it. I think because it's so personally connected to women's identity and self-confidence, there's

a bit more of personal assurance involved. I try to build their confidence, to let them know that they look great, and you wouldn't necessarily do that if you were teaching a ballet course or something where it's a lot more strict, where you're really focusing on the form, and wrong and right, and you're not paying attention to how they feel or how they're experiencing the teaching. In my class, because it's training, but it also goes into female empowerment, I try to keep it extremely positive. So nobody does anything "bad" or "wrong" or "incorrect," but I try to bring in more grace and improve the places where their body isn't picking it up as quickly.

*So you're emphasizing self-expression, and you're starting with something in them and helping them stylize it rather than having them copy something that's external.*

Yes, for the most part. Except maybe pole dancing, which is much more skill oriented. There they are learning specific techniques, and there's a very particular way the pole makes contact with the body and how to support yourself. One could study pole dancing with me for six months and still be an intermediate because you have to build core strength as well as upper body strength. But in the other classes there's a lot more room for self-expression, and in the basic intro to exotic dance course, I really encourage people to express themselves through the movements. They need to understand that what I'm doing is just a starting point, and if they follow certain guidelines, they can make up their own moves and use music to express themselves.

*How many of your students are taking the courses so they can perform professionally?*

I'd say about 15 percent. Sometimes they come to me specifically for pole-dance skills. So it's a small percentage. It's not my target market.

*Of all the courses one can choose, why do people choose exotic dancing?*

It's exciting because it really pumps you up and puts you into a sweat. It's a great adrenaline rush. I'm teaching a feminine form of exotic dancing, so it invites the women to reconnect with their femininity. Typically, if she's a professional woman, that has been locked inside. If she's a mom, it's been put away. So a big piece of it is reconnecting with her feminine nature. And combining that with fitness—it's just a lot more fun. There's the motivation that it looks good and she can perform it for a partner. There are a lot of layers to why it's a little more exciting than an aerobics class.

*You speak of exotic dancing in terms of women's empowerment; some feminists see it otherwise and would speak of "objectification."*

Sure, sure. It's a great old argument. I used to march against pornography when I was a young political activist. So I understand the argument. But I feel really lucky in the Bay Area because there's been a lot of education around sex-positive feminism—which is the movement I like to associate myself with—which is not to deny our sexuality, but to honor it and to be able to have a choice in how we want to share it.

I have experienced being objectified in public and in the workforce, where it felt like an assault. In the strip club it felt like an appropriate avenue to be seen as a sexual commodity, particularly because there is a structure to contain it, and there is the financial gain. My personal experience was that the patrons often felt that they were the ones being exploited for their sexual needs. We often saw them as walking wallets we could easily exploit once we got them turned on—sadly. We also experienced them as human—sometimes lonely or fragile, men seeking female touch and love. And then there were the less desperate patrons (sometimes very good looking) that were extremely appreciative and respectful.

*Did you have a teacher or were you self-taught?*

There were no classes in exotic dancing then. But I did have some role models. My cousin secretly was an exotic dancer. I spoke with her. I also had a good friend who encouraged me. She was an artist and I was a visual artist with over nine years of art school. And then I found the community of women who worked in the clubs, and they were wonderful. There was a wonderful sisterhood of strippers.

*So you learned the dancing on your own . . .*

I went to strip clubs and watched dancers. And I studied some modern dance in college, and I later studied contemporary belly dancing. When you work in a club—say you work an eight-hour shift—you're not always dancing, so you sit and watch other dancers. And a lot of it was just my natural ability to move—I used to go club dancing about three times a week when I was in my early twenties. So some of it was watching and some of it was borrowing from other forms of dance.

*Can you describe some of your student success stories?*

She comes to me at a place where she's completely disconnected from her sexuality. She's a professional woman, successful, she has a career and family, but there's just some place where she dropped off in terms of her connection to her sexuality. She's lost a piece of herself somewhere down the road.

So she starts with me, and there's this out-of-body clumsiness. She's not quite getting it. There's a disconnect. Through taking my classes she finally starts to connect to that graceful, feminine essence, and she starts walking differently and starts experiencing herself moving through space differently and experiencing other people responding to her in a different way so that she just feels a little juicier, a little more sexy, more attractive, and a little more alive.

So this joy starts to unfold. Her movement starts to feel more languid and more natural. In the class, she's no longer copying movements but she starts to embody movement, and I see that juicy place, like when women fall into the zone. I love it when I see that in my class. Sometimes it's the whole group and sometimes it's just a few. They drop into that place where the air becomes thicker, and there's this mesmerizing quality that their movement starts to take on, and we all start to appreciate how beautiful and sexy their movement is. It wakes them up to a place that's just such a far place from where they started. It wakes them up to a place where they feel a little more joy and happiness in life.

*How did they become disconnected from their sexuality in the first place?*

For mothers, it may not seem appropriate to be in their sexual identity when they're being moms. Some women do it, and I love meeting moms who do not separate their sexual identity from their motherhood. But for some, they think that's what they're supposed to do—become "Mommy." And even to their husbands they become "Mommy." They just take on that mommy role—which is wonderful, but there's something missing after a little while. And with their careers, they take on that strong, "taking care of things" identity, that more masculine part of their identity, to the point where they don't have that relationship that keeps them juicy. So I'm one of the tools that women can use for coming back to that part of themselves, for reintegrating it. I start off a lot of my workshops by saying, "This is nothing outside of you. This is inside of you." Women are naturally sexual, naturally sensual. But for some reason or other, we have to close it down just in order to survive in different environments.

*So when your teaching is at its most successful, the student undergoes a kind of metamorphosis?*

Yes, and I see that a lot and I'm always surprised. They might come into my intro to exotic dance class at one in the afternoon and they are stiff and nervous, and by the time they leave, they're standing different and they're excited and they're looking forward to dancing at home in front of a mirror—or sharing it if that's something that feels good. They leave with a glow.

*"The people who went before us are our teachers."*

# Tlahuitollini (Ernesto Colín Álvarez)

## SPANISH TEACHER, AZTEC DANCE TEACHER

*Tlahuitollini teaches Aztec dance and culture with Calpulli Tonalehqueh in San Jose, California. He has also taught high-school Spanish in Los Angeles, and he currently mentors beginning teachers in Stanford's teacher-ed program. At thirty, he is one of the two youngest teachers interviewed for this book. In conversation, he exudes a strong, gentle, and soulful passion.*

I am very humbled by the invitation to be interviewed for your book. I feel that I am very young, and I have a long way to go as a teacher.

*Maybe you could speak first about teaching Aztec dance.*

I teach Aztec dance and culture in an Aztec dance circle. I've been an Aztec dancer for fourteen years. My doctoral dissertation is about the teaching and learning of Aztec dance.

It is part of the Aztec heritage that people organized their lives through a system called *calpulli*. The *calpulli* was a cooperative of families in which people pooled their collective resources to do agriculture and everything that was required for life.

Every *calpulli* had a system of formal and informal education. People taught their children in their homes, informally, but the *calpulli* also organized a system of formal schooling. It was public, compulsory, and time tested. Children were taught through song and dance, everything from myths and legends to mathematics.

Today in the United States, there are still *calpulli* that teach Aztec dance, language, arts, and song. At the *calpulli* where I teach, a group of parents meet and talk to each other about how to raise their children in an Aztec way.

My Aztec dance group is really active and intentional about trying to investigate, learn about, remember, and innovate and recreate the traditional ways. The way teaching and learning happen in our Aztec dance group is a new iteration of the way things were done in Mexico for thousands of years. We have a child-rearing group, a class that does scholarly research on Aztec culture, dance classes—starting with a beginner's class, a song class, and a class in Aztec art that does leather work, feather work, pottery, and beadwork. So in this group learning happens everywhere you look.

We teach Aztec dance through immersion, and some would say through remembering. When we do Aztec dance, it's done in concentric circles. The circles are organized in terms of recognition, status, and experience. The people in the circles closest to the center are more experienced dancers. In the center there's an altar with the four elements represented—earth, air, fire, and water. There are also drums in the center. The circles closest to the center are made up of the most experienced dancers; they are the most confident in their movements and they know how to lead the dances. The circles outside them are less experienced folks, and then the outer circles are the least experienced. As a result, you have lots of teachers. Nobody tells you anything in terms of how to do it step by step—you just dance—but you always have models. That's also an effective mechanism for teaching because the people in front of you are your cues in terms of what step is coming next and how it should be done. And there are always people to your left and your right to show you as well. So it's learning by immersion.

There isn't pressure in terms of right versus wrong or success versus failure. There's a lot of talk about just coming with an open heart. There's always talk like, "We all had our first day. We were all there at some point. And we all learned to get better. Just listen. Just move. Just try."

We also feel that human beings have in their bodies natural inclinations toward patterns, mathematics, rhythms, music, and dancing. Human beings are natural dancers. I don't want to call it magical, but there's something very natural about the patterns. Human beings are very receptive to the patterns and learn them very quickly.

Aztec dance works in counts of four and eight. There are base moves that are followed by ornamental moves, so the dance progresses in patterns. So the first time you might stumble through it, but then the second time it comes around, you know what's coming and you can do it. It's sort of like forming words with an alphabet. Aztec dance is the same. There are maybe 50 basic moves but about 360 Aztec dances, so every dance is just a different arrangement of those 50 moves, just as with different arrangements of the letters in an alphabet you can make different words.

There's also something in Aztec dance that we don't talk much about in Western culture, and that's the idea of ancestors, of spirit, of energy. There's something that happens in Aztec dance when people are connected in a circle, moving in the same way, and giving of their own energy—when they're sharing sights and sounds and the smell of the incense. It's a harmony that happens with the movement and the sound and the ceremony. There's an energy that gets created that sweeps you up. The whole circle moves you—you get enveloped—and if you tune in and focus, you get lifted by the energy. It's in your own body and in your own history, so it's like remembering how to be in that way.

We believe that our ancestors are very present—that when you die, you don't really die, you just get transformed into energy. So the people who did dance before are present all around us, and they help guide us. They help maintain the harmony. The people who went before us are our teachers.

*When you taught high-school Spanish and now when you mentor new teachers, do you draw heavily on Aztec culture, or is there a complete separation between that teaching tradition and this one?*

I'd like to think that it's not completely separate, because the Aztec tradition is so much a part of me and of what I value. If I'm going to be genuine in the way I teach, some of that will emerge. But I'm not sure I can articulate what part of the ethos of Aztec dance teaching actually enters into my teaching and mentoring in public education.

That being said, my work in the formal education system is responsive to other needs—responsive to state standards, written requirements for a teaching credential, requirements for the degree, to the way the school system is set up. If you're trying to help people be successful in that realm, you have to know how the system works and give them the tools to be successful in that system. In that way I would say there is a separation between the Aztec teaching and teaching in the public education system.

*How did you decide to teach?*

When I went to college, I was a double major in Chicano studies and Spanish. I've always been passionate about the Mexican American experience. The Chicano studies major was very interdisciplinary—so we studied the Mexican American experience in terms of art, civil rights, history, labor, activism, education, psychology, the justice system, literature, and poetry. I was enthralled by everything having to do with my culture and my identity.

There's a message that's very frequent in Chicano studies—that you're always part of a community, and there's an emphasis on giving back to your community. There are not many minorities in higher education, there are not that many Chicanos getting college degrees, and there are a lot of people who get pushed out of school or who drop out. If we have made it this far, it's because other people have sacrificed—people who went before us, who fought in the civil rights movement. You get inculcated with that idea of giving back. If I had to point to something that led to my being a teacher, it would be that. I really bought into that idea of giving back to our community. My work-study job in college was in the department of education, so I was around the professors of education. I decided to teach as a way of giving back. And I wanted to teach people like me: working class, immigrant, Mexican-American students. I was qualified to teach Spanish, but I wanted to teach a particular kind of Spanish—Spanish for native speakers—where I teach them how to write, and teach them about their literature and their culture.

So after I received my BA, I taught Spanish for heritage language speakers in a public high school, and then I helped start and I taught in an ethnocentric Latino charter school in Los Angeles. It was a small school that served the working-class Mexican immigrant community, and its curriculum was tailored to meet the needs of those students.

*In that experience, did it seem to you that teaching was more of an art or a science?*
Yes, I've heard that debate.

People are drawn to someone who is passionate. I've always been on fire with my own culture, my own history, my own people, and so I was always thirsty for knowledge and learning. I was passionate about where I was, and I was really happy with teaching. It was where I wanted to be.

I knew my content area, and through my degree programs I was competent in the rules and methods and standards and the nuts and bolts. But all of that was coupled with passion. I was young and energetic, and I was caring. I wasn't far removed from the students' experiences. I was a reflection of them. The students were able to see me as a role model because I was just an older version of them, and I was confident and successful. I had been to college.

We often talk about cultural mismatch between teachers and their students. But for me it was no mismatch. I liked the same music that they liked, I could make them all laugh because I had all the idioms—I knew the slang, I knew the jokes. My family was like theirs. I had the connections to Mexico. All of those things were a match.

But beyond that, I really did care about them. I don't know that I could say that for a lot of my colleagues. I taught in a school where there were ninety teachers. A lot of those teachers had been there for decades, and a lot of them were really jaded. They had stopped caring. A lot of them, I'm not afraid to say, were just collecting a paycheck. There were teachers who would photocopy crossword puzzles, tell the students to do them, and then go sit in the back of the classroom and read the newspaper—or would throw on a video and tell the students to be quiet.

The students sniff you out real quick. They know if you care about them or not. And they'll tune you out or let you in. I was genuine about caring about them as human beings. When I started teaching I was twenty-one, and some of my students were eighteen. I was also soccer coach. I walked around during lunchtime. I showed up at the Friday night football games. And that carries a lot of juice. It almost didn't matter what I said. They liked me because I cared.

One of my mentors at the high school told me, "Students will remember only about 10 percent of what you try to teach them about the curriculum, but what they don't forget is how you treat them. Whether they are first grade or fifth grade or ninth grade" . . . and he had taught all three . . . "what they want is somebody who cares about them."

One thing that no one can prepare you for in teacher training is the absolute, immense power you have as a teacher. Sometimes it's a delayed kind of thing, where you see students years later and you didn't even know how you touched their lives, and they'll tell you that you saved their life with one thing you said. Students will come back and tell me I was their inspiration for going to college or studying Spanish or starting Aztec dance. There are also moments in which you save lives. I can think of students for whom I was the first person they told about sexual abuse in their home, and I had to call child protective services.

There are students who have tragic stories, and you are the lifeline. There are students whose parents are heroin addicts, students who are living on the streets, students who are fourteen-year-old prostitutes and nobody knows about it. There are students who are gay or lesbian and in the closet, and are just tormented by coming out, and you help them come out and then the weight is off their shoulders. You can help move them. There are a lot of students like that who have come to me and I've helped—maybe by pointing them in the direction of resources, or just by being there to listen, or just cry with them, or whatever.

# 8 | *Teaching at the Bottom and on the Edge*

*"The humanities teaches us what we value and believe."*

# Jeannette Riley

## TEACHER, THE CLEMENTE PROGRAM

*Jeannette Riley is an associate professor at the University of Massachusetts, Dartmouth, where she teaches courses in English and women's studies. For the past three years, she has also taught in the Bard College Clemente Course in the Humanities. The program teaches a humanities program consisting of classes in art, literature, moral philosophy, and U.S. history to adults who are economically and educationally disadvantaged. The program was piloted in 1995 in Manhattan, and it has now been taught over a hundred times in fourteen states. It charges no tuition, and books, transportation expenses, and child care are furnished. It was about her teaching in the Clemente Program that we spoke.*

The Clemente Program is all about the humanities. Students come for eight months, and during that eight months they take a class in U.S. history, a class in moral philosophy, a class in art history, and a class in literature. There are also writing classes mixed in as well. We have also added public speaking as a part of all of our classes because we recognized that by helping students gain their voices, it was paying off in their ability to think about the things they read—not just in our classes but on a daily basis. The hope is that through exposing them to the humanities we are not just helping their critical thinking abilities, but we are also exposing them to things that can enrich their lives.

The Clemente Program is not based on the expectation that the participants will go on to college, though they can earn up to six college credits through Bard for transfer to a college they might attend. But it's mostly meant to give them a sense of self.

*You've taught the course three times now. How do you think it works?*

Like any adult-education class, there are definite challenges. The Clemente courses start with high numbers—anywhere from twenty-five to thirty students—and by the end of the year we are down to about fifteen students. When you're bringing in people who are underserved, many are facing economic issues, family issues, and health issues that may prevent them from being successful in the course, no matter how many resources you give them.

On a good note, for the people who do make it through, I think the program is tremendously successful. It changes people's lives.

We just had our graduation the other night, and we watched twelve of our students who have found their voices, who feel that they have power and agency. Many of them are now looking to get into community college or even UMass–Dartmouth. So for those who make it through the whole program, it's really a transforming experience.

*Some people would say that the highest priority for the disadvantaged is something more practical, even vocational in nature . . .*

We can all go out and learn practical skills, vocational skills. We can learn how to be a plumber or an electrician. I think the humanities teaches us what we value and believe, and it teaches us how to think about the issues that face us in our society every day, and it gives us language with which to talk about it. I also think the humanities offers us a way to learn throughout our entire lives.

I have a student—Gilbert—from two years ago who came back for this year's graduation. Gilbert reads poetry on a daily basis now. He had never read poetry before in his life. Suddenly for him, poetry is a way of thinking about his self, of making sense of things he experiences in the world, and it's giving him pleasure. The humanities can help people sort through how they see the world and how they experience the world. That's a real value for people.

*Are there particular works that students have especially responded to?*

I remember with my second class I brought in a poem by Jimmy Santiago Baca. A lot of our students are minorities, and I brought them one of Baca's poems talking about how immigrants are perceived in America. We have a large first-generation immigrant population here [*New Bedford, Massachusetts*], and last year we went through a major federal raid on a local factory that pulled in a lot of immigrants. This is a major issue here. I think what they found in Baca's poem was a way to talk about immigration and to make sense of it and to express the emotions that come up with that issue.

And this year I saw students really connect with Langston Hughes's poem "Theme for English B." Hughes talks about race in that poem, as well as education and the value of education, and more particularly how we learn from one another and the way the white instructor learns from the black students. In the same way, the student is learning from the instructor. The way in which America is made up of a mix of people with different experiences and different levels of education really resonated with them. They can see themselves becoming part of larger conversations, and that they have a place at the table.

*I assume that there are also classical works in your curriculum. Do they respond well to that?*

We do Plato, Kant, and Mill in the philosophy class, and I do Shakespeare in the literature class. I try to mix it with contemporary works so they can see how themes carry across the ages.

What they say about the philosophy when they encounter it is that they think it's the hardest thing they've ever read in their lives, and by the end of the class they have an understanding of logic and reasoning and the larger questions philosophers ask. We really focus on the idea of philosophy asking questions: how does one live the good life, how does one make ethical decisions that require hard thinking about what one is going to do and how one is going to do it.

Just the other day at our graduation one student said, "Now if I hear someone mention Socrates or Plato, I know what they're talking about and I don't have to feel like I'm on the outside looking in." I think that's really powerful, too.

*Do you ever feel that gaining this education makes them feel alienated from the neighborhood or their family?*

That's an interesting question. We do assessments throughout the course, and I have never had students mention to me that they felt alienated from their community; in fact, I see their family and friends really gather around them and support them. We had the largest turnout of family and friends ever for this year's graduation. I think the community sees it as something really valuable.

*Is the class taught as a discussion-oriented seminar?*

Yes, absolutely. It is designed to engage the students into being able to look at texts, talk about them critically, and then write about them critically, as well as do oral presentations.

*How does teaching in the Clemente Program compare to teaching undergrads at UMass–Dartmouth?*

The Clemente Course is like a 100-level general humanities course in college. In terms of similarity, you see the lights go on for students when they start to understand or see things in texts that they didn't realize were there. There's the excitement of building their skills and being able to engage in the conversation.

One of the key differences is the preparation and writing skills. The Clemente students often struggle more with the writing, and they lack the confidence that undergrads usually have. Teaching adults for me is always more challenging, but also more fun. Maybe because you're teaching people who are thirty or forty years old and they're much more able to engage with you at an adult level. The challenges are that some have been out of school so long that you're really having to do some remedial work with their writing, and you really have to help them learn to think at a higher level than perhaps they're used to, and so you find yourself having to repeat yourself a lot and backtrack. Often you have to think of new ways to do something in order to reach them.

*Does an example come to mind of some new way you've done something?*

I brought in to the Clemente program New Criticism [*a literary theory emphasizing close reading of the text*]. I really took them through that idea of "close reading": looking at formal elements, looking at linguistic devices, mapping out the text itself and how it works. That very objective, concrete approach was more effective than just sitting them down and trying to have a conversation about a text. I found that really preparing them from the ground up, with terminology, made a difference.

Another thing in the Clemente Program that's been particularly successful is I use a riff of Robert Pinsky's Favorite Poem Project [*a project in which Americans submit their favorite poems, initiated by U.S. Poet Laureate Robert Pinsky in 1997*]. I have the students select a poem and make an oral presentation to the class on how the poem speaks to their Clemente experience. That assignment has really reso-nated for students.

### Are there other students who come to mind?

I think one of the amazing things about Clemente Program is that in every graduat-ing class, you feel some connection to each student who has made it through. And just because my literature class ends four months in, it does not mean that I am not showing up throughout everyone else's classes. I'm helping on portfolio nights; I might show up with food one night. You feel a real affinity with these people when they come up to get their certificates on that night. So in many ways, they all stand out to me.

If I had to talk about one, this year we had a student Beth, an older African American woman who came in and wasn't sure she was going to do this, wasn't sure why she was there, and was very, very quiet in the beginning. A couple of weeks in, Beth started talking more and talking more, and by the end of the eight months, the class had elected her as one of our graduation speakers. She had really become a spokesperson for the class. Not only was she really engaged with the material but she was a leader of our community. When she spoke at graduation she brought a new poem and talked about Clemente and put into words what a lot of her class-mates wanted to say abut the program. The faculty sits there at graduation and at some point during that ceremony we are in tears because we are so moved by what has happened to these students.

### You spoke of how the program helps them find their voice. Does it also help them learn to listen, and listen not just to their peers but to great works whose authors may be far removed from them in time and circumstance?

Absolutely. And I think the way we get that accomplished is most often not by the written texts. We work throughout the year to bring them to various cultural events. This year, for example, we took them to a production done by the Black Rap Repertory based on Toni Morrison's *The Bluest Eye*. The students were just blown away. These are people who don't have any money and on the way out they were donating to the theater. We've also taken them to Shakespeare productions and to local museums. They started to see these cultural events as things that are open to them, and that they could take their kids to and enjoy and share. That's part of the listening that they have gained, and I think it's a great thing.

The other day one of my colleagues started our graduation by talking about how the Clemente Program is about change and transformation. I really do think that's one of the most powerful elements of it. Clemente is not focused on proving ourselves by having huge numbers of people graduate. With ten or twelve a year graduating, we've now had about forty-five graduate. Each one of these people has gone back to the community and brought his or her knowledge. I think that's how change can take place in a community. I'm thinking of Margaret Mead's statement, "Never doubt that a small group of individuals can change the world; it's the only thing that ever has." I think Clemente is a part of that, and that's what I love about it.

*One might say that literature, philosophy, and art don't necessarily have anything to do with contemporary social issues. They can, but they don't have to. How much do social issues shape the class discussions?*

I don't think our discussions in the classroom are about change; the discussions in the classroom focus on the texts that we're reading. I think the important change that takes place is within the students. They find a language: they find the ability to talk about these works of art, and then they transfer that ability to look at their world and talk about that world. I think that's where the change can take place. Last year, I had a student named Marlene who came in one night, two and a half months into the literature part of the course, and she was really angry. We asked why she was angry and she said, "I can't pick up the newspaper now, I can't walk down the street without thinking critically about what I'm seeing. It's no longer just this blur to me. I'm looking at everything now and analyzing it." I think that's a great tool that you can give somebody.

*"We are all children in a certain sense."*

# Betty Martin

### TEACHER IN WOMEN'S PRISON

*I grew up in a small town in Kentucky, and as soon as I heard Betty Martin's voice—her soft, mellifluous drawl and her gentle, humble manner—I felt I was back home.*

*After retiring from teaching in a public elementary school, she started teaching women at the Dr. Eddie Warrior Correctional Facility in Taft, Oklahoma. The cur-*

*riculum is the creation of NewLife Behavior, a non-denominational Christian minis-*
*try based in Texas. We spoke on a Thursday afternoon. The next morning she was to*
*teach her weekly class at the prison.*

After my first husband died, one of the elders in our church knew that I was a retired teacher, and he asked me if I would help in the prison ministry. I said sure. I've
been doing it now for ten years.

Currently, we have a class of twenty-two women. It's a thirteen-week class. This
is a faith-based program. We have a structured curriculum to follow, but we also try
to get the women talking, to give their own views on things, and to feel a part of the
class. It's not just a Bible study, it's a study of behavior and, well, of how to change
your life, to live a better life. It's an awfully good course.

There are a lot of scriptures used in the lesson. We will read those scriptures as
we go through the lesson. There is a lot in the course about the family, family roles,
and relationships. A lot of them realize that they have come from dysfunctional
families. And they want to know what to do to better their family.

All of the classes try to give them self-confidence. So many of the women are
from broken homes, and many of them have low self-esteem. We try to encourage
them to realize that they are people of value and that God loves them, that they
should love themselves, and that they have something to contribute. They may
have messed up but they're still of value; they're good people who did some bad
things.

*Hate the sin but love the sinner . . .*
Yes, that's right.

*Do all of these women even have families? I assume some do not.*
[*Sadly.*] There are some who have no family at all. Either their families have dis-
owned them or some of them just had no family. Some of them don't have anybody
outside the prison walls to help them or give them anything. So to them—we care,
and I think that means a lot to them. We're there every week, and we also have
church worship services twice a month. They are very appreciative of what we do
and that we're there for them, to teach them.

A lot of them have children that their parents or grandparents are taking care
of, and they worry a lot about that. Some of them have husbands. Some of them are
single. We have women from age nineteen to sixty-seven.

*The women sign up for your course voluntarily. Are they Christians already?*
Most of them believe in God, but often they have not lived by Christian principles.
Some of them don't know a lot about being a Christian. A lot are looking for help.
Our program tries to teach them what the Bible says about being a Christian and
living a Christian life. I think the women realize there's a better life.

*When you first started teaching in this program, I imagine you were seeing a side of life you weren't accustomed to.*

Yes, I was. I certainly was. At first, I was a little apprehensive. But I realized that they're just people—young people, most of them—who have done something against society that caused them to be incarcerated. We've had several people who have come into the prison ministry that were really afraid, and I've told them, "There's no need to be afraid." Because most of these women are wanting to turn their lives around.

Of course, I realize that maybe some aren't as sincere, but we can't judge that. We have to accept them for what they are and what they are trying to be.

I've been doing it now for ten years, and it's a blessing to me. It's something that I look forward to.

*In what way is it a blessing to you?*

It's a blessing in that I can see these women growing and changing their lives and feeling good about themselves. They say we're a blessing to them, but we say they're a blessing to us.

I have since remarried, and my husband also teaches in the prison. He teaches a course on Christians against substance abuse. Many of the women are in for drug abuse, or for selling drugs, or for stealing money to buy drugs.

*It seems that drugs are involved in the lives of so many of the people who end up incarcerated.*

Yes, and a lot of these women have been used by their boyfriends or husbands or lovers or whatever for drug money. And it's the women who have gotten into trouble.

*In these ten years, are there ways you have improved as a teacher in this program?*

I think I've changed in how I look at the women. I feel like I'm probably more understanding. Not as judgmental, maybe. And in the teaching, I've learned to involve them more in the discussion and give them a chance to share how they feel, and share some of the things they've been through.

*It seems this program is very successful. But there must also be failures.*

Yes, sometimes someone will drop out. Or we have had a few that get out of prison and then come back. But the recidivism rate is lower for the people who have taken these classes. There have been studies that show that. And these NewLife Behavior classes are now being taught in a lot of different states.

But we have had a couple that have come back. One of them said that when she went back home, she thought she was going to be able to change her friends and be a good influence on them and help them. But she found that it didn't work. Before long, she was back into her old habits. One thing that our program stresses is that you have to change the people that you're with. You have to change your playground.

I have had two of my former students that I taught in elementary school come through the prison. That was hard, especially one that I had been close to. She was so embarrassed. But she has now served her time, gone through a work program, and she has a good job and is going on with her life. But that was a very hard experience.

Once in a while someone will drop out. Or they will be moved to lower security. This is a medium-security prison, and sometimes they get moved to a minimum-security facility. But that's a plus, because that gives them greater flexibility, and sometimes it means they are closer to their homes.

*Are there particular students who come to mind as success stories?*

There are a couple, actually, that come to my mind first. One had such low self-esteem that she would not even look you in the eye. By the time she had gone through the program, she felt better about herself, she felt like she was worth something, and that she could accomplish something.

There was another woman who had very poor reading skills. We were able to get her an "easy read" Bible, and she had someone to help her with it, and we saw her grow a lot.

*If someone has low self-esteem, how do you turn that around?*

There are a lot of things in the curriculum that teach them through Bible stories that God loves them. And God says they need to love their neighbor as themselves—so you've got to love yourself, too. We use a lot of examples like the woman at the well—stories about times Jesus approached somebody who didn't have a good life, but he cared about them.

You can see them change as they go through the class. It's just wonderful to see the women change. You can tell it on their faces—that's what always amazes me.

*How do their faces look different?*

It's a softening, I think. It's like, "Hey, I'm worth something, you know, I'm not so bad after all." It's amazing to me. It's in their eyes, too. It's a sense of feeling better about themselves and accepting God in their lives. In some of them it's almost a glow.

I've taught in a lot of different situations, from a city school to a country school where I had three grades—fourth, fifth, and sixth—in one room. And that was a good experience, but this is different. This is very rewarding.

I think this prison ministry is very good and very beneficial to the inmates. I'm just thankful that I've had an opportunity to be involved in it.

*This must be very different, but does it also seem the same? Do you feel like you're just back in your old classroom again?*

[*Laughs.*] It does. It really does. Being a teacher, you're still dealing with those different personalities. A lot of these inmates are children in grown-up bodies. I don't mean to sound condescending, because I think we are all children in a certain sense. Most of us just want to be loved and cared for and to realize that we amount to something.

"*Teaching is really about being human.*"

# Shaina Traisman

## MEDITATION AND YOGA TEACHER IN JAILS AND PRISONS

*Shaina Traisman teaches yoga and meditation to prisoners in the Seattle area. She is the founder of Yoga Behind Bars, a non-profit organization that trains other teachers and now has yoga programs at a jail, a prison, and two detention centers in the Seattle area. She first discovered yoga when she was eighteen, and she took a teacher-training program in yoga when she was twenty-two. She is now twenty-nine, and she has been teaching incarcerated people for six years. Students themselves as well as guards at the facilities report positive changes in the inmates as a result of the yoga classes.*

I have between five and fifteen in a class. They are there voluntarily. A typical class focuses on meditation as well as the physical postures in yoga. A lot of the class is focused on meditation because we are really trying to work with people's mental patterns and trying to give people new ways of dealing with confrontation and with problems in their lives. When we train our own volunteer teachers, we emphasize that they focus a lot on meditation and yogic philosophy, and not just the postures. People respond really well to the meditation. It tends to be what they remember the most, because it has a positive impact on a lot of people.

A class is usually an hour and fifteen minutes. On the outside, classes are an hour and a half, but on the inside I cut them a little shorter because the attention spans tend to be shorter. By "inside," I mean in jail or prison. A lot of times on the inside—or just with teaching in general—you have to use your intuition and get a feel for the class and what people are receptive to. Sometimes you even have to throw out your whole agenda and just work with what's going on in the class.

The biggest difference between classes on the outside and classes on the inside is that a lot of the people on the inside have pretty major injuries in their lives and often quite a lack of body awareness. So you're teaching them the fundamentals of how to connect with their body—how to connect with their emotional state—in a whole new way. You're beginning at a very basic level but at the same time not depriving them of the depth of the practice and the spiritual side of it.

The other difference is that on the inside it is very important to be as real as possible. People are going to be a lot more receptive to you if you're not just playing a certain role but connecting with them on a real level. So I share stories with them about how yoga helped me. I use humility a lot. I tell them about how at times I have failed to apply yogic principles in my life. Sometimes I tell my students that if it weren't for yoga, I would be a complete neurotic mess: somebody who bounces from one thought to the next, who can never commit to anything.

So yoga really changed my life, and that is why I feel so inclined to share it with people—all people, but especially people who are in crisis situations or feeling like they need something to ground themselves. Because yoga did that for me in a time when I was going through a lot. I talk about my own struggles, so that I come across as being human. Teaching is really about being human.

These people aren't judging you, and if you go in there without judging them, and you're just on the same level, and you're just sharing information with them and sharing a little piece of yourself, then you really get that in return, and it's very rewarding.

*How did you decide to offer yoga classes in jail?*

When I was going through my teacher training program in yoga, I attended a workshop on political prisoners, and I met a man who had just come out of six years in prison—four of those years in solitary confinement—and he was so closed off and in pain. The workshop was part of a camp for political activists, and I was doing volunteer bodywork at the camp. This man approached me, and after thirty minutes of simple bodywork, he experienced a great deal of healing, a great opening up in an enormous way. At the camp he had been acting out a lot, causing trouble, and even these very open-minded people were thinking, "I can't really handle him." But after the session, he really softened and opened up. So I thought, this population of people—that is, prisoners—really has a great need. Then back in Seattle I contacted the volunteer coordinator at the jail, and I went from there.

*Can you describe the meditation part of teaching? I'm not sure I really understand what meditation is.*

I keep it pretty simple. A basic meditation would be just guiding people to take the witness seat in their mind. That's what I call it. I give them a visualization—like, imagine that there's a nice comfy seat in the front of your mind. Go ahead and sit down in that seat. Just notice what you're thinking about. Without judging it, just take some mental notes. The main principle is that you can't silence the mind until you understand what the mind has to say. Meditation is the practice of getting to know yourself a little better.

Often we think the same thoughts throughout the day; our thoughts loop around. So we start to intervene with that process. One of the first stages is accountability. You start to be accountable for your thoughts and actions. This is one of the reasons I think meditation is so important in this work. There's a deepening of self-awareness. Change starts to occur. It doesn't happen all at once. It's a full process. That's the basics of meditation.

Sometimes we focus on a forgiveness meditation. That tends to have a really good response because it's very freeing for them to ask forgiveness—first from themselves, and then to mentally forgive other people for things that have been inflicted on them. Most people who commit a crime are in there for some sort of imbalance in their psyche or for learned behavior. Sometimes the reason a person commits a crime has a lot to do with what's been done to them in the past. Through meditation they are learning how to understand that more fully: how to be accountable and not view themselves just as victims who then perpetuate a certain pattern without taking responsibility. It's a simple process of getting to know yourself better.

It's a myth that you just sit down and your mind is calm and peaceful. Even if you're an advanced practitioner, it can take some time to get to that place. There are a lot of different ways to meditate, and it can seem very daunting to people. So I just tell people, "If you just sit down to meditate, you don't need to follow these techniques and do it perfectly. You just sit down and say, 'I'm going to be conscious and aware of my thoughts for the next ten minutes.' And that's it—you're meditating." That's a good place to start.

*What is it that makes yoga especially effective—as opposed to jogging, for example?*
I start with meditation and then I introduce the yoga movements and postures as a sort of moving meditation. So first we do breath work—you know, getting in touch with your breathing. In meditation, breath is a helpful tool for focusing the mind. Then I encourage them to use the breath throughout the physical part of the practice as a means to really focus. If the mind starts to wander, just come back to the breath. In that sense, it's a moving meditation. You're always being aware of where your thoughts are and you're trying to draw them back to the breath and to the moment and to what you're doing in your body. Because if you're just thinking, and your ego is just telling you that you want to do all the postures as best you can, and you're pushing yourself and not paying attention to how the body's responding, you're going to have a propensity to get injured. People get to know their bodies really well this way. So it's a constant checking in, and increasing your own self-awareness. In Sanskrit that's called *svadhyaya* or self-study. So even when you're just doing a physical posture, you're still observing yourself, still taking that witness seat.

*Is there a particular student who comes to mind as a success story?*
[*She pauses.*] Five or six people flood into my mind. But the first one I thought of is a woman who had been a heroin addict, in and out of jail her whole life. She came into my class, and the first class she attended, she could barely focus. She had sores all over her face. She would try to do a pose and have to lie down, and then she would curl up into a ball and start trembling.

*So she was still in withdrawal . . .*

Yes, and technically she should have been in a special unit, and I did not understand why she wasn't. It seemed like she had managed to disguise it so she would not be isolated. Toward the end of that first class, she even had to run to the bathroom and throw up. I finally said, "Why don't you just go back and lie down and take care of yourself. But please come back next week."

Each week she came back, and she got better and better, and she became the strongest student in the class.

She went around recruiting, telling everybody in the jail that yoga had saved her life. By the end of the summer, the class was overflowing. She told everyone she was never going to do heroin again, she was never going to be in jail again, and she couldn't wait to get out, and she was going to keep doing yoga.

Each week she would come to me with a new revelation she had realized, or a new strength she had gained within herself through the practice of yoga. She was practicing every day by the end of the summer. She went from having no strength or muscle tone to being really strong—from having no willpower or self-confidence to being this vibrant, beautiful person.

*That's an inspiring story. And so she practiced on her own between classes?*

Yes. She didn't have access to a yoga mat, but it didn't matter. She would just do some meditation and some key postures each day, and after a while, she asked me to come up with a specific routine for her, and I spent some time thinking about what would be best for her. Each week I would give her more information. She was very motivated to have her own practice. By the end of the summer she had a whole stack of handouts.

*There must also be failures.*

Yeah. In most classes there will be one or two people who it feels that you're not quite getting through to. Often it will be someone who has a very difficult time paying attention. Or maybe they just wanted to try something new but then don't really want to be there. But still I try to check in with them and let them know they're doing a good job. I try to be very encouraging. It's important not to discriminate against them, because sometimes they are the ones who really need it the most.

But not everyone is going to like it, and that's fine, too. Usually people do like it if they give it a chance, but it's not for everybody. Sometimes people have a resistance when they come in and they realize that there's a spiritual aspect to the practice. Sometimes people will ask, "Is this a religion? Because I'm Christian, and if this is a religion, then I'm out of here." So I just reiterate that it's a spiritual practice and that no matter what religion you are, it applies.

Every once in a while, someone will act out. But I have a little spiel at the beginning of every class where I remind people to respect themselves, to respect one another, and to respect the teacher and the practice. If they can't do that, they have to leave the class—though that hardly ever happens. Usually if there's any kind of problem, other people in the class will speak up and say, "Hey, can you stop interrupting because it's taking away from my experience." Or sometimes it's not that polite. [*She laughs.*]

*Are you a better teacher now than you were when you started six years ago?*
God, yes.

*How have you changed? How have you improved?*
The main thing is just comfort level. When I first started, there was a bit of stage fright. Just not being entirely comfortable in front of people—having everybody stare at me. Now I feel a lot more comfortable. My classes are a lot more fluid. I'm not just experimenting with my teaching style, but I'm more versed in what I'm doing. No matter what kind of teacher you are, it takes some time to find your groove, to find your own style and just get comfortable.

*It sounds very rewarding . . .*
What we do is karma yoga—selfless service. What that means is that you just give without needing anything back, from the bottom of your heart. I really think that good teachers do that. A good teacher is doing it because he or she believes not only in the youth, but also in people and what they can do with knowledge. With all of my favorite teachers, I've always gotten that sense from them—that their heart was 100 percent in it. I feel that teaching is that: it's selfless service. I feel very blessed to be in this role. It's so rewarding. It's the best payoff that I could ever ask for.

*"I teach women how to save their own lives."*

# Rhodessa Jones

## TEACHER IN WOMEN'S JAILS

*Rhodessa Jones is an actress, singer, dancer, director, and writer. She is founder and director of the Medea Project: Theater for Incarcerated Women. A winner of numerous awards, she has lectured and given workshops around the world. She grew up in Florida as the daughter of migrant workers. She is a woman of regal bearing, and her voice is vibrant, expressive, full of soul.*

I was hired by the California Arts Council fifteen years ago to go into the city jail and teach aerobics to incarcerated women. In retrospect, I think it was because they didn't know what else to do. So they thought, "We'll get Rhodessa Jones. She's a dancer, she's a mover." Aerobics was the buzz of the day. For me, as an artist getting this call, I was ugly-mystified. What has that got to do with rehabilitation?

So I answered the call. I said, "OK, I'll do it." To their credit, I think the California Arts Council wanted to do something that would speak to the women in a very contemporary way. Martha Graham, the great choreographer, always said that people from California believe anything's possible.

I went in, and right away, I knew these women were not interested in aerobics for real. But because I'm an actress, I thought, "OK, how do I get their attention?"

I just improvised every day for the first month. I strutted in there looking very fashionable—looking like Danielle from *Solid Gold*, which was a television show around that time. I had just turned forty, and they were just fascinated. And I was black, and most of the women were black or Latina. So the black and brown women sat up and took notice.

For me, it was a way to create a positive, enlightening environment in a place like that. It was OK that they looked at me. It was OK that they came over and asked me who I was. They started saying, "The gym teacher's really wild. She's off the chain." So they followed me to the gym. Then I simply performed. I had a series of exercises called "sound and movement" that I do with actors, non-actors, children, adults, teenagers. It's a way to get people breathing and talking and being present. If we can really be present, then we can go anywhere. I can establish the safe environment as a teacher and a leader if I can get everybody to focus up.

What I had to do that first month was to perform. At forty, I was in great shape. I'm doing walkovers, handstands, backbends, bridges, splits . . . and I'm talking about my own life. I'm merely telling the story of my life. I'm taking them on the journey that has brought me to this place, to this jail, in this city, on Wednesday morning at eleven o'clock. In the course of that, I talked about having a baby at sixteen. I talked about my own dance with drugs and dangerous men. I talked about my own experience of looking for love in all the wrong places. And they were mesmerized. They were mesmerized by all the things I could do and all the things I was willing to share.

It nudged their memory. You know—the cheerleaders, the dancers. There was even a contender for Miss Black California who had gotten strung out on cocaine and was in for murder. My purpose was to take people out of this space where, "I'm a ho, I'm a dope fiend, I'm a crackhead, I'm a speed freak, I'm a thief." These are titles that people lay upon themselves. And I'm saying, "You were so much more before this. Before this, who were you? Who were you, and where were you, and what was going on before life started to hurt?" I reminded these women of who they used to be. And they started wanting to show me what they remembered physically of who they had been. All of a sudden it was like we were all home girls, just kickin' it.

And I'm noting all this stuff. I kept journals. I was like, OK, if I'm going to attempt to teach, communicate, investigate—if I'm going to somehow impress them with the fact that they are sitting at the center of the culture of women with an artist/

activist (though at that time I didn't know I was an activist)—I've got to figure out what I can teach them in a place like this. What can we share in a place like this?

I probably had a lot of the stuff in my head and in my heart, but when I started teaching in places like jails it became really important to keep a measure of what I did every day. Because it demanded that I be as flexible and as fluid as possible.

So out of that experience, I learned immediately that I had to create a circle of intimacy. I love circles, and I think that any teacher understands that in a circle, anybody can come or go. There's no hierarchy. The circle makes a lot of sense to me.

*You mean literally a circle?*

Yes, sitting or standing in a circle. Always. Because we see each other. Then anyone might step into the middle of the circle to speak—especially when there are problems.

I have been very fortunate that they would lay this stuff at my door. Someone might say, "I don't like her. I'm pissed off at her. I can't be in class today."

I'll say, "Are you willing to come and talk about it?" And all of a sudden, a whole other teaching avenue opens up. I say, "Because in the real world, honey, you can't go around slapping and hitting and shooting people, or cutting off your own nose to spite your face just because you don't want to be in the same room with them. So let's burn through this."

Sometimes it's people who have been very close to each other, and then somebody felt betrayed. And whatever is dropped, as the teacher, you pick it up—delicately.

I remember one woman crying and being very upset, and the other woman not wanting to be in the same space with her, and it came down to a tube of lipstick.

The woman had let everyone use her lipstick except this one other woman. The two women were playing house—they were a couple—and the first woman thought the second wouldn't want to wear lipstick because she was playing the male role, the butch, in the relationship. It was fascinating to get down past the tears . . . and also to remind people of pain.

I remember another incident where a young woman was talking about something horrific that had happened to her. She had been abducted and raped by a man who had been stalking her at school. So she's telling this, crying, shaking, hyperventilating.

Another woman is impatient with listening to this story and says, "Oh, that's not nothing. Let me tell you what happened to me." And then as a teacher, I say, "Wait, wait, wait. What do you mean? How can you sit here—and we've all been crying—and say that this woman's story is nothing? Everyone's story is valid. Everybody's pain is priceless. And I just need to say in this moment to everybody that I am sorry that all of these terrible things have happened to you. But don't ever say that that ain't nothing. Because she's giving it up in this moment."

I could see that the woman who was telling the story, who was going to resort to anger and withdrawing, was all of a sudden listening to the fact that it was valid.

Just being able to reiterate this horrible thing that had happened to her was valid. And good for us all. I don't think anybody had ever said to that woman, "I'm sorry." I don't know if she had ever told anybody before.

As a teacher, you're watching for this place where, as they say in hip-hop, you "drop some knowledge." And also where you've opened up another avenue for thought. Two or three days later, the young woman who had said "that ain't nothing" came back and in our circle said, "I have something I want to say to Alice. I'm sorry that I said 'that ain't nothing.' And I never said I'm sorry to any bitch about anything. I don't mean no disrespect, but I've never apologized for anything. But Miss Jones, you're right. And Alice, I'm sorry, and I'm sorry that that happened to you."

Then she broke down and started crying. And I'm like, wow.

In these institutions you have to wade through all this incredible posturing. The air is so thick you can cut it with a knife. Everybody's wearing this armor that says "Don't touch me. Don't mess with me." They have all seen and been to such strange places.

As an artist who is being an art teacher, I have found visual arts valuable. Finding a way to stream words together in the name of poetry has been priceless, you know, with this population. Because most of these people have met the devil, and they have found him to be a very dull dude.

Now as any teacher will tell you, you're going to learn as much as you're attempting to impart. And I tell you, it changed my life to be working with incarcerated populations—mainly women. It made me much more grateful . . . it makes me practice gratitude. I really do.

*So until you were forty, you had never worked in jails?*

No. I had been with the California Arts Council, but I had worked with kindergarteners. But then I jumped right in. I wanted to try it, especially because it was in jails.

I have eight brothers, so I knew something about the incarceration systems in America. My brother Richard—may he rest in peace—was at Attica when it all came down. [*Attica is a maximum-security prison in New York. What "came down" was a 1971 riot of over a thousand prisoners in which thirty-nine people were killed, twenty-nine of them inmates.*] And then I have two brothers who are law enforcement people.

My brother Richard was on the chain gang at Raeford State Prison [*Florida*] when he was fifteen. He was my favorite. He had two older brothers, and back in the day, they were dashing—they were the Jones boys. Richard was their younger brother, as much as nine years younger. But he wanted to run with them. He wanted to be considered a man. And he was going to be harder. My older brothers were men who liked a lot of women—they had a lot of women. But Richard was a brutal pimp and did some terrible things to women in the name of maintaining his own armor and his own legacy as a man.

*It sounds like part of your success rests in knowing when to listen and when to step in and be the mentor, to say, "Don't ever say 'that's nothing.'"*
You're absolutely right. I had to learn how to do that.

*How did you learn it? Trial and error?*
Yes. And I'd miss so much. And I'd end up blowing up myself. I'd turn into my mother at her worst. [*Laughs.*] I had some very interesting students from the outside who worked with me. I overheard one of them say to a reporter, "We don't see ourselves as us versus them. Because we're all women, we're all struggling with the same issues. So there's no us versus them. It's we."

I remember when somebody would say her kids had been taken away or whatever, and I'd take a deep breath and say, "OK, that's terrible, [*calmly*] but what are we going to do about it?" versus [*here she shouts, miming agitation*] "What are we going to do about it? You gotta stop doing drugs! You gotta stop doing that!"

[*She speaks calmly again.*] "What are we going to do about reclaiming our children, our families, our communities? What are we going to do about helping our elders grow old peacefully and not have them taking care of our children while we are in jail?"

But it took me trial and error. It took me being very vigilant about my journal—to the point of being honest about when I would blow it. "Today I didn't listen so good. Today I shouldn't have blown up at that person." I lost some people. Some people didn't come back because I was too heavy handed. They didn't want to be in my kind of terse, loud, over-the-top, emotional tirades—which I did a lot of in the beginning. So yeah, I had to learn to know when to move. I had to learn to listen, too, to really listen.

*People have been through so much. They've come through rivers and mountains. If someone arrives and says, "You know what happened to me?" and she decides you're the repository, you've already come miles. How do you start a dialog to be helpful and meaningful?*
I think great teachers do it in a lot of ways, too. The academy, secondary schools, grade schools . . . I think teachers in those places exude a fierce humanity. A great teacher does. It's just part of the makeup of a great teacher. Humanity. And young people recognize it—they really do.

*What would you say that you teach?*
I teach women how to save their own lives through the creative process. What that means is to give them the legs on which to stand as they move back into their communities, back with their families. Give them some basic tools for countering where they've been. Now I'm not going to say that I've saved that many. Because the culture has to be interested, and benign neglect is everywhere.

I try getting them to give voice to where they've been, to stand up and claim where they've been. Then as the artist, creator, goddess, gangsta mamma, I've also got to be willing to catch them when they start to stumble and fall. It's very spiritual work for me, because I have to call on spirit. Not that I'm religious, but it's like, "OK, Spirit, I've opened this gate. Everybody's wailing. What do I do?" And always, something really beautiful comes through.

They trust me. I can walk in and my energy is such that they trust me. But am I ready? Am I ready for the floodgates? For the rage that might happen?

*The reasons that people are incarcerated are complex, but would it be right at all to say they're there for want of a teacher at some point in their lives?*

Oh, yes, truly. Yes. And this generation, the ones who are lost are truly lost. Because what happened was the fall of those structures—church, school, home.

You know there's that great song by Stevie Wonder—

Show me how to do like you,
Show me how to do it.

During the civil rights era, black people didn't go to jail—except a few, and the ones who were railroaded into jail. People did go to school. They did go to college. They did go to church. There were familiar structures—neighborhoods, community. And all of that started to fall with the success of the civil rights movement. Anybody who could moved to suburbia. They left the inner city.

And in the course of that, families fell apart. Church fell apart. The educational systems as we knew them fell apart. The government infrastructure fell apart. The inner cities started crumbling. So yes, for the lack of all kinds of teachers. . . .

# 9 | *Teaching the Protectors*

*"Everything you teach you have to take seriously. If you don't, it could be someone's life."*

# Gunnery Sergeant Daniel Fuson

## DRILL INSTRUCTOR, MARINE CORPS

*Daniel Fuson grew up in Vicksburg, Mississippi, and joined the Marine Corps in 1997. Currently stationed at Paris Island in South Carolina, he teaches the basic warrior training course to recruits, and he also trains other marines to be drill instructors.*

*Paris Island gives marine recruits their first phase of training, after which they go on to further training at another site.*

I teach the basic warrior training package to recruits. It's a twelve-week cycle. I teach one group for twelve weeks, and then another comes in. A drill instructor has to teach a recruit everything he or she needs to know about living in the field—first aid, how to wear the packs—the basics of what recruits need to know in combat. Everything they need to know—we will actually show that to them so they can see it through us first before they have to do it themselves. The final part of their training is the Crucible. That's where everything comes together. [*The Crucible is the fifty-four-hour culmination of recruit training. It is a physically and mentally challenging event that involves food and sleep deprivation and the completion of various tests and obstacles throughout a forty-eight-mile course in which recruits carry forty-eight pounds in addition to their rifles.*]

*So a lot of your teaching method is showing by example.*
I would say that is the biggest thing that we do. Absolutely. Of course, we also have the lecture method, so we teach some material in a classroom environment in a standard way. For example, one of the things I teach is first aid. We teach everything from head wounds, how to suck out chest wounds, abdominal wounds, and heat- and cold-related illnesses. That will be lecture and also hands-on.

*I would think that a big challenge is to teach them in such a way that they can do it all in the field, when it's not a training exercise but real. Even real combat.*

Absolutely. One of the things we do is—during our PT [*physical training*] sessions, we'll take one student out and say, "You're going down today for heat exhaustion." So as a simulation, he'll go down, and the other students don't know that this is a mockup. So the recruits will have to react as if it's real. The other thing we do is that a lot of the marines who teach here have combat experience, so we'll let them share those real-life experiences, and that helps out quite a bit.

*Do you ever have recruits who you think are not going to make it—or don't make it?*

Most recruits who come here can make it, and the vast majority do make it through. But at the very beginning of training, they're definitely taken by surprise. It's that old analogy—you don't know what a fire feels like until you touch it yourself.

A lot of them come here and they really want to be a marine, but they get here and they start second-guessing themselves. So multiple times during the training cycle, you'll have recruits come up to you and basically tell you they don't want to be here. How do you combat that? For me, when I was a senior drill instructor, I would sit the recruit down man to man, human being to human being, and ask him what he came here for. I might call the recruiter and let him talk to his recruiter. At points I might let him talk to his mother and father on the phone. I'd let him talk to someone who had guided him through his life. Normally, that was pretty much all it took—a little more assurance that he did the right thing, reconfirming the fact of why he came in, why it's a good thing, and that he *can* do it. It means a lot to recruits, and they'll get re-motivated and continue on.

*The view that the public gets about marine training—through movies and so on—is that it's really, really rough. Is there also a supportive or even gentle side to it—or is it all rough?*

I'm not going to say it's rough. Is it designed to be stressful and to keep the recruits moving and keep them thinking? Absolutely.

Is there a side to it where, uh—I guess you could say a softer side? Yes.

One of the things the recruits have an opportunity to do is, every Sunday, go to church. We don't tell them they have to go to church, but we do emphasize spiritual development, whatever their religion is. It doesn't even mean they have to believe in God—maybe it's just believing in themselves, going there, getting recharged, talking to someone who is positive, who can uplift them, so to speak. There is definitely that aspect of it.

Is it always a drill instructor in your face yelling all the time? Absolutely not. We have our core values time where a drill instructor sits down with recruits, and they talk about some life experiences, talk about doing what's right.

So Hollywood will portray recruit training in a way to help people buy the movie, but it's not always like the way they portray it.

*Aside from teaching recruits as a drill instructor, you also teach marines to be drill instructors, is that right?*

Yes, as a squad instructor. I have twelve marines and basically I mentor them, so to speak. That's 75 percent of my day. I'll take them through the training environment, explain what recruits are doing, how drill instructors are training those recruits. I explain the full process to them. I'm the person who helps them through this training, so that when they become drill instructors themselves they understand what they're doing. I teach them how to teach the recruits, how to evaluate them. Again, it's leading them by example. It's not me standing on the platform teaching. They're taught the basics that way, but the vast majority of our leadership experience in the marines is having things shown to us, by example.

They have to have an overall perspective of what they're doing. They have to understand the objectives of the recruit training process. That's one of the biggest things I have to get them to understand—those objectives. What is the intent of this training?

*In the years you've been teaching, as a drill instructor or a squad instructor, are there ways you've changed as a teacher? Or are you basically the same as when you started?*

[*He laughs.*] I'm definitely not the same as when I started.

I've really learned how to read individuals. I've learned how to calm down and listen to other individuals. I know that I don't always have all the answers. I know that. I believe any teacher who believes he does have all the answers is going down the road toward failing. I know there's always a continual process for me to learn. I've definitely changed.

*Some people might be surprised to hear a marine drill instructor say he's learned to listen.*

Oh, yeah. You've got to listen. Don't get me wrong—you're definitely going to be telling them what to do throughout the day. But if you don't listen to their feedback . . . At the very end of the cycle, I'll ask the recruits, "What did you find to be really challenging? What could this drill instructor possibly have done so that you would have learned this or that better?"

And the same thing is done in drill-instructor school. After every class, we have instructor evaluation forms done and we read them. And we use it. If we didn't use it, what was the purpose of asking?

You definitely have to listen to the people you're teaching. They're not idiots. They're full-grown men and women. And they've had good teachers, from first grade up, and they've had bad instructors. The only way you're going to make yourself better as a teacher is by listening to them—at appropriate times, of course. Listen to them, and change, if need be. Otherwise, you're just going to suck your entire life, I suppose.

*Are there any recruits you remember especially vividly?*

Yeah. [*He laughs, and he mentions the recruit's name.*] My first cycle as a senior drill instructor. He was so pigeon-toed that he had a hard time walking. He was uncoordinated. He had no physical stamina. He did not appear to be very bright—at least not right off the bat. I don't know how he even passed the physical to come in.

Halfway through the cycle, this recruit started blossoming. He really did. By the end of training, he was not the best recruit—I mean, he didn't pass every test with a 100 percent and he didn't run the fastest. In fact, he was near the bottom. But the heart this individual had was amazing. Never once did he ever complain or give up. It was amazing to watch him in his transformation from that kid who had just graduated high school to a marine. He was one of my favorite recruits ever to watch.

### What led you to become a teacher in the Marine Corps?

For me, it was about the fact that I absolutely love being in the Marine Corps. The Marine Corps has done quite a bit for me. I had no direction in life. If I had gone to college out of high school, I probably would have just flunked out. So when I went to the Marine Corps, I became very disciplined. It opened doors to me, I was able to travel, and I met outstanding, wonderful individuals.

So I wanted to give back to the Marine Corps. Being a drill instructor was a way I could give back. I could teach these individuals who had no clue about the Marine Corps through my own experiences. I could teach them, help them, guide them, and mentor them. To be honest with you, I absolutely love mentoring and guiding marines. I love learning from them, and I love teaching them. So it's an absolute privilege to teach not only the recruits, but also to teach these marines here. It's just something that I've found very joyful—that I'm able to give back to the Marine Corps, to be one of those individuals that I looked up to when I was eighteen years old and just coming up.

### Did you have a teacher along the way who influenced you?

I did. I have many people in the Marine Corps that I look up to, depending on the circumstance. But there was one I always looked up to—and he probably never even knew it. He was the one that whenever I was questioning myself, I always thought, "Would he do this or that?" His name was Robert Owens. He was in the Marine Corps with me. He was a gunnery sergeant. He was always the one setting the example. I'll remember when he was in front of us and he showed us this way or that way.

Teaching in the marines is a time-consuming process, and you can't afford to half-ass it. You have to put everything you have into it, because you never know when these recruits, soon to be marines, are going to have to go back to their training to save the lives of those around them. That's always what's in the back of your head. Everything revolves around the mission—to fight and win the battles. Everything you teach you have to take seriously. If you don't, it could be someone's life.

*"You have to always have a beginner's mind."*

# Rob Magao

## MARTIAL-ARTS TEACHER TO CIVILIANS AND LAW ENFORCEMENT PERSONNEL

*Rob Magao is a police detective and a S.W.A.T. team member in Connecticut. He also teaches in-service training classes to fourteen police departments, classes at the police academy, and courses to federal, military, and counter-terrorist units. In addition, he teaches a variety of civilian martial-arts and self-defense classes to students ranging from children to adults. He has over twenty years of martial-arts experience and holds black belts in Bushido Jujitsu and Goju Ryu Karate. He is a certified Advanced L.O.C.K.U.P. Arrest and Control Instructor, Ground Combat Instructor, Handcuffing Instructor, Baton Instructor, and Simulation Scenario Instructor.*

*How did you originally learn martial arts yourself?*

I grew up in eastern Connecticut with my grandparents and my mother. My dad wasn't around after I was about twelve. I had started doing judo in the fourth grade, and then the instructor became ill and the class stopped. Later, when I was a teenager, I was riding my bike down the road one day and I saw a sign that had some Japanese kanji on it. I didn't know what it said, but I thought the place was probably a martial-arts school. So I knocked on the door and asked the woman who answered if there was a martial-arts class there. Without answering, she told me to come the next day. I had to go back several times, and I later learned that her husband, the teacher, had been there all of those times, but he wanted to see if I was really serious. It was a traditional karate class, very serious, and I joined, and that instructor really changed my whole life.

He found me at a time when my father had gone, my grandfather was getting sick, my mother was pretty depressed, and my aunt who was living with us had cancer. I was in a pretty tough spot, and I really didn't have a lot to fall back on. Karate gave me an outlet. I started training with him. After a couple of years he allowed me to teach some of the beginners in basic techniques. So he started building me as an instructor.

I still do that to this day with my students. I believe that if they start teaching something soon, as the years go by they are not only learning techniques, but they're learning to teach. By the time they're ready to receive their black belt, they've developed a way to teach just as they've developed a way to fight.

He was such an inspiration to me that I felt I wanted to teach some day. And I've never stopped training. Even when I was going through the police academy, I trained on the weekends.

### How do you teach martial arts? Is it mostly that you demonstrate and then the student attempts it?

Yes, basically. I usually have them come and watch a class first, and then I get them on the mat. I don't separate classes by beginner-intermediate-advanced, because I think the beginners learn by watching people who are more advanced. They see examples to follow, and they see where they can go in their training. And the advanced students learn by teaching the people who are new.

People come in with a wide variety of skill levels and fitness levels. Some are in fantastic shape, but some haven't worked out in years, so I have to mediate what I give them. But I take everybody in and treat everybody the same. The first thing I do is ask every student why he or she is here—what are the student's goals, what does he or she want to attain by training. Then I ask myself whether I can help this person. If I think I can, then I'll do whatever I can to lead them down the path and get them stronger and fitter—mentally, spiritually, and physically. If I think I'm not the right person for them, I start researching who I know that can help this person. A lot of times, I have to be mature enough as an instructor to know that I'm not the best person for this student.

There are various systems of martial arts. Some are very traditional and date back thousands of years and are based on certain ways of doing things that have been handed down for many generations—and nothing has changed. Everything is left the way it was thousands of years ago. Then there are modern systems that have adapted and changed. I try to mix both. In fact, one of the mottos of our school is, "Where traditional martial arts and modern self-protection meet."

I think it's important to understand the history behind what we do, but at the same time, we live in a different world now. We don't live in feudal Japan. The threats that people face today—muggings, carjackings, terrorist attacks—didn't happen a hundred years ago. For example, handgun attacks—they weren't something you had to worry about in the 1400s.

So if someone comes to me and wants to learn a traditional system—learn the customs, some of the language—that's something I'm not really qualified to teach them.

My whole thing is modern-day self-defense. There's a motivational speaker who says that everybody is one of three types. Most people are sheep, going about their business. One percent of the population are predators—wolves looking for prey. And then some are sheepdogs, protecting. Those are the police and military. The mentality I teach people is that you have to be a sheepdog. Whether you're a cop or not, you have to go about your life alert. I don't mean being paranoid. But you have to always be paying attention.

At any moment, your life can be taken from you—in a second. I've had many people die right in my arms. The last person they ever saw was me. They always say, "What happened?" They don't even know what happened. They didn't see it coming.

As an instructor you have a huge responsibility teaching martial arts. The last thing I ever want to do is take somebody in that has a bad attitude or has some type of negative goal as to why he or she is learning. If you look at 9/11, some of the terrorists who rushed the cockpit and attacked the airline personnel had gone to a school in Florida and learned martial arts. They had learned to take people out as quickly as possible. So one of the things I require of anyone who comes into my school—if the person is not a sworn law enforcement person or if one of my students cannot vouch for the person—is a criminal history check.

*How much of a spiritual element is there in the teaching you do?*
That's one thing I try to be cautious of, because Hollywood has tried to mix spirituality—or even religion—with martial arts. I believe that you shouldn't mix the two because they're completely different.

To me, martial arts is spiritual only in the sense that you're constantly pushing yourself. Also, in competition, it's just you. You don't have any teammates to blame. I see it all the time when people get attacked, and there will be ten or fifteen people watching, and not one person will help. Later, they'll say, "Oh, I thought that other person was going to help." What I try to teach people is that you have to be strong and in shape physically, because when you get into a struggle, your heart is going to be in your mouth, you're going to be shaking, you're going to lose your fine motor skills.

Have you ever had someone pull out in front of you when you were driving down the road?

*Oh, yes. It's quite an adrenaline rush.*
Well, multiply that times a thousand and that's what it's like to be assaulted. When a stranger walks up to you at an ATM and sticks a gun in your face, that's what it's like. If you don't have the spirituality to believe in yourself, to be focused, to be strong in mind, body, and spirit, you're going to freeze. A lot of times people think, "Oh, I'll rise to the occasion." That's a lot of baloney. You'll fall to the level of your training—you won't rise to anything. That's what I've been taught my whole life. You won't overcome something unless, through your training, you've prepared yourself for it.

*So for you, the key to what you call spirituality is actually training.*
Exactly. It's every time you train really hard and push yourself and try to become better. It's hard to explain, but the more you train, the more you realize how much more you have to learn—if that makes any sense. And if some people reach a point

where they think they don't need to learn any more, they've lost it. You have to always have a beginner's mind. You have to go into everything, no matter how many years you've been doing it, and have the same focus you had when you started, the same drive, the same desire. That kind of spirituality only comes from loving something, from it truly being a passion. For me, that's the spirituality of it: never giving in, never quitting, always being focused, doing it every day—religiously, so to speak—and pushing yourself to get better. You're pushing yourself not just to get better on the mat, but to get better as a person, and eventually to give back and to teach others. That's also the spirituality for me, constantly giving to others what I have learned, passing on my knowledge to them.

That's where I think a lot of martial-arts schools have lost it. You walk into 90 percent of the martial-arts schools and you'll see the students bowing religiously to the instructor or calling him master or head sensei, and it's a forced respect. You won't even see the instructor really teaching half of the time. He's just barking orders at the students and the students are doing it. They never get to see what the teacher is capable of, because the teacher is afraid that he may lose to one of his students and look bad.

I'm of a completely different cloth. I believe instead of forced respect, it should be earned respect. People will follow a true leader—or teacher—because they want to, not because they have to. I prove to my students every single class why I am their teacher. I do every push-up and every sit-up. I grapple with one after another after another. And God forbid that one of them should submit me sometime, but as far as I'm concerned, that would be the ultimate compliment for me as a teacher because I taught the student to do that. If I took them from knowing nothing three or four years ago to now being able to challenge me, that's the ultimate compliment. My goal for any students who walk through the door is for some day, if they stay with me long enough, that they would surpass me, be better than I am. Just like I want my children to grow up some day and have a better house, a better job, a better life than I do.

*When you think back over your civilian students, are there any who stand out in your memory?*

Absolutely. There's one who very much comes to mind. About eight years ago a friend came to me and said he had a relative, only thirteen years old, who had a really bad upbringing and he got hooked on drugs and committed an armed robbery. My friend, who is a police officer, and was the kid's uncle, thought this kid could be turned around. The kid had been taken away from his home and was living with his uncle now.

I've always had this rule that I wouldn't teach martial arts to anybody who had been in trouble, but he brought the kid and for the first six months I just made him run with me—every day. He ran, and ran, and ran. I kept pushing, and he never gave up. He got clean—he had been doing fifteen bags of heroin a day and he looked like he was dying. I could see that he wanted to change. He continued working out with me, and I started to see that he was basically a good kid.

So I started training him in martial arts. He got healthier, his skin tone changed, his attitude changed. He started talking and became more outgoing. He continued training with me.

He's now in his early twenties. He got an associate degree from college and he works as a paramedic on an ambulance. He still trains with me, and he's turned his life around. He had had no positive role model in his life, no one to tell him that he could do it. And now he's out there helping people every night. He's told me many times that if it weren't for his uncle and me and his martial-arts training, he doesn't know where he'd be—probably in jail or dead.

*We've been talking mostly about your teaching of martial arts to civilians. Could you tell me about your teaching to law enforcement officers?*

Every year one of our lieutenants who runs the training comes up with in-service courses that have to be taught, and one of those is always something tactical. He'll come to me and another guy I teach with, and then we'll come up with the course we're going to teach.

For example, we did school shootings one year, where we talked about an active shooter in a school and how to respond to it, and what to do to ensure the safety of everybody in the building. The class will start with me showing videos of actual school shootings. We study how the shooters come in, how they're dressed, their body language, the weapons they have. Then we study how we could resolve something like that.

Then from there we go to a facility that's a vacant school or office building, and we'll set up a live simulation with role-players. The officers will get the call and come in armed with simunition guns—real firearms where we've taken out the barrel and exchanged it for a barrel that shoots something like paintballs. So they use all the things they've been trained on: how to enter the building, how to form up as a team, how to go down the hallway, how to enter a room, how to communicate with the suspect if they see him, how to get hostages out. So we physically put them through the scenario. There might be smoke, loud noises, flashes going off. We try to create the environment they'd have to perform in, should this ever happen to them. Then after the live exercise, we come back to the classroom and review everything we did.

Reality-based training is everything. You can sit in a classroom all day long, but when you strap the equipment on and go through the door and see somebody holding a gun to some woman's head, and physically react and do what you're trained to do—that's all the difference in the world. When you physically have to do it under pressure, there's nothing like it.

*And you also train police officers in hand-to-hand techniques, more in line with your martial-arts work?*

Yes. First of all, if you take the average police officer and take away all of the equipment on his gun belt, and ask him to do what he's sworn to do . . . well, a lot of them can't, to be honest with you. I try to explain to them: How many times has an officer pulled his gun only to have it jam? Or the Taser didn't work? Or the pepper spray doesn't affect this person? And now you're in a physical struggle. Can you do what you have to do? A lot of them are very surprised to find out that they can't.

It's a perishable skill. If you are not doing hand-to-hand, martial-arts-type training consistently, every week, you will lose it, and under stress you will not be able to do what you need to do. When someone gets in your face and the fists start flying, you're not going to be able to do what you were taught unless you consistently do it. Police officers in some jurisdictions have to do that weekly, in some jurisdictions it might be daily. I know in my jurisdiction, there's not a week that goes by that I don't have to put my hands on somebody and take him or her under control.

I try to tell them, don't depend on the tools on your gun belt. You may not be able to get to them in time, or they may fail. And if that's the case, you're left with you. Can you stop this person? And that's really the reason I learned martial arts. I learned martial arts so I could stop people and protect others, and really, so I could stop someone without hurting the person. I don't want to hurt anybody, but I also don't want that person to hurt others or do more damage than he or she has.

*I think you've already answered a question I was going to ask—how you teach people to perform under extreme stress. But it sounds like the key is repetitive training.*
Absolutely. In fact, students come into my martial-arts studio and they want to learn all the fancy stuff they saw on television, and I try to explain to them that this is going to be years of doing the same things over and over and over again, thousands of times. Because that's how you get better at something—constantly doing it until it's instinctual, until you can do it without thinking.

*What do you think are the keys to success in your teaching?*
I use a lot of humor. I have students who tell me I should have been a stand-up comic. Laughter goes a long way. It reduces tension; it brings people together. It shows that you have a human side. If you can make them smile, you can hold their attention and they'll learn a lot more. Teaching and learning should be fun.

Students have to like the person they're going to learn from or they're not going to learn very much. A lot of it is a chemistry that I have with the students. Chemistry is something I don't think you can teach; you can get better at it, but it takes practice. It's like a relationship—you have to put energy into it.

I think a huge key is that you have to remember what it's like to be a student—remember what it's like to walk in there the first day and feel a little intimidated or nervous. And you have to remember that without them, you have nothing. Without the students, there is no school.

*"Your training saves your life."*

# Vince Dunn

## TEACHER OF FIREFIGHTING

*Vince Dunn served for over forty years in the New York City Fire Department. He served seven years as a firefighter, nine years as a company officer, and twenty-five years as a chief officer. He was commander of the midtown Manhattan division from 1984 to 1999. He began teaching in 1975, and he has taught within the department as well as at Manhattan College, John Jay College, and the National Fire Academy. He gives workshops and seminars around the country, and he is the author of four textbooks on firefighting and a regular contributor to* Firehouse *and* WNYF: With New York Firefighters *magazines. He speaks with passion and great enthusiasm, in a heavy New York accent.*

To become a firefighter in New York, and in most big cities, you have to pass a physical exam, and a written exam, and a medical exam. Firefighting is labor-intensive work, so you have to be physically fit, with upper body strength and leg strength and wind strength. That's very important for a firefighter. Then you go to training—what we call rookie school. That might be for six months.

The training there is both classroom work, with written tests, and hands-on training. A lot of the hands-on training is in a burn building. In the burn building, they actually light fires and develop smoke, and the new firefighters go into these smoke-filled buildings. They learn how to extinguish fires and they learn how to search. One of the things about firefighting is you have to learn to work without sight. When you put on a mask and go into a smoke-filled room, you're practically blind. So firefighters over the years acquire the ability to feel their way through a burning building. The training in these burn buildings is very dangerous. New firefighters have actually died in these fires. It's an important type of training, but it's also a dangerous type of training, so we have to closely supervise the firefighters. It's very sad when we lose a firefighter in a training fire, but it happens.

Like I said, it's manual work, so firefighters have to learn a lot of manual skills: stretching hose, raising ladders, directing hose streams, tying knots, cutting roofs, forcing open doors, bridging an alleyway with a ladder. They learn these by actual hands-on training. You learn to tie a hose strap—that's what you tie around a hose to attach it to a railing or a fire escape to keep it from falling down when it's charged with water.

After you get out of rookie school, mentoring is a big thing in the fire service. When you're a new firefighter, a veteran firefighter usually takes you under his wing. Also, what they do throughout the country is send the firefighters back periodically for what we call performance training. We evaluate the firefighters every year so they keep up their ability. We bring them back and send them through smoke rooms to search for and rescue mannequins. We build mazes that help them train to work in darkness and in unusual locations.

Other than that, every week in the fire service we do hands-on training in the firehouses. We tie knots, raise ladders, practice sliding off of roofs in rescue work. We put on masks and blacken them to practice searching for mannequins. They really should call us smokefighters, not firefighters, because we rarely see fire.

We also do drills in the fire service. I used to work in midtown Manhattan where there are lots of high-rises. Thank God, we don't get too many major high-rise fires, but when we do get them, they are horrendous. So we would get permission from a high-rise building owner to take over their building on a Saturday or Sunday morning, and we would call a drill with a hundred firefighters and fifteen fire companies. We'd have smoke machines and fill up a floor with artificial smoke. Everyone would dress up, fully masked, and they'd come into the lobby and we'd assign everyone. We'd assign two engines to get a hose line up to a floor, two engines to get a hose to back up that first hose line. They'd stretch hose lines up the stairwells to the floors. We wouldn't turn on the water, of course, but they would carry hose lines up to the smoke-filled floor. We'd assign two truck companies to get a team to search and rescue. We'd have mannequins on the floors in smoke-filled areas and we'd have an elevator stuck with victims between floors.

The drill takes maybe an hour and at the end everybody would be soaking wet. Afterward we'd go down to an auditorium where every officer would get up and explain what he had done. So one would say, "I was the second arriving officer and this was our assignment." Then each battalion chief would do the same. It was the most elaborate hands-on training I was ever involved in.

As you become an officer and a chief, you do more classroom work with lectures and so on because you're talking about ideas and strategies. When the upper ranks continue their training, it's more classroom work.

*In a lot of areas of life, someone receives training and then applies it on the job. But it strikes me that what's so challenging about fighting a fire is that when it comes time to apply the training, it's in an emergency, adrenaline-rush kind of situation. How do you train people to remain calm enough to do their job well?*

Well, that's a very good point. That's a big part of emergency work, whether it's military or police or firefighting. You have to keep calm. What we know in the fire service is that if you train, if you do the hands-on training in these smoke rooms, then in an emergency situation, you'll start thinking, "What do I have to do? Step one, I have to stretch the hose line to that spot. Step two, I have get my mask on properly." So if you've got good training, during that emergency, you block everything out and try not to get swept up in the chaos all around you—everybody's shouting, there's smoke and you can't see much, flames are jumping from floor to floor. Your mind is focused only on your training. You focus, focus, focus, on everything you do.

Every individual task you do becomes paramount—find the hydrant, get the mask on, flank out enough hose that you can dance in on the fire, force entry on the door, get the water flowing in the hose line, point the nozzle, turn the valve, direct the hose stream over your head when you enter the burning area. Inch by inch you crawl into that room . . . possibly two rooms, three rooms . . . you don't see much. Hot water is coming down on the your head; you look for the glow of flame through the smoke. Possibly you do see the glow and you direct the hose stream on it—cool down the upper reaches of the room, sweep the floor area to cool that off. You keep moving forward, moving forward. Then you think the heat is subsiding, and you go to a nearby window with the hose—possibly put out a fog stream pattern and blow out all the smoke. And then you know you have extinguished the fire.

Of course, sometimes you can't extinguish the fire. Sometimes you can't get into that room because there's so much heat and fire blowing. You may have to retreat and set up aerial streams and fight the fire from the outside. These are the things you've learned in that smoke house, in that burn building. That's why that hands-on training is so important. If you have not been training, you will not have the discipline or the concentration at that particular time. We call that the moment of truth.

*Do you find that your writing helps your teaching—or vice versa?*
I went to college on the GI Bill. I had joined the navy at seventeen. I went to college first in 1959. Then later in 1976 I went back for my master's and I told the professor I didn't like taking classes with young kids, so he said I could do a tutorial and write papers for him. He was a PhD, but he didn't know anything about the fire service, so I had to describe and explain things very carefully because I couldn't just use jargon. That freed me up somehow.

I remember how I got started. I got assigned to the Bronx in 1977, and I remember going to this fire—it was a horrendous fire, an arson fire, a collapsed building. So I did some additional research and wrote an article. Then there was a terrible tragedy—August 2, 1978—and six firefighters died from a collapsed wall at a fire. So my articles got published because they were relevant, and eventually I wrote a book, *Collapse of Burning Buildings*, and now it's a book I use in some of the classes I teach.

When I was making up lesson plans for my teaching at Manhattan College, I said to myself, "These lesson plans are like articles. Or each one could be a chapter in a book." So I developed a whole course in fire protection design. So teaching really started me writing. I started writing for my department magazine. There was no money involved, but I felt I just had to write.

Almost all of my writing is primary research. I write about flashover and backdraft explosions and building collapse. I measure how far walls fall out when they collapse. I go out there and I look at how fires grow and I see how buildings explode. I go back after the fire and check things. I check the gas to see if it caused the explosion. I take pictures.

*It sounds like you have a great passion to learn. Is it fair to say that out of that passion to learn comes the passion to teach?*

I have to say, I was a terrible student as a kid. So you know how the passion to learn came? In the fire service, to get promoted you have to take preparatory classes for the tests, and I would watch these fire chiefs up there talking in the classroom, and then I would see them at fires, and I was in awe of them. So the passion came from watching these guys—many of them just working-class guys who only finished high school—teach classes.

Then I took these classes at Queens College, psych and biology and sociology. In each one of the classes, these professors are telling you about generations and centuries of knowledge—I mean, God Almighty, these academic subjects—and I used to sit in these classrooms and listen to these guys . . . and they got to me. When I got the ability to teach and write, then I got the bug, I got the passion.

I have to say, my formative years were not really spent in the firehouse. My formative ideas came from college—from the college teachers and from the fire chiefs teaching those preparatory classes. I did not hang out in the firehouses. I worked there, but I did not hang out there. My formative influence was City University and those instructors there. To this day, I can't tell you how much I admire them—both the college instructors and the chiefs and captains in those preparatory courses. So I got the passion to learn from other instructors. And then I went on to start teaching myself.

Let me tell you something. I am terrified of teaching. The greatest fear I ever felt was standing up in front of an audience.

*That's quite a statement from a guy who has spent his life walking into burning buildings.*

I know—it sounds funny. But nothing terrifies me as much as teaching. It's true. I'm not a born teacher. The night before I speak at a seminar, I feel sickening fear. I always thought, maybe I should take something for this. I never did, thank God. Instead, I faced the fear. To this day, the fear is still there. Once the words come out, I'm OK and people say I'm good at it, but the fear is there.

Writing I love. I tell you, these positive ions go through my body when I'm writing. I love writing. I wrote my first book in 1988, and now I'm revising it twenty years later.

*As a teacher of firefighters for many years, what is the one thing you want a firefighter to remember when going into a bad situation?*

The main thing I would always tell them is to train. Your training saves your life. There's no question about it.

The other thing I really want to say—and it's been the secret to my life—is to think about what you do. For the first twenty years in the fire service, I didn't think about anything. I would go into these burning buildings and run in and run out and do all these things, and then when it was over, I'd come back and say "Whew" and have a few laughs back in the firehouse. Then I'd put it out of my mind and go home and have dinner with the wife.

Then all of a sudden, when I became a deputy chief and got assigned to the Bronx and had a lot of people under my command, I said, "Wait a minute. I am responsible for them." And then I started to think about what I did.

Once you start thinking about what you do, you start writing, and you start teaching. You think, "So what exactly happened here today? That's what happened today? Whoa! And then we did what?" It was tremendous event that happened, and then in writing I would try to create it.

We had this fire, and we put the fire out, and during the fire a part of the floor collapsed, and a chimney fell over and almost hit a guy—that's pretty interesting. And then after I thought about what I did, I wrote about it, and when you write about it, it becomes much more dramatic or real.

One day, I remember rescuing a battalion chief. I had to go up a ladder and rescue him from the roof of a building. He was trapped up there. It was Easter Sunday, early morning. I took him down and gave him a hug—and this is a rough guy—and I'm sure he went that morning and ate dinner with his family and never said a word.

But I went home and I wrote an article about him getting trapped there. Over the years, I've written maybe fifty articles, and that's from thinking about what I did. Most people in the police, fire, military do not think about what they do. So the most important lesson I would tell anybody is to think about what you do, to come back—and I know it sounds corny—and write it down, and then maybe use it as a training aid for a young rookie firefighter. Once you start to think about what you do, then you realize everything.

*"It has to be about the student."*

# Kathy Mitchell

## TEACHER, FBI ACADEMY

*Kathy Mitchell has been in law enforcement for thirty-five years, and she has been a special agent with the FBI for twenty. She currently teaches at the FBI Academy on its 385-acre campus in Quantico, Virginia.*

I've done a variety of teaching here. I've taught new agents. I've taught in our police executive school. But predominantly what I'm known for around here—and I've worked very hard to build a reputation in—is teaching people within the FBI (and other law enforcement personnel) how to teach. Instructor and faculty development happens to be my forte, and that's something I've worked really hard to develop. Teaching is a skill I don't believe everyone has an innate talent for, but needs to be educated in, so that they can do a better job instructing others. I've also been invited to speak to Interpol, over in Lyon, France.

*So you're like the education department in the FBI, teaching the teachers to teach.*
You're right. That's a good way to sum it up.

I've built an instructor-development program here. About five or six years ago, I identified a problem here—we didn't teach our people how to teach. So I put together a school of sorts for instructor development. It is a forty-hour course that is built around adult learning principles. We do it in one week, and they're working hard: from the moment they come in to the last day. When they leave with a certificate, I feel confident that they have been able to demonstrate to me that within the context of the classroom they can apply what they have learned.

A good many of them that I've heard back from through the years say that they really did take the time to apply the skills we teach, and they've been far more successful in the classroom than they ever had before.

*What do you believe are the qualities that make for a good teacher that you try to develop in these instructors at the FBI?*
Because we are not an academic institution—our job is law enforcement and national security—it's my job to bring the educational element to the instructors here. I have to start fairly basic.

One of the most profound principles is that it has to be about the student. That's a huge concept and one that sometimes people have trouble putting their arms around. It has to be about the learner. Whether you're teaching a new agent or someone who's been in law enforcement for twenty-five years, it has to be about what they need and what they have to leave with in order to do their job better.

Another principle that I profess is that there is a huge difference between presenting to an audience and actually teaching an audience. That point is often missed, and many people find it difficult to differentiate between the two. I define a presentation as something that is one way—you have information that others need and you are going to deliver that information to them. How they use that information once they leave is up to them. As an instructor you've done your job; you've delivered the information. That's what a presentation is.

As a teacher, you need more than that. You give them that information, but you expect something in return. You need to see that they have learned it, that they're able to apply it, and they need to give some indication that they are going to change their behavior to do something better. So teaching is a two-way street—as opposed to presenting, which is a one-way process. That's the other concept that people sometimes find difficult to grasp.

Another thing I truly believe in is interactive and experiential learning. There has to be some level of practical application attached to it. Adult learners are going to make up their minds about what they need to know, as opposed to what you're telling them they need to know.

At one point we brought back all of our advanced instructors to be recertified. There were rumblings, of course—"I've been teaching for twenty years and now you're going to make me do this . . ." But everybody came back, and one of the things I stressed was interactive learning. One of the activities I put into the program was that they had to do a ten-minute interactive presentation. They could choose any topic. They'd never done that before. They were saying, "What are you, kidding me?" But they probably had more fun doing that than anything they had done. We had people teaching us how to throw baseballs and what the proper etiquette for sushi is. You name it, they did it. Someone did how to wax a surfboard. The point was that they needed to learn how to be interactive, and they needed to teach their students how to be interactive. That exercise made the biggest impact on them, because when they went back to teach the new instructor-development program, they did have the capacity to be more interactive and build experiential learning activities.

Another principle that I try to foster is that of leadership. Instructors need to think of themselves as leaders, and all too often, they don't. When you look at the characteristics identified with a good leader, they often mirror the characteristics of a good teacher. So why not think of yourself as a leader, because you are making a difference and you are leading these people through whatever you're teaching in order for them to move on to bigger and better things. And I think they do grasp this concept.

*In your own teaching of agents in training, could you give an example of an experiential method of teaching?*

One of the things we have here is what we call the integrative case scenario. That is the practical application side of investigative methods. As part of our curriculum here, we teach fifteen to twenty different types of investigative methods that can be used. And of course, our investigative-methods curriculum is intertwined with other curricula, like interview and interrogation and legal aspects.

So we put together a scenario where they investigate a fictitious event. Right now we use a case of disaster fraud. A hurricane hits, and we investigate suspected fraud. It starts as a financial investigation and it builds to a witness tampering case, where there are also weapons and things like that. We have established the scenario so they get to develop sources, they do consensual monitorings—where they wire people to tape conversations—and they do a variety of different things. They have little pieces of everything, and it culminates in a practical exercise where everything comes together. And they put together search warrants and arrest the subjects, bring them in, collect evidence at the scene, interrogate the suspects—and then all of this culminates in a hearing in a moot court. They apply the things they've learned in a macro context. That's one of the biggest interactive pieces we have.

As a smaller activity, one of my instructors here who teaches financial statutes has put together a case study based on a Ponzi scheme. It involves the sale of fraudulent diamonds, infomercials, money laundering, and all sorts of things. She identifies people in the class to be the bad guys, the victims, and the agents. By the time the case has played out, the students understand which statutes apply and where the different violations have taken place, what they can charge and what they can't charge, how they use money laundering statutes, whether there is any way they can seize assets. So at the end they have a clear idea of the statutes and how they can apply them, as opposed to if they had just sat there and heard her drone on about Title 18 and its various statutes.

*One thing that must be challenging is that, as I understand it, within the FBI Academy, the subjects being taught are very diverse—everything from firearms to driving to law to techniques of criminal investigation.*

Absolutely. But while the teacher's areas are very different, the principles of adult education are still the same. How they apply those principles to their areas of instruction is where the challenge lies. So what I have to do is bring them to the table and say, "You're a really good marksman, and you're a good firearms instructor in terms of being able to articulate to others how to shoot the weapons. But do you really know what it means to teach a class and know how to reach each individual shooter?" Because not everybody is capable of shooting at the same level, and it might not be because they lack the physical skills to do it. They've actually done studies where there might be some physical differences between men and women, but also men and women process information differently, which makes it more difficult to become more proficient in firearms. So do these instructors recognize that difference? And do they know how to reach those people in an effective way? What I try to do through the certification class is teach them how to be effective in the classroom regardless of where their classroom is. The subjects our instructors teach are diverse, but the fundamentals of teaching adults are the same. I have to get our instructors to recognize that those fundamentals are just as important for someone teaching investigative techniques as they are for someone teaching firearms or physical defense tactics.

*This is a theme that has come up in a number of these interviews—the difference between knowing how to do something yourself and being able to teach someone else to do it.*

Absolutely. And this is one of the battles I've had to fight here. They want to bring in people who have solved the big cases—the thought is, "They know how to do it, they'll be able to tell others how to do it."

Not everybody has that talent to be able to translate his or her knowledge into a form so that others can learn it. Sometimes those who are the best at what they do are really the worst to put in front of a classroom, because their knowledge is so ingrained in their heads that they either forget or don't know how to break it down so that others can follow the steps to that end point. So I argued against focusing purely on subject-matter experts. Certainly, they do need expertise in their area, but the truly great FBI agents or analysts may not always be the best to come in as instructors.

*What first got you interested in teaching?*

I was a police officer for thirteen years before joining the FBI, and I've always been interested in teaching law enforcement. Law enforcement has been my life, but my educational background was in journalism and criminal justice. What first sparked my teaching interest is that when I was a police officer in Colorado, we had a program where we would go in and work with the eighth-grade civics classes, teaching them for a whole semester in what we called "street law." At the end of the term they'd have a moot court where they'd have a judge and prosecutor and so on. I became involved in that program and saw how that made a difference with a lot of kids who were at risk. I really enjoyed teaching it, so when I became an agent with the FBI, as soon as I became eligible, I went through the police-instructor school so I could start teaching.

I feel that this is where it all starts—here at the FBI Academy—so it's a place where I can give back to the organization and have an impact on the future of the organization. I've been here almost ten years out of my twenty years with the FBI, and I really enjoy it.

Because I didn't have an education background, there were some things in which I felt woefully inadequate as an instructor. So even though I already had a master's degree in criminal justice, I went through a two-year program at the University of Virginia and received a master's degree in education. It was probably one of the best things I ever did. What I took from that program was what allowed me to structure the instructor-development program here at the FBI Academy. Now I'm at the end of my doctoral program and I'm finishing my dissertation in adult learning.

*In my own lifetime, opportunities for women in law enforcement have expanded quite a bit. Has your own career been largely free of problems in that regard, or has it been a struggle at times?*

As a female in a male-dominated field, I've had a wide variety of experiences, both good and bad. Part of the reason I'm even with the FBI is that I worked for a small police department in northern Colorado, where I was the only female officer for thirteen years, and I was not going anywhere. I wanted to go into the detective division, but that was the men's club, and there was no way I was going to be allowed in there. When that realization hit, I said, "I'm going to move on to bigger and better things," and that's when I joined the FBI. The FBI has opened a lot of doors for me. I have not experienced some of the discrimination or some of the problems that some other women have, but I think I've been lucky in that respect. I think discrimination is still out there, and I think it will continue to be out there until society changes its opinion as to how far women should go in any male-dominated profession. So it's getting better, but there are still struggles.

# 10 | Teaching in the Corridors of Power

*"Teaching is about inspiring."*

# Michael Ansa

CORPORATE CONSULTANT

*Michael Ansa works for a consulting firm specializing in designing and executing "learning events" for businesses. Born and raised in Ghana, he moved to the United States for college. Before becoming a consultant, he worked as a counselor in hospice care, as a high-school English teacher, and later as a school administrator.*

*As a consultant, he works with businesses in the United States and around the world. When we spoke, he had most recently worked in Chicago, Germany, and Angola. The following week he was to leave for Singapore. He is a handsome, charismatic man who speaks English without a trace of an accent.*

Everything I do I learned from being a teacher. I think this work demands three things I learned from teaching. One, the ability to ask really good questions. You can't just ask any old question; you've got to ask the right one. And then when you get the response, you've got to do something with it. Two, the ability to listen. And three, the ability to move from abstract to concrete and back to abstract again, really fluidly. I thought everybody could do this, but everybody can't. Those are three things I learned from teaching, and also from working in hospice as well. Those are the three areas you really need to be solid on if you're going to go into any kind of consulting—or teaching.

*What do you teach? A history teacher teaches history, a chemistry teacher teaches chemistry, but as a corporate consultant, what do you teach?*

I teach leadership. But what does that really mean? I teach people how to motivate others. I teach consciousness around what deficits one might have as a leader. I teach people how to be good coaches. I teach how to solve problems with people in a way that develops them. Within that there are many iterations, but it's generally leadership that I teach.

*And within those areas, are there certain basic principles you find that you are teaching?*

My company was founded by two people as an outgrowth of work they were doing in communities during the civil rights era back in the 1960s. The whole idea of collaboration and community action was new then. They were thinking about how we get people to talk to one another, especially across interest groups, and not just in some fuzzy way, but as a model, almost a science. So they came up with a method. It was related to managing meetings, to getting people to collaborate who didn't necessarily agree or have the same style or approach. All of our intellectual property has grown from that work. So we have models—both elaborate and simple—around collaboration.

Consulting is less a body of knowledge; it's really about approach and process, and that's what I've learned here.

*So in a way, what you're doing is meta-teaching; that is, you're teaching people how to teach—or how to coach—others.*
Yes, or even we teach people how to coach coaches.

**For someone who wasn't familiar with the work you and your company do, would it be accurate to say that what you teach is the sort of thing that might be taught in certain courses in business schools?**
I would say yes, and the field is called organizational development or organizational behavior. You don't need that, however, to do this work. I think what you need is to stay current on research and current thinking in the field, and to be able to do those three things I mentioned. In addition to those three things, there's a big people side to this work—the ability to be facile and creative in sometimes tense situations with very different kinds of people, the ability within minutes to read what might be needed as an intervention, or as a proposal, or a solution for that client. We also say that what you're getting from the client—the dynamic, sometimes the difficulty in understanding, or the difficulty in communication—might be endemic to the organization. When you're having difficulty working with the client, it's probably because of something within that system. If you can understand what that "something" is, your chances are better of succeeding with the client.

*Though we've been calling what you do teaching, is there also a sense in which it's a form of therapy?*
[*Laughs.*] I have colleagues who would disagree with that. My angle to this work is group dynamics. I believe that organizations are just exponential replications of the individual within the organization. So the whole idea of culture is around that exponential growth. When people get together, they create a culture, and so you have to understand individual psychology in order to understand group psychology. And that's a window into understanding—it's not the only window, and some people look at this in strictly a business perspective. But I always say that who you are as an individual is different than who you become in a group, and so it's really important to understand who we become in groups. When I'm working within

an organization, I want to understand the group dynamic or the organizational dynamic. It's infinitely superior to walking in cold with just what the client has told you about what the business issue is.

*If you are teaching leadership, is there a hunger in our culture for leadership?*
I think most organizations within the United States and the world are lacking in that kind of leadership. People are promoted to leadership because they are good technicians. But that's not what it takes to be a good leader. So if you enter an organization and are good at your job, they promote you and promote you, but the same things that made you good at shuffling files and doing your work are not the same things that make you good as a leader. So there is a dearth of leaders.

A leader must have the emotional intelligence as well as the strategic intelligence to run the organization, and he or she must have a moral compass so that people know the leader gives a crap. I think if you look at organizations now, people know that the guys at the top—and they are usually guys—are in it for themselves. They're going to getting a big cut if they leave. And, you know, the small guy or woman at the desk is not really on their radar. I think very few leaders are really able to speak to all the people. But real leaders, when they speak, people believe what they're saying and know that they care beyond the bottom line.

*One thing that makes you unique among the people interviewed in this book is that you don't teach in one place, or even in one country. You teach all over the world. Do you find in your teaching that people are basically the same, or are they different according to their culture?*
Both are true—which is sort of the cop-out answer, but that's my answer. I think what has made me successful is that I approach global work with a level of humility. I approach it with questioning, and I am constantly thinking about the appropriateness to the audience. I am not one of these folks who believe that you have to learn everything about a culture to be there. Or that there's some kind of magic wand or key to doing work in China, for example. I think Chinese people, or Africans, like everybody else, take a look at you and say, "Is this guy going to fuck with me or is he really the real deal? Does he really care?" And if they can answer that question "yes," I think you're in better shape. And that's how I approach global work.

In this era it helps that I'm African and not American, to be honest. Because—and most of America doesn't know this—the world really doesn't like us very much. And now, more than before, I'm very quick to say that I was raised in Africa because it gets me a lot of points. In recent years America has lost a lot of credibility and respect in the world.

So are people the same? I think people are the same in that they want to be respected, they want to know that you really care, they want to know you're safe. And if they can say yes, yes, yes, to those, they can hear what you have to say. They might even like it and take it on. But if you're walking in as the expert—as the American expert—especially in Europe and the Middle East, you will fail.

*In ancient Athens, there were teachers called the Sophists who helped young men get ahead. In Plato's dialogs, the Sophists were held up for derision because their goal was to teach the tools to practical success, not truth or moral betterment. Do you ever question your work as a consultant, worry that you're just helping corporations maximize profits?*

For me, the question is no longer business or non-profit because I don't think it's that simple, and I don't think we would survive as a globe without businesses. We all wear, eat, and live in products of businesses. So I'm no longer that black and white about it. At the same time, I think social responsibility is a moral mandate that we have. So within this firm, we believe in what we call the three Ps—people, planet, and profits. So we focus on organizations that are mindful and are doing something in terms of people development, environmental responsibility, and the bottom line. For example, there are organizations we will not work with. If you are making arms, we will not work with you. We are really drawn to companies who are doing a lot for their people. That's why I'm not at other big consulting firms. This is a firm that really believes in that stuff.

*So to paraphrase Mao, this is the long march through the corporations in order to better the world?*

Yes.

*So what does it mean to teach? Does it mean to change people?*

Forget the change part. Teaching is about inspiring. Teaching is about validating people's experience and giving them other hooks—other places to hook their experience. Sometimes it's a text. Sometimes it's a model. I think the best teachers give people a language for what they already know. I really mean that. My best teachers have done that for me. Sometimes they have shown me something new, but what I remember them for are the ways in which they gave words, body, and a frame to what was already true for me. And when I can do that as a consultant, that's when I'm most effective.

> *"That's how you help the next generation—by passing the knowledge on."*

# Emil Jones

## POLITICAL MENTOR

*Emil Jones is the president of the Illinois State Senate. A one-time Chicago masonry inspector, Jones made his first foray into politics as a volunteer for the 1960 presidential campaign of John F. Kennedy. In 1972, he was elected to the*

*Illinois House of Representatives, then to the state senate in 1982. As a mentor to Barack Obama, he came under intense scrutiny during the campaign, and his critics portray him as an old-time machine politician.*

*We spoke in August of 2008, a few weeks before the Democratic National Convention, in his office in the James Thompson Center, one of Chicago's architectural marvels. He speaks slowly in a gravelly bass voice.*

*It seems that one of the goals you've set for yourself as a political leader is to mentor younger people coming up in politics. Is that true?*

Basically, yes.

*If you look back on how you've mentored people, are there certain lessons or general ideas you find that you've tried to teach?*

Sometimes people look at politicians and politics as something off and different. It's not. It's just a way of life. It's not something that is all different or foreign. It's the same applications that you apply working in any profession; it's the same processes.

When I first got elected to public office, I was mentored by a senior member to get to know lawmakers that don't look like you, or who are from different regions. And that's what I did. I learned all about the farming community, I learned quite a bit about the coal mines in Illinois. I got to know the legislators who represented those particular areas. After you learn all that, you try to find a commonality between some of the interests you may have and some of the interests they may have, and you can be rather effective that way.

It's a constant learning experience. Books I read in college—*The Prince,* written by Machiavelli during the Renaissance era, and *The Art of War,* written over two thousand years ago by Sun Tzu—still apply. If you read those, then you're better able to function.

*Do you still go back and reread those books?*

Yes, simply because sometimes . . . you're constantly in a decision-making position, deciding which way to go on a particular issue or how you're going to deal with your membership. So it's always been a good reference to look to in helping you to make those decisions.

Folks sometimes assume that you know it all just because you're in an elected position, but you have to admit to yourself that you don't. And since you don't, then you try to go out and acquire all the knowledge you can about various subject matters and surround yourself with smart people. If you surround yourself with smart people, then you're going to learn quite a bit. But if you don't do that, then you're in trouble.

Machiavelli said, how do you judge the brains of a leader? Look at who he has around him. If he has smart people around him, then he must be smart because he chose them. You should surround yourself with the brightest people you can get.

One thing a person must not be fearful of is having other persons around with a lot of knowledge. You must be secure in your position. Too often politicians are insecure. Don't worry if you have someone who is bright and smart—you should be glad you have him.

*It sounds like a lot of what you try to teach younger people is to stay open to learning.*
Right. The General Assembly down in Springfield—it's just like a college campus. And on a college campus, you've got different groups—you can call them cliques—they get together, and you must get to know them as individuals. You can be quite effective if you immerse yourself in the activities of other members. You have people from different backgrounds, different cultures . . . like the one that just left here—Ira Silverstein [*the state senator representing the Eighth District of Illinois, who had been chatting with Emil Jones when I arrived*]. He's Jewish. I learned quite a bit from Ira. He's an Orthodox Jew. So I make sure that I respect his religion. I won't call sessions on days that are religious holidays for him, out of respect for his culture. These are the kinds of things you constantly learn.

*One of the people you have mentored is Barack Obama. What in particular did you teach him?*
I knew Barack Obama when he first came to Chicago and began working as a community organizer. I believe that was in 1985. I did not know this until I read his book and he was already elected to the state senate, but he had come to protest at my office. They wanted my involvement. I had seen them out in the street and I had invited them into my office to discuss the issue of school dropouts. I liked the group and I had the same concerns, so we developed a good working relationship.

When he was elected to the state senate, he came in to see me and he said to me, "You and I know each other, and you know I like to work hard. So feel free to give me any tough assignments and I'll do my best to carry them out."

I suggested to him that he could be more effective in this body if he got to know the lawmakers on both sides of the aisle and also from the various regions of the state. I told him not to hang around the people from his own community. I told him to get to know downstate legislators, and he did it. So I was passing on to him the knowledge that I had acquired.

*As the years went on, were there other themes in your mentoring of Barack?*
Well, to be more pragmatic. You can come in with idealistic views about changing the way government operates, but you've got to be pragmatic—for example, on proposed ethics legislation. I assigned him to be my point person on campaign finance reform and the draft legislation was so far-reaching that he had lot of opposition on both sides of the aisle, and even from members of his own caucus. In order for him to pass that, it would have to be changed in certain ways. So he understood that, and he worked with them and made the necessary adjustments to get it passed. I

told him something is not going to pass just because you want it to pass or because you think it's good. You must understand and respect the views of the members who will be called upon to vote for this. So I tried to mentor him in that process— learning to compromise, but at the same time not really losing the main focus or thrust of the legislation that you are proposing.

*Is there ever a danger in compromising so much that you—*

As long as you don't compromise your principles. You may not get everything that you want. For example, on the ethics legislation that Barack pushed, lawmakers would usually have fund-raisers while we were in session. He wanted to change that so you could not hold fund-raisers while the legislature is in session. There was a lot of opposition to that. So now we can not hold fund-raisers while the legislature is in session—in the capitol, that is. So that's a basic principle that he did not compromise on. On some things you just don't compromise your principles.

*When someone mentors someone in politics, who usually initiates the relationships, the mentor or the one being mentored?*

It's based more or less on personalities. The younger person would come in all starry-eyed, but if one of the older members happens to like the individual, he or she will pull them aside and explain to them that this is how you get it done.

There was another individual who came to Springfield, and he would jump on the floor, ranting and raving. One of my colleagues pulled him aside and said, "See that press box? There's no one sitting there. If you are trying to get news coverage, you're wasting your time. So you're just talking to the members and you're not being effective." And that was that. It's things like that that the older members will sometimes convey to the younger members.

*If you had to give Barack a piece of advice at this point, what would it be? [We were speaking a few weeks before the Democratic National Convention of 2008.]*

Don't change. Barack is a very intelligent individual, but he doesn't like the gutter politics, all the dirty attacks. That's not Barack. He doesn't like that, and he never did. The times I've talked with him, we talk about those things. He always tries to keep above the fray. Even in his race against Hillary Clinton, there were those who said, "Why doesn't he attack more?" But he doesn't like that part. He'd rather stick with the issues. He gives more credit to the electorate as having the intelligence and the sense to know what's really going on.

*What are the other principles you find yourself teaching?*

You asked me about the books, and one quote I have on my wall from Sun Tzu is, "Don't depend upon the enemy not coming; rather, be prepared for the enemy when he does come." There will always be those challenges coming, so you must always be prepared. You must constantly be prepared. I tell this to my friends, my colleagues, and those I mentor. Someone who has a piece of legislation will say, "I haven't got any opposition. There is no one against it." I'll say, "But there is someone against it, and you must be prepared for that." You must prepare for when the attack does come—and it will come.

In the legislature they have a program for new members, and they give them an orientation. But there are many things you're not going to learn in the orientation. I found that out in my first term as state representative. That knowledge you need may even come from a clerk who has been around a while. So get to know people. When you get to know people, you're going to learn quite a bit. That's what I try to pass on.

I'm working with the Paul Simon Institute at Southern Illinois University, and we're dealing with intergenerational teaching. People can work on a job for many years, and then they retire and they take all the knowledge they acquired over those years with them. It's lost. So we're working to get them involved in teaching to younger people and passing on the knowledge they have acquired. That's how you help the next generation—by passing the knowledge on.

*So inclusion, communication, human relationships—it sounds like those are your mentoring themes.*

Yeah, but inclusion is the most important ingredient. A well-informed body can be more effective. I tell the members that when I call them—I try to give them all the information I can possibly give them. Then we sit down and discuss it. When they're involved in that process, then they feel that it's part of them, and they in turn respond in a more positive manner.

I tell my members you've got to involve other persons in the process you may not like. You'll be more effective that way. We had some major legislation dealing with the death penalty here in Illinois. I told Barack—he sat on the judiciary committee—"It's your job to get this done." The attempt to pass the legislation before had failed, and there was a lot of opposition to the reform legislation from law enforcement, prosecutors. He had to sit down with those individuals who were in opposition and make them a part of the reform legislation that was being drafted. By bringing them in and including them in that process, he was able to successfully pass the legislation. It was almost a unanimous vote in the senate. If he had not brought them in, the legislation would not have passed. So inclusion was very important.

*So Barack was a good student.*

Yeah, he was a good student. He's a very intelligent person—very bright.

[*The phone rang and Senator Jones told his secretary he would be with his next appointment presently. When he hung up, his answering machine signaled he had a message by playing the musical theme from the film* The Godfather.]

*That music reminds me. Is the story true that Barack Obama has referred to you as his political godfather?*

Yes.

I liked the movie. It wasn't a criminal story; it was a story of human life and how you respond to issues.

Barack came in to see me one day and he said, "As senate president, you have a lot of power."

I said, "You tell me what kind of power you think I have."

He said, "You have the power to make a United States senator."

I said, "If I have that kind of power, do you know of anyone I can make a senator?"

He said, "Me."

During the course of the campaign, there were a couple of members who were not supporting him, and he called me about them. I told him I'd see what I could do about it. I talked to the individuals, and one was hostile. But I got them to turn around and then they were very supportive of Barack and his candidacy.

*How did you get them to turn around?*

[*Laughs.*] I knew that question was coming. Barack asked the same question.

So they became very enthusiastically involved, and Barack asked me how I did it. I told him, "I made them an offer . . ."

*. . . they couldn't refuse? [We both laugh.]*

I told him, "You don't want to know," and I let it go at that.

So after he won the primary, there was a big unity breakfast, and Barack was thanking everyone. And when he got to me, he said "A special thanks goes to my political godfather." So the national media picked it up, and that's how that got out there.

I have godchildren. I'm Catholic. I've got a godmother, godfather. In that context, a godparent is someone who looks out for an individual, who will be there for that person. And that's the context in which Barack looks at me as a godfather.

*[I thanked him for the interview and told him I would be sure to send him a copy of the book.]*

Books are very interesting. You know, I was in Italy—I believe it was Florence—where the priests are buried in the church, and you know who's buried there with them? Niccolò Machiavelli. I was shocked.

Some people think he's very sinister. But why is he buried with the priests?

When he wrote that book [*The Prince*], he was in exile. He had gone into politics, but he found out that's not the way it worked.

In college my humanities course was the most interesting course. I liked it so much that things stuck with me. It was at Loop College [*later renamed Harold Washington College in honor of Chicago's first African American mayor*]. The teacher was really good. He taught poetry, prose, Shakespeare . . . *Hamlet* . . . "To thine own self be true." Don't lie to yourself. Too often politicians lie to themselves. Always be truthful to yourself. As long as you're truthful to yourself, you'll be quite successful.

*That's good advice in any realm of life.*

Politics is just like any realm of life.

*"I'm a midwife of change."*

# Michael Bell

## CORPORATE CONSULTANT

*Michael Bell is a consultant who works with both businesses and non-profit organizations. He is the co-founder, president, and CEO of InPartnership Consulting, and he also gives workshops in the Rockwood Leadership Program, an organization devoted to developing leaders in progressive social causes.*

Leadership is about an individual's ability to inspire, motivate, and enroll others through his or her sense of purpose in a shared vision. I believe that real leadership happens from the inside out, so it's about our ability to align our heart and head and spirit in service of the work we want to do in the world. The fuel for real leadership is about the ability to connect to a sense of purpose—what am I here to do in this lifetime? Connecting with purpose is the fuel for real leadership.

*You teach in a number of contexts—semester-long courses as well as workshops. In a workshop what might you do? How do you teach leadership in a week-long workshop?*

There's a lot of work that happens in preparation. At least fifteen of your colleagues will evaluate you. They actually complete an individual assessment of your leadership. These come from a lot of people—people who work for you, your peers, senior leaders, people who manage you or the board that elected you president. So you've got a total picture of the impact you're having in the world as a leader. Then you have to write an individual essay about what you want to work on, why are you coming to such a program, what season are you in as a leader.

Then we sit down—the team and myself—and we read through everything. By the time I get there, I have a pretty intimate knowledge of the kind of leader you are and the kind of impact you are having as a leader. I have a plan for the week, for how we are going to challenge you, how we are going to work with you on both building your strengths and taking an uncensored look at your challenges, what you need to work on. Part of the gift we want to give someone in a setting like that is the gift of truth—of authentic dialogue. We do that by taking them through an arc (we have a kind of architecture for the program).

We start with purpose. What is it you are here in the world to do? We connect you with purpose, and we have a series of exercises for that. We take the high-dive approach with folks working on leadership so we basically jump off right away and get you out of your comfort zone, into a conversation about purpose.

From there we move into a conversation on vision. What is your noblest aspiration? What would be different in the world as a result of your work? Then we move into a conversation on values. What are the values that you bring to your work? What are the beliefs and values that are the foundation you stand on? What are the filters you use to see the world? What were your early messages about the world that shape your reactions to others, even as they walk into a room—whether it be an employee, a funder, or a volunteer?

From there we look at your communication skills. We actually have you look at your assessments, the rich feedback. That's usually the point at which people are a little disoriented. There's always a gap between the impact you think you're having out there in the world and how others see you. It's in that moment that what can take place is something called transformative learning. It's not learning where you add to what you already know, but it's learning where you transform how you see the world, how you see yourself and how you approach your work with others. So we try to use that moment to strip away all the myths and fantasies and lies about yourself to give you an unfiltered, uncensored view of how the world sees you. If you have enough humility to step into the truth of that, that's where we can coach you and give you some more tools to be a better leader.

*It sounds like there is a certain ideology of leadership built into this. We've all known those leaders who have a "my way or the highway" approach, who do not seem to care what their employees think of them . . .*
Right. Command and control.

*Do you run up against that, or do people who come to your group know what you're about?*
I should disclose that in my company until about five years ago, I only worked with Fortune 25, for-profit organizations, and I covered the United States and Europe, and we worked mostly with global corporations: banking, oil, large manufacturing corporations. Mercedes-Benz, Shell, Chrysler, Sun Microsystems, IBM, and Kellogg were some of our clients.

*Can these names be mentioned?*
Sure.

I think the leadership models that work are not the command and control models. The leadership models that work are models where we create an environment that is rich in information, where leaders foster collaboration—as opposed to command and control, need-to-know environments, with low levels of emotional literacy. There's a lot of research that says those environments don't work. They certainly don't work with generations X and Y. Everyone wants an environment where he or she is respected—any generation. Everyone wants an environment where one feels the work that is being done connects to his or her values. Whatever generation you're working with, folks are really not that comfortable with change—change is not easy.

So it's very important for leaders to create the conditions for all the different types of people at work, whatever your differences might be—whether it be age, gender, or race. Leaders are there to be in service to their employees and create the conditions for their employees to be successful. The old leadership model that you're describing was, "I create the conditions. The conditions work for me. If they don't work for anyone else, they can go find another job." We really don't see those kinds of leaders being successful anymore—whether I'm in London or Kalamazoo or Dallas or Dubai. Those kinds of leaders aren't going to be successful in today's workplace.

The complexity of the workplace now requires that we move beyond individual treatment to teams. How can we work together? In fostering an environment where teams are front and center as opposed to individuals, we need to consider how to create an environment where what we're promoting is not individual achievement but collaboration, cooperation, co-powering, and empowerment. So as the generations change, and the complexity of the work environment changes, there are new models of working together that are required to get the work done in a global environment.

Also the demographics are different. The workplace of the forties, fifties, and sixties was homogeneous—predominately male, predominantly white, between twenty-five and fifty-five. That model has changed. From now until 2015, 86 percent of the new entrants into the workplace will be women and people of color. So even if I am a white manager in the workplace, the question becomes, am I ready to manage, motivate, and enroll that next generation of leaders that's coming into the workplace? And what it requires in addition to great management skills is cultural competence. Do I have the cultural competence to work well across differences?

*In your teaching, it sounds like part of what you do is hold up a mirror. That must be tough, because I imagine there are some people who don't like what they see—or they won't see it. How do you get them to see it?*

I laughingly say that I get paid to tell people that their baby is ugly. I have to gently, authentically, in a way that you can hear it, say, "Let's take a closer look at the baby and see what are our strengths and what are our weaknesses and how can we prepare this thing that you love so much for the real world that's out there." I'd say about 40 percent of the time when I come back with that picture—in all of its beauty and all of its ugliness—to the leadership team, people will say, "We didn't sign up for this. You charged us a lot of money to give us news we didn't want to hear." I say, "Thank you very much. Let me know when you want to do something about this." And I leave. So I really have to be committed to telling the truth and letting them know that what they're getting from me is an uncensored, authentic, data-driven picture of what is. And that's the moment where people have to choose.

I'm really a midwife. I'm a midwife of change in individuals, groups, teams, and organizations. They're going to have to make choices about what they're willing to do. Are you willing to make the changes that will make you a better leader, that will make this team a more effective leadership team? Are you willing to make this organization ready to be successful in the world that's coming?

*Have you acquired techniques or tricks that enable people to see things about themselves they may not want to see?*

I don't think it's a technique and I don't think it's a trick. I think that what you need to do is gather the facts. There's nothing more compelling than bringing together the picture they've created themselves. It's not what I think about you, but what the people who live here and work here say about you. There's nothing more compelling, because I didn't say it, I didn't make it up, I didn't insert my opinion. I just assembled all the information that is around you that we've now put together into a picture. So the power resides in the truth—as in "truth" with a small "t."

*What makes you good at this?*

I'm the son of a mortician. It's been in my family for a hundred years. I grew up watching families walk through the door to bury their child, their brother, their sister, their parents, and I listened to regrets. "I wish we had done this, I wish we had said that. I wish we had . . . I wish we had . . ." It made me at a very young age want to say, "Why didn't you? Why did you wait?" So I have a very deep sense of the power of now. Why would we wait to fix something we need to fix, or say something we need to say, or do something we need to do? So it's brought a kind of deep resolve to not sugarcoat the truth. Because the truth is over there in the casket—they're not coming back.

I'm the oldest son. I'm supposed to be at home running our family business. My father was very invested in my going to Cornell. So I got to Cornell and there were really a lot of very talented African Americans there, so I was stepping into this legacy where I was connecting to all the black families around the country where I was going to be part of that next generation of leaders.

And lo and behold, I get to Cornell and realize that I'm gay. And in the process of realizing that, I had to let go of all my dreams and expectations and the legacy I was going to step into. I just couldn't step back into rural, southern, Christian Virginia and be who I was as a gay man. I was either going to have to be that southern, Christian, African American person who wasn't gay, or be gay. I needed to figure out who I was going to be in this more authentic iteration of myself. I had to fashion a life for myself that took all the experiences of my childhood, all of the lessons learned, but that wasn't the life that I had planned for myself and certainly wasn't the life that my parents had planned for me.

I was fortunate enough to have a set of parents who despite all of their background really embraced me, who I was, the fact that I was gay . . . and I never lost a strong connection with my parents. But I did have to fashion a new life for myself. I kept having to walk down my path very courageously. Having had to do it myself, I've created the conditions where I can help others do it.

*Do you have former teachers who have been especially influential?*

The two biggest influences were my parents. My mother was a teacher, and both my parents had a very strong set of values that drove their work. And it was about using privilege and education to create opportunities for others and to role model that for others.

> *"I think it has been essential that the concepts that we teach are reinforced by the social network."*

# Hannah Riley Bowles

## PROFESSOR, EXECUTIVE EDUCATION PROGRAMS

*Hannah Riley Bowles is an associate professor of public policy at Harvard University, where she teaches in the Kennedy School's Executive Education program. She has a DBA from the Harvard Business School, an MPP from the Kennedy School, and an AB from Smith College. Her research focuses on gender in negotiation and leadership. In 2003, she won the Manuel Carballo Award for Excellence in Teaching.*

*She teaches a number of courses in the Kennedy School's Executive Education program. We spoke about her teaching in the Women and Power program, of which she is faculty chairperson. The course takes place once a year, in May, and lasts for a week.*

We designed the Women and Power program at the Kennedy School, and our first session was in 2002. It was created to provide some additional executive training for women who were deeply in their careers but hadn't yet reached the pinnacle of their careers.

We recruit women from the private sector, the non-profit sector, and the government/military sector. For the women in the private sector, they need to have demonstrated some form of public leadership—philanthropy, having run for office, serving on non-profit boards, or things like that.

I'm the faculty director. I design the curriculum and then I teach six classes throughout the week. I focus my classes on general leadership topics, but I also intersperse that with discussions of gender. I also talk about my research, which is focused on gender and negotiation, and also on the paths women have taken to senior leadership positions.

I use primarily the case method, and so do the other faculty in the program. We use simulations and case method discussions, and we also have some evening speakers.

The case method allows for inductive analysis. So it's not just that you're telling people what they should think about something, but you give them a problem, and through their own analysis, and through discussion, the key teaching points emerge. They're building the lessons themselves as they analyze, individually and collectively, the specific problem. I always try to choose cases that will illuminate some general theoretical principles, so that you're not just discussing what this one manager did in this one specific situation, but you ask how you can generalize from that one particular case.

The limitations of the case method are that sometimes people don't ever get to that general point. They have trouble recognizing a general dynamic in a new situation because they so closely associate the general dynamic with the details for the case. This is something that a teacher can avoid by explicitly drawing connections to other cases so that people are thinking comparatively.

### Are the cases fictional or real?

Most of the cases are real. The ones that are fictional are a compilation of real-life cases. The simulation and negotiation exercises are abstractions of things that happened in the real world.

For example, one thing we do is watch the first ten minutes of a thirty-minute video of a fictional business situation in which the protagonist in the case is trying to lead an initiative and is rather flat-footed at first about doing it. We stop the video after the first ten minutes and ask the class how he's doing. What has he done well? What has he done poorly? Then we show them the second ten minutes and I introduce them to some negotiation-analysis concepts to get them thinking about how he can build the coalition he needs to build. Then we watch the final segment and we do an analysis of what happened, and I use that to bring up some other theoretical concepts.

Another example is a real case based on the chairmanship of Myrlie Evers-Williams at the NAACP following a period of crisis for the organization. To open that case, I use some classic readings on the distinctive challenges of leading within institutions as opposed to organizations, an institution being a value-laden organization that has evolved over time, and may have cherished practices and people who really identify personally with the institution. A lot of the executives I work with in the Women and Power program are leading in institutions or working with people who lead in institutions, so we can have a broader initial conversation about the challenges, barriers, and opportunities of leading in an institution as opposed to an organization. Then we look specifically at the case of the NAACP, and we talk about what caused the crisis and what types of things Myrlie Evers-Williams did to try to turn it around. I use an analysis of that case to get us deeper into the conversation about institutions and leadership.

In the Women and Power program the size of the group is about fifty, so the challenge from a teaching perspective is to facilitate the discussion in such a way that you get a conversation going among the members of the group, rather than having a series of student comments back to the teacher.

*Is part of the rationale for the program to try to help women break through that glass ceiling?*

Oh sure. Some of the women are at the top and they're here to think about what this last stage of the career is going to look like, but one of the most wonderful things about the program is that when the women stand up and introduce themselves at the first session, it's almost like a flame ignites. There's a sense of excitement that they are so rich with peers. Many of the women who have achieved really senior positions just don't have a lot of female peers. So they come into this class and all of a sudden there are fifty other women who are not from their own organization or from their town. It's a really diverse group: everything from a senior university administrator from Texas to a woman from Saudi Arabia who is the president of a women's college. There are military women and corporate executives. But they see in one another ambition and extraordinary achievement and competence, so they really connect with each other. A huge part of the week is giving them the space to connect with one another.

Some of the women have just had babies and some are pregnant and they're trying to figure out that stage of their lives. Others are—or are about to become— empty nesters. And then another set of women may be dealing with their husbands' retirements, and they're thinking about their own retirement and trying to figure that out. It's important to facilitate conversations that validate all the life stages and give them space to talk about that.

Every morning we divide them into groups of three or four, and each woman presents a real case of what she's going through. The other women in her group will give her feedback and help her problem solve through it. Overwhelmingly, that has been one of the most meaningful experiences of the week.

One other thing I should share with you is that from the first year the women were so excited by this program that they created an alumni program.

*What is the long-term effect of the program on the people who went through it? The vitality of the alum group indicates that it's pretty positive.*

We don't have great systematic data on this yet. I'm sure that my own data is skewed because I'm more likely to hear from the well-satisfied people than from those who just had the experience and then it faded from memory. But I think the takeaways are multiple.

One is this network. I think the women benefit from it and invest in it. There are women who tell me proudly that they've helped others get jobs or given important career advice, and they feel very good about what they're giving to the group as well as what they're receiving.

Pedagogically, for me the goal of the program is to give them new insights into what they do. There's a professor at the Graduate School of Education, Jerome Kagan, who talks about the goal of education in elementary school through college as making the unfamiliar familiar—so what we're trying to do is teach young people about the world. But when you get into professional education, particularly executive education, what you're trying to do is make the familiar unfamiliar; you're trying to give people frameworks for looking at what they do on a regular basis through a different lens. Hopefully, with that new lens they'll gain some new insight and maybe even change their practices or develop a new strategic approach that they might otherwise not have pursued.

One of the women who went through our program tells the story of how she was joining a kind of old boys' club partnership, and when she was entering our program, they were saying, "You're going to have to earn your way for a while until you are actually a partner." She had always been an entrepreneur and always owned part of her company, so she wanted an ownership stake in this new firm. So she really used the negotiation stuff that we covered in the program and she got a lot of support from other women in the program, and she went back and successfully negotiated a great deal. She has stayed with them for some time now and really helped them to rebuild at a time when they had become a firm that was a little stale—and she really brought new energy to it.

So I think the success of our program is a coupling of both the concepts and strategies we teach and the networking. Also, it's risky to change. A lot of these women are thinking about their careers and leadership challenges—should I go for something that's much bigger than what I'm doing now? It takes courage to do really new things. So I think it has been essential that the concepts that we teach are reinforced by the social network.

*You won a very prestigious teaching award—you must be doing some things right. What are the keys to your success as a teacher?*

I prepare really hard. I put a lot of effort into preparing . . . but preparing in itself isn't enough.

I really care about communicating ideas and communicating them in a way that's interesting and engaging—where smart people will find them interesting and stimulating and relevant to their lives. I care a lot about that.

I also try very hard to make my course content grounded in research and relevant to practice, so that these exercises are not just fun or an opportunity for navel gazing or something like that. I will say to the students that I'm using this because there's really good research on it and I'm going to tell you what the research says. And now let's talk about why this is relevant to practice and why it's relevant to you.

I think another reason I got that teaching award is that I put a lot of effort into writing or adapting materials that display a broad array of leadership examples demographically. So I might have a gay woman protagonist negotiating with an Asian man. If you're looking for leadership examples, it's a lot easier to come up with a lot of white men, particularly within our society. Because we overwhelmingly see white men in those positions, we draw these naïve associations between the attributes of white men and leadership abilities. This is why the Obama example is blowing young black men's minds, the idea that "this could be me, and there are things about me that could translate into being a leader."

I think there are a lot of students who deeply appreciate my teaching general principles and showing that they apply to a diversity of types of people. I have had young women in my class say that in their previous courses in leadership they looked at cases with male leaders and thought, "I don't know if this applies to me."

So I put in a lot more time on my courses than someone who's on a research track. [*Laughs.*] But I find it gratifying.

> *"The best way to teach is to arrange things so that people are learning."*

# George Shultz

## POLITICAL MENTOR

*George Shultz has had a long and distinguished career in education, business, and politics. He taught at M.I.T. and the University of Chicago and held a number of positions in government, including four cabinet positions. He served as secretary of labor, secretary of the treasury, and director of the Office of Management and Budget before becoming President Reagan's secretary of state, a position he held from 1982 to 1989.*

*Since 1989, he has been active as a writer, corporate board member, and policy advisor to Republican administrations at the state and federal levels. He has received numerous awards for his years of service, among them the Reagan Distinguished American Award, the Elliot Richardson Prize for Excellence and Integrity in Public Service, and the John Witherspoon Medal for Distinguished Statesmanship. He is Thomas W. and Susan B. Ford Distinguished Fellow at the Hoover Institution.*

There are people who run for office, and they're in politics. There are people who sit around in universities and write policy papers and have views about political issues, and sometimes they're very influential, like Milton Friedman. Then there are people who are in between, like me. I have been part of the university, and I've also been a cabinet appointee. As a cabinet officer, you're appointed by the president, confirmed by the Senate, so you're not quite in politics but at the same time, you're not in the ivory tower, either. You're in between. So that's where I sit.

When you wrote me about your book, I thought you might be interested in my own experience in, and view about, teaching.

The first time I found myself in that position was an odd one. I was a football player at Princeton—this was before World War II—and I came back for my senior year in the best physical condition I think I've ever been in. I thought it was going to be my year.

I got clipped in the back of my knee before the season started. It damaged my knee badly, and I never played again. So they asked if I'd like to be the coach of the freshman backfield. In those days there was a freshman team and a varsity. We had a talented group, and I had come to understand how backfields operate. They were about the same age as me, really, so we just sort of worked together.

As I look back, it dawned on me that the best way to teach is to arrange things so that people are learning. They don't think of you as a teacher; they find that when you're around, they learn something, and they like that. And of course you like that.

I feel that as an adult, I've been a teacher all my life, even though in a job like secretary of state, people would say that's not a teaching job. But actually, it always seemed to me that in administering things, whether in a university or a company or in the government, if you can create an atmosphere around you where everybody, including you, is learning, you're going to have a hot group. You're going to have to send them home at night because everybody enjoys learning. So I always sought to create that kind of an atmosphere, and it paid off for me handsomely, because I was able to attract some very able people to be my associates.

People always say, "What's the best background for going into government?" Well, for me, being a teacher, so to speak, with that attitude about teaching, was very good preparation.

And then I was a dean at the University of Chicago before I went into government, and that job was good preparation because if you're a dean, you have a lot of responsibility and practically no authority. You have a central administration you have to cope with to get money. You have students whom you can't order to learn so you have to arrange an atmosphere where they do. You have faculty, and if you're a dean, faculty people are real nice one on one, but you get them together in a meeting and they're nearly impossible, so you can't order them around. You can't order the alumni to give you money. So your job is persuasion. That's what you're trying to do—you're trying to help people learn how to achieve the objectives of the organization.

And when you're in government and you're a cabinet officer, you've got the same problems. You've got the White House you've got to cope with, and then you've got the Congress; you can't spend any money unless they appropriate it for you. And they're tough. You've got all these constituencies and you have a lot of responsibility, but again, your authority comes fundamentally from the legitimacy of what you're doing and from your ability to persuade people.

*You are frequently mentioned as mentoring others, Secretary of State Condoleezza Rice, for one.*

As far as mentoring is concerned, when you have any administrative position, or even if you don't and you're somewhere like here [*he gestures around him; we're in his office at the Hoover Institution*], and people like Condi Rice are getting ready to go do something, they'll come around, and we'll talk about it. So I'll mention some of these things from my experience. Number one is what I just told you about the importance of creating an atmosphere of learning, so that people will want to work in your environment and you'll attract first-class people.

There was a wonderful man named Bryce Harlow—probably the most skillful and thoughtful congressional relations person I ever knew—who took me under his wing when I was secretary of labor. He said, and I think this is so important in mentoring, "Never make a commitment unless you are sure and determined to carry it out. And if you make a commitment and it turns out to be hard to carry it out, just break your neck to carry it out—because that's your credibility." It's easy to make commitments; it's hard to carry them out. Don't make them so easily because as he said, and these are the words that stuck in my mind, "Trust is the coin of the realm." When people learn that they can trust you, and that when you say you will do something you will deliver, then you get somewhere. You've got to maintain a high level of credibility.

So on any important job, you've got to work very hard at it. It requires tremendous physical and intellectual energy and staying power.

I remember an experience I had with Ronald Reagan. I think he instinctively had the same kind of attitude I did about teaching, but he didn't have the same kind of experiences. When I was secretary of state, Reagan made an important decision in the area of foreign policy—I don't remember what it was—and I was given the job of announcing the decision and explaining it. I remember I took great pains to write a speech, and when I brought it to him, he picked it up and read it and said, "It's perfect." Then there was a pregnant pause, and he said, "Of course, if I was doing it, I wouldn't do it this way."

So he made some notes on it for about four minutes and then handed it back to me. At one place he had written "story" on it. I looked at it and I realized he had personalized it. So he said, "You've written this speech to be printed in the *New York Times* and as a State Department bulletin, but when I give a speech, I give it to people. Where you're trying to make a point that's maybe a little abstract, tell a story so that people can put themselves into it. Then they get it."

And I thought to myself, "This guy is an instinctive teacher. He wants the people on the other end of the television camera to learn something."

*You talk about building an atmosphere of learning, and as we know, there are offices and institutions that have no such atmosphere. What are the qualities that contribute to this "atmosphere of learning"?*

Well, one of them is that you share the problem. Whatever you're dealing with, you've got to know, "What's the problem?" And then you let everyone know what it is.

Another is that everyone's views are welcome to be heard. That doesn't mean you get your way, but you get to express your views, to be part of the argument, and out of that comes some decision. As a result of that process, you are involved and you support the decision even if you don't fully agree. It has a legitimacy to it that it doesn't have if it's just been dictated to you. I'm not saying that dictatorial regimes don't work sometimes, but I never felt they were valid, and I've also seen a lot that didn't work at all because the people who have to carry things out aren't invested in it. So I think that's a big characteristic of the atmosphere of learning.

*Early in your career you were a professor at M.I.T. and the University of Chicago. Do you think your classroom teaching experiences shaped the way you did jobs you were to have later on?*

Absolutely. People say, "Only in business is there a bottom line." I don't agree with that at all. It may be more elusive but it's there. What you're trying to achieve when you're in the classroom is that when you get through, they've learned something. That's your bottom line—that they've learned something. I used to hate to get the bluebooks and correct the exams and find that some weren't good. You want the people to do well because that shows they got something out of it, but if you read bluebooks where people just didn't get it at all, something is wrong here, because the kids are able.

If you've had the experience of being a teacher at good places—and maybe even not-so-good places—you have had a great source of satisfaction.

*"You're asking people to think of the world as it might be."*

# David King

## DIRECTOR, PROGRAM FOR NEWLY ELECTED MEMBERS OF CONGRESS

*David King is the faculty director of Harvard's Program for Newly Elected Members of Congress, run through the Institute of Politics. He has overseen similar programs for the State Duma of the Russian Federation, and he has advised on legislative design issues in South Korea, Nicaragua, Chile, and Bolivia. He is lecturer in public policy at Harvard University's John F. Kennedy School of Government.*

*When a man or woman is elected to the Congress, a flurry of activity begins. The office lottery is held, a flood of applications from people seeking staff positions pours in, and the Democrats and Republicans each hold orientations for the newly elected members. In late November or early December, Harvard's Program for Newly Elected Members of Congress is held over a four-day period. All newly elected members are invited, and typically between 65 and 80 percent attend.*

*We spoke about the program King directs and also about the mentoring that goes on in Congress.*

People come to Congress with very different experiences. The model experience is that they have been a member of a state legislature. Because they will come with an average age of late forties, they have a lot of experience, so you're not going to teach them or even presume to teach them about something they've just run their campaign about. For example, if a campaign is run for the most part around health care policy or education policy, what are we going to do other than confirm their own biases? And people hear what they want to hear.

So the program is divided into several sections. One is an overview of the entire budget process—how it really works, and what kind of devastating trouble we are in. We follow that with an overview from members of the House Appropriations Committee staff on how you actually get money out of the system to help you get re-elected . . . and basically to perpetuate the system that they've just learned is a disaster. With those two bookends, we hope that there will be a discussion about what is responsible in the long run.

We cover the way the President's Office and the Office of Legislative Affairs work. The president will interact with individual members: What can you expect? What can you ask for? What can you never ask for? How does that actually work for the majority and the minority? There are some nuts and bolts issues like that that I think they enjoy.

The general frame that I've used since 1996 is not to play to their short-term interests, and not to refer to the kinds of things that they would have run on, but to acknowledge that they will probably be in office for twenty years and take the long-run view. We map out—from the very best scholars that we can find, not just at Harvard but from any institution in the United States—what the world will look like in twenty years in terms of genetic research, population growth, the economic impact of globalization, environmental affairs. And what can we do right now, or in the next ten years or fifteen years, that will move the needle in one direction or another? They need to think of themselves not as short-term members and short-term holders of the public trust but as long-term guardians of a broad national and international interest.

Focusing on twenty years takes them out of the election they've just been through. It is engaging in a way that they can ask questions they wouldn't otherwise ask. What are the emerging technologies? What are the political ramifications of Spanish becoming the dominant language in seven states?

The third area is around actually surviving with each other—building friendships and keeping your family together. One of the sessions includes current members of Congress where they describe their relationships with their spouses and with their children. It's a closed session, and it's very frank. Among members of Congress, there are problems of infidelity, and the divorce rates or disaffection rates are very high. How do you keep your marriage together and make sure you're there for your children's birthdays when you're working ridiculous hours and you have people telling you at every turn how great you are? So hearing from members who have been through that for years is very helpful.

The other thing that we find most useful is that members get to talk to each other. There's a formal introduction but very informally done, where every member will stand up and spend five minutes talking about why they ran for office and what they hope to do and really, who they are. Usually it will be a presentation of themselves, of where they truly come from, what they hold in their hearts, how they organize their thoughts about the world. Democrats, Republicans, North, South, East, West—they have so much in common. Everyone who comes to Congress could make far more money out in the private sector. They don't come there for the money. They usually don't come for the power. They come because they want to make a difference. Voters don't believe that. But when they're in a room with other members speaking from the heart, they hear that, and it's much more meaningful. That becomes the first moment where new members from across the aisle get to hear from their colleagues. Before that, the only time in this short post-election period when Republicans and Democrats are together is for the office lottery.

So that's what we do.

### When people leave the program, do they seem to have felt that it was valuable?

The evaluations we get are through the roof, and they allow us to continue year after year. We will use the members of the 110th Congress to recruit members of the 111th and encourage them to come to Harvard. And we maintain contact with these members for years to come.

We've had some great teachers. The reason that they're good teachers is that they engage the imagination. There's a certain "oh, my goodness" quality to it. In engaging the imagination, you're asking people to think of the world as it might be and taking them outside of their comfort zone—which is always a good way to teach.

### As you observe over the years the members of Congress who have come through your program, do you feel in terms of your goals that the vaccination took?

That's a difficult problem. First, it's hard to measure whether or not the vaccination really takes. I think that for most members it does not. What does take is that they know these other colleagues fairly well. But the House leadership is now so strong, so controlling of committee assignments and campaign finance rewards, that these approaches to bipartisanship that we offer are usually fairly disappointing.

An entirely predictable conversation at the end of our program is that members will pledge, almost with tears in their eyes, that they will not be sucked in to the polarization of Washington, that they will be able to work together, that they will meet as a class. And sometimes, for some members, it actually works. But for the most part, in order to get ahead in Congress, you have to play ball with the leadership. And until the leadership sees the benefits of bipartisanship, they will continue to create a polarized environment with the new members.

So we do the best we can, and hope for the best. But year in and year out, we do little that actually diminishes polarization in Congress.

*Once newly elected members of Congress take office, is there much mentoring that goes on, either formal or informal?*

It is almost entirely informal yet very predictable. Most of the time a member of Congress will have very little information about what he or she is voting on. Members will become an expert in one issue, so they major in one issue and they'll minor in two. That's the standard language you'll hear on Capitol Hill.

"What's your major?"

"I major in transportation policy."

"What's your minor?"

"K–12 education and the environmental impact of wetlands."

If that's your major and two minors, there's an awful lot you're not covering. And those areas are going to be reflected in the committees you're on. In all the other issues that come before Congress, you have to choose cue-givers. You are a cue-taker on almost every issue and you have to choose your cue-givers.

So from day one in Congress, you're looking for people who think like you, who represent districts like yours, who know a lot about a policy area that you don't know about—and they are going to be your cue-givers. There's no instantaneous voting in Congress—or any state legislature. So the cue-givers vote first, and if you're majoring in an area that has something up for vote, you're going to vote early, knowing that you're a cue-giver for others. If you're a cue-taker, you'll delay voting to see how the cue-giver votes.

You'll also look to the senior member of your congressional delegation. And it will be his job to mentor the new members of Congress from his state. So mentoring is informal, it is usually within the party, and it tends to be structured around cue-giving and cue-taking. And it relies on the senior member of a congressional delegation.

Then there are two structural organizations within the caucuses that also help to create a mentoring relationship. One is the whip system. You can think of it as a large web with the chief party whip at the top and then deputy whips, and then regional whips. Regional whips are assigned specific members in their region to get to know. It's a way for the whip to understand how these newer members are actually thinking. And when they want to "whip" a vote, the whip structure will go out there and find out how members are thinking.

The whip needs to know that member's district extremely well, but the whip's job is not merely to tell members how to vote or find out how they're going to vote; the whip's subsidiary job is to make sure that member survives and does not do something to hurt his or her re-election chances. So if you are my whip, and I'm a new member, and I don't know a lot about an issue, your job as the whip is to say, "Listen, the leadership wants a yes vote on this, but I think that because you have such and such in your district, you should vote no." So this structure produces something like mentoring.

The other structure that produces something like mentoring is called either the Committee on Committees on the Republican side or the Policy and Steering Committee on the Democratic side. These committees help assign members to committees. So if I've been on committee A, but want to move up to committee B, I have to work with these groups—and mentoring takes place in that context.

Also, you need to remember that these folks in Congress are about as affable and gregarious and extroverted as you're ever going to find. So they naturally find mentors.

*It strikes me that one of the most important goals of your program is to move members toward long-term thinking. It seems that so many of the serious challenges in America—from issues of ecology to the budget deficit—are due in part to the fact that the time frame of political leaders is six months out, not five or ten or twenty years.*

Yes, that's right. Incentives in politics are short term, but interests are long term. The most direct and beneficial way promote long-term thinking is to have representatives' constituents thinking about the long term. If we have constituents thinking and talking about global warming, then members of Congress will respond, because the next election will partly be judged on what've they've done for the long-term interest. So the problem for the country is how we engender a public that thinks long term and expects their representatives to do likewise.

One of the problems about representation is that we want people in office who are just like us, except a little more noble; just like us, except a little more honest; just like us, except a little smarter. That's not how democracy works. What we get in our elected officials is people who are just like us.

And unless we can *ask* for long-term thinking, for less partisanship, for more dialog, we can't expect it from our representatives—because they're just like us.

*Working on this book, I find myself looking at everything in terms of teaching. And it strikes me that what you're suggesting is that in this country we need to be serious about teaching our people to be conscientious democratic citizens.*

I think that's exactly right. I hope and pray that happens.

# Acknowledgments

I wish to thank these fifty-one great teachers who gave generously of their time and energy in granting me interviews.

I am grateful to my wife, Jenna Chan Smoot, for her love and support, and to my friend Jack Metzgar for his encouragement.

I am indebted to the late Studs Terkel and his lifelong example of finding wisdom from listening to people.

I owe a debt of gratitude to my agent, Jon Sternfeld, for believing.

And I am grateful to my own students—past and present—for being who they are.

BILL SMOOT has been a teacher—at levels ranging from sixth grade to university—for thirty years. He has taught at Northwestern University, University of Hawaii–Hilo, and Miami University, where he received the Outstanding Faculty Award. He currently teaches English at a Bay Area prep school, the Castilleja School, where he has received the Outstanding Teacher Award. His short stories and essays have appeared in *Georgia Review, Literary Review, Western Humanities Review, Crab Orchard Review,* and the *Nation.*